SCANDINAVIAN
PHRASEBOOK

Scandinavian phrasebook
3rd edition – February 2001
First published – December 1992

Published by
Lonely Planet Publications Pty Ltd ABN 36 005 607 983
90 Maribyrnong St, Footscray, Victoria 3011, Australia

Lonely Planet Offices
Australia Locked Bag 1, Footscray, Victoria 3011
USA 150 Linden St, Oakland CA 94607
UK 72-82 Rosebery Ave, London, EC1R 4RW
France 1 rue du Dahomey, 75011 Paris

Cover illustration
by Brendan Dempsey, based on an original illustration by Patrick Marris,
A horse is a horse, of course of course

ISBN 1 74104 603 3

10 9 8 7 6 5 3 2 1

Printed through The Bookmaker International Ltd
Printed in China

About the Authors

Birgitte Hou Olsen updated the Danish chapter, based on a chapter by Peter A. Crozier.

Bergljót av Skardi wrote the Faroese chapter. She is 50 years old and teaches Faroese and English at the high school in her home town Tórshavn in the Faroe Islands.

Gerald Porter updated the Finnish chapter, based on an original chapter by Markus Lehtipuu. He's English but has lived in Finland for many years. He is at present lecturing in the English department at the University of Vaasa.

Icelandic was updated by Margrét Eggertsdóttir, based on a chapter by Ingibjörg Árnadóttir. Margrét was born in Reykjavik in 1960. At present she is a lecturer in Icelandic language and literature at the University of Copenhagen.

The Norwegian chapter was updated by Runa Eilertsen and Daniel Cash. Daniel is Australian but has lived in Norway. He currently works for a Melbourne-based newspaper. Runa is a native-born Norwegian who lives in Oslo. This chapter was developed from an original chapter by Doekes Lulofs.

Anna Herbst updated the Swedish chapter, based on an original chapter by Pär Sörme. Anna is Swedish but has lived in Australia since 1986. She has taught English and Swedish language and literature in secondary school, adult education and university in Sweden and Australia, and English and media subjects at university in China. She has also worked in broadcasting and once made a living as a folksinger.

From the Authors

Birgitte Hou Olsen wishes to thank Karin Vidstrup Monk from Lonely Planet for a creative and fruitful working relationship during the entire process.

Bergljót av Skardi wishes to thank her colleague Guðrun Gaard for passing the phrasebook job on to her. Also a big thank you to Hans Marius Johannessen for suggestions and advice.

Gerald Porter wants to record his thanks to Sirkku Aaltonen for love and constant guidance.

Margrét Eggertsdóttir would like to thank Professor Robert Cook at the University of Iceland for his contribution to the chapter on body language, showing his clear insight into what characterises the Icelanders.

Runa Eilertsen would like to thank Daniel Cash.

Anna Herbst would like to thank Dino Bressan for being most helpful in allowing her to test the phonetic transcriptions on him.

From the Publisher

Thanks go to Christian Becker-Christensen and Jan Katlev for their invaluable linguistic advice and also to Wenche Eriksen and Natasha Sayer for their assistance on the Norwegian chapter.

Patrick Marris illustrated the book and the cover and still managed to find the time to help Yukiyoshi Kamimura lay out some of the chapters. Fabrice Rocher supervised layout. Karin Vidstrup Monk edited, proofed and oversaw the whole process. Emma Koch edited, Fleur Goding proofed and Natasha Velleley produced the map.

CONTENTS

SWEDISH 307

INTRODUCTION

Although it's not widely known outside Europe, the term 'Scandinavia' actually refers only to Denmark, Norway and Sweden while 'the Nordic countries' include Scandinavia plus Finland, Iceland and the Faroe Islands. This phrasebook covers all six languages and is thus really two in one: a Scandinavian phrasebook and a Nordic phrasebook!

To add to the confusion, five of the six languages – Danish, Swedish, Norwegian, Icelandic and Faroese – are referred to as the Scandinavian languages and they all form the northern branch of the Germanic languages tree. Finnish is the exception, being from a different family tree altogether. The Scandinavian languages have all descended from Old Norse, the language of the Vikings, while Finnish is related to Estonian and (more remotely) Hungarian.

However, luckily for English-speakers, these five languages are cousins of English and you'll be able to recognise quite a few words, eg, dør/dör for 'door' and hus/hús for 'house'. One big advantage of Danish, Swedish, Norwegian, Faroese and Icelandic being so closely related is that once you've got the hang of one language, the others should seem quite familiar.

This book provides the basics for you to get around while making the most of all the Nordic countries have to offer. English is spoken very widely (and very well!) throughout these countries but if you take the time to learn at least a few phrases in the local language you'll find that you're more than rewarded for your efforts.

SCANDINAVIAN & NORDIC

Arctic
Ocean

Faxaflói ○ Reykjavik

ICELAND

Heimaey

**FAROE
ISLANDS**

Tórshavn

0   150   300 km
0   90   180 mi

*Shetland
Islands*

*Orkney
Islands*

Bergen

Outer Hebrides

*Atlantic
Ocean*

Scotland

*North
Sea*

Stavanger

Northern
Ireland

Isle of
Man

IRELAND

BRITAIN

St George's Channel

Wales

England

Frisian Islands

NETHERLANDS

Map 11

INTRODUCTION

EUROPE

Barents Sea

Norwegian Sea

Lofoten Islands

Inarijärvi

Oulu
Oulujärvi

FINLAND

Kemi

SWEDEN

Kitka
Pyhäselkä

Gulf of
Bothnia

Tampere
Kallavesi
Päijänne
Saimaa

Trondheim

NORWAY

Oslo

Turku
Helsinki

Åland

Gulf of Finland

RUSSIAN
FEDERATION

Mälaren

Stockholm

ESTONIA

Vänern

Gulf of
Riga

Skagerrak

Vättern

Gothenburg

Gotland

LATVIA

Jutland

Öland

DENMARK

Helsingborg

Copenhagen
Malmö

Baltic
Sea

LITHUANIA

Zealand
Funen
Bornholm

RUSSIAN
FEDERATION

BELARUS

GERMANY

POLAND

INTRODUCTION

HOW TO USE THIS PHRASEBOOK
Transliterations

Simplified transliterations have been provided in blue throughout this book. Italic is used to indicate where to place stress in a word.

Polite Forms

When a language has polite and informal forms of the singular pronoun 'you', the polite form has been used in most cases. However, you'll come across the informal form of 'you' in some phrases, such as those for talking with children.

Arthur or Martha?

When there are both feminine and masculine forms of a word, it's indicated in either of two ways, with the feminine form always appearing first:

- with a slash separating the feminine form and masculine ending (which is added to the feminine form) of a word:

  hot   **hait/-oor**   *heit/-ur* (f/m)

- when the distinction between masculine and feminine is more complex, each word is given in full, separated with a slash:

  cold   **kerld/kuhld-oor**   *køld/kaldur* (f/m)

These distinctions occur mostly in Faroese and Icelandic, but you may see them pop up in the other languages from time to time.

Finally

Don't be concerned if you feel you can't memorise words. You'll find the most essential words and phrases in the Quick Reference section at the start of each chapter. You could also try tagging a few pages for other key phrases.

ABBREVIATIONS USED IN THIS BOOK

col	colloquial	n	neuter
f	feminine	pl	plural
inf	informal	pol	polite
m	masculine	sg	singular

PRONUNCIATION GUIDE

Below is a general pronunciation guide of the sounds that are common to the languages in this book, outlining in blue our representation of each sound, used in the simplified transliterations throughout the book. In addition, each language chapter contains a section about pronunciation particular to that language. It's a good idea to have a look at this as well, as it explains any sounds that might be slightly different in that language, or not found in any of the other languages.

Vowels

ah	as the 'a' in 'father'
uh	as the 'u' in 'cut'
a	as the 'a' in 'act'
eh	as the 'e' in 'bet'
ee	as the 'ee' in 'seethe'
i	as the 'i' in 'hit'
ü	a bit like the 'e' in British English 'dew' – try pursing your lips and saying 'ee'
o	a short 'o' as in 'pot'
oh	as the 'o' in 'note'
oo	a long 'oo' as in 'cool'
u	a short 'oo' as in 'foot'
ö	as the 'e' in 'summer'
or	as the 'or' in 'for', with less emphasis on the 'r'
er	as the 'er' in 'fern' but shorter, without the 'r'

INTRODUCTION

Diphthongs

ae	as the 'ea' in 'bear'
ay	as the 'ay' in 'day'
ai	as the sound of 'eye'
oy	the 'oy' as in 'toy'
ow	as the 'ou' in 'out'

Semiconsonants

w	as in 'wet'
y	as in 'yet'

Consonants

g	always a hard 'g' as in 'get', never as in 'gentle'
s	always as in 'kiss', never as in 'treasure'
sh	as in 'ship'
ch	as in 'chew'
dj	as the 'j' in 'jaw'
th	as the 'th' in 'lather'
h	as the 'h' in 'horse'
ng	as in 'sing'
ngn	as the meeting of sounds in 'hang-nail'
rr	a trilled 'r'
rt	as the 'rt' in American English 'start'
rd	as the 'rd' in American English 'weird'
rn	as the 'rn' in American English 'earn'
rl	as the 'rl' in American English 'earl'
dn	as the 'dn' in 'hadn't'
dl	as the 'dl' in 'saddle'

All other consonants are pronounced as in English.

DANISH

QUICK REFERENCE

DANISH

Hello.	hai/ghor-*da*	Hej/Goddag. (inf/pol)
Goodbye.	hai hai/fah-*vehl*	Hej hej/Farvel. (inf/pol)
Yes./No.	ya/nai	Ja./Nej.
Excuse me.	*ān*-sgül	Undskyld.
Sorry.	*ān*-sgül/bi-*kla*-ah	Undskyld/Beklager.
Thank you.	tahg	Tak.
That's fine.	di ehŕ ee *or*-dehn.	Det er i orden.
You're welcome.	sehl tahg	Selv tak.

I'd like a ...	yai vi *gehŕ*-neh ha en ...	Jeg vil gerne have en ...
one-way ticket	*ehng*-gild-bi-lehd	enkeltbillet
return ticket	ŕeh-*tooŕ*-bi-lehd	returbillet

I (don't) understand.
  yai fo-*sdor* (ig)   Jeg forstår (ikke).
Do you speak English?
  ta-lah dee *ehng*-ehlsg?   Taler De engelsk? (pol)
Where is ...?
  vor ehŕ ...?   Hvor er ...?
Go straight ahead.
  gä *li*-eh ooth   Gå lige ud.
Turn left/right.
  dŕai ti *vehns*-dŕah/   Drej til venstre/
  hoy-yah.   højre.
Do you have any rooms
available?
  hah ee *lith*-ee *vehŕ*-sah? Har I ledige værelser?
I'm looking for a public toilet.
  yai *li*-thah *ehŕ*-dah id   Jeg leder efter et
  o-fehnd-leed toy-*lehd*   offentligt toilet.

1	in	en	6	sehgs	seks
2	tor	to	7	sü-w	syv
3	tŕeh	tre	8	ā-deh	otte
4	feeŕ	fire	9	nee	ni
5	fehm	fem	10	tee	ti

DANISH

Danish belongs to the North Germanic language group, together with Swedish, Norwegian, Icelandic and Faeroese.

Consequently, written Danish bears a strong resemblance to these languages. Spoken Danish, on the other hand, has evolved in a different direction, introducing sounds and pronunciation not found elsewhere.

Danish has a polite form of address, using the personal pronouns **De** and **Dem**. The words and phrases in this chapter are mostly in the familar form using **du** and **dig**, except where it's more appropriate to use the formal form. In general, use the formal form when speaking to senior citizens and officials, and the familiar form the rest of the time.

As Danish is not broadly spoken and few visitors take the time or effort to learn it, most Danes speak English. However, an effort to learn at least the basics is well received. It's a good idea to memorise the words for 'thank you', 'goodbye', 'hello' and 'I'm sorry'. This minimum effort will be appreciated, and with an increased command of the language you'll be rewarded by gaining a greater insight into Denmark and the Danes.

The pronunciation of each word and phrase in this chapter is transcribed using a simplified phonetic system, so with not too much effort it should be possible to grasp the basic sentence structure and begin creating your own sentences.

PRIMARY STRESS

In Danish the stress is usually placed on the
first syllable, or on the first letter of the word.

PRONUNCIATION

Danish varies from island to island as well as from north to south, with each region having its distinct dialect. The translation and pronunciation presented here follows the form of Danish known as **Nudansk**, (literally 'Now Danish'). This is the form of Danish spoken in Copenhagen, and understood throughout the country.

Stressed syllables in multi-syllable words are printed here in italic type, and longer syllables have been split into more manageable lengths.

Danes do not necessarily pronounce what they write. The pronunciation of letters varies depending on the word, and written vowels and/or consonants will sometimes 'disappear' completely in the pronunciation. Unfortunately there are no hard and fast rules as to how any given letter is to be pronounced. In general, the best advice for good pronunciation is to listen and learn. Good luck!

Danish varies from the general pronunciation guide, given at the front of this book, in only two respects:

Vowels

Danish	Guide	Sounds
u(n), å, o	ā	a long rounded 'a' as in 'walk'

Consonants

r	ŕ	rolled in the throat

PRONOUNS					
SG			**PL**		
I	yai	*jeg*	we	vee	*vi*
you	doo	*du*	you (pl)	ee	*I*
he	han	*han*	they	dee	*de*
she	hoon	*hun*			
it	dehn (di)	*den (det)*			

GREETINGS & CIVILITIES
Useful Phrases

Hello.
  hai/daow/ghor-*da*   *Hej/Dav/Goddag.* (inf/pol)
Goodbye.
  hai hai/fah-*vehl*   *Hej hej/Farvel.* (inf/pol)
Yes./No.
  ya/nai   *Ja./Nej.*
Excuse me.
  ān-sgül   *Undskyld.*
May I? Do you mind?
  mā yai? *ti*-la-thah dee?   *Må jeg? Tillader De?* (pol)
Sorry. (excuse me, forgive me)
  ān-sgül/bi-*kla*-ah   *Undskyld/Beklager.*
Thank you.
  tahg   *Tak.*
Many thanks.
  mahng-eh tahg   *Mange tak.*
That's fine. You're welcome.
  di ehŕ ee *oŕ*-dehn. sehl tahg   *Det er i orden. Selv tak.*

Greetings

Good morning.
  gor *morn*   *God morgen.*
Good afternoon.
  gor *ehf*-dah-mi-da   *God eftermiddag.*
Good evening/night.
  gor-*ahf*-dehn/go-*nad*   *Godaften./Godnat.*
How are you?
  voŕ-*dan* gor di?   *Hvordan går det?*
Well, thanks.
  god tahg   *Godt, tak.*

DANISH

Forms of Address

Madam/Mrs	ffoo	*fru*
Sir/Mr	hehŕ	*herr (hr.)*
Miss	fŕer-gehn	*frøken*
companion	kahm-ah-ŕahd	*kammerat*
friend	vehn	*ven*

SMALL TALK
Meeting People

What is your name?
  va *hi*-thah doo/dee?   *Hvad hedder du/De?* (inf/pol)
My name is ...
  mid naown ehŕ ...   *Mit navn er ...*
I'd like to introduce you to ...
  yai vi *gehŕ*-neh   *Jeg vil gerne*
  pŕehsehn-*ti*-ah dai for ...   *præsentere dig for ...*
I'm pleased to meet you.
  di ehŕ *hüg*-lid ad *tŕah*-feh   *Det er hyggeligt at træffe*
  dehm/*mer*-theh dai   *Dem/møde dig.* (pol/inf)

Nationalities

Where are you from?
  vor *kom*-ah doo *fŕah*?   *Hvor kommer du fra?*

I'm from ...	yai ehŕ fŕah ...	*Jeg er fra ...*
Australia	aow-*sdŕahl*-yehn	*Australien*
Canada	*ka*-na-da	*Kanada*
Denmark	*dan*-mahg	*Danmark*
England	*ehng*-lan	*England*
Ireland	*eeŕ*-lan	*Irland*
New Zealand	nü *si*-lan	*New Zealand*
Scotland	*sgod*-lan	*Skotland*
the USA	oo ehs a	*USA*
Wales	*wa*-ehls	*Wales*

Age
How old are you?
    vor *gah*-mehl ehŕ doo?   *Hvor gammel er du?*
I'm ... years old.
    yai ehŕ ... or *gah*-mehl   *Jeg er ... år gammel.*

Occupations

What do you do?	va *la*-wah doo?	*Hvad laver du?*
I'm (a/an) ...;	yai ehŕ ...;	*Jeg er ...;*
I work as (a/an) ...	yai *ah*-bai-dah som ...	*Jeg arbejder som ...*
artist	*kãnsd*-nah	*kunstner*
business person	fo-*ŕahd*-nings-dŕeeoo-neh	*forretnings-drivende*
doctor	*leh*-eh	*læge*
engineer	ing-shin-*yer*	*ingeniør*
farmer	*bã*-neh	*bonde*
journalist	shã-na-*lisd*	*journalist*
lawyer	ath-vor-*kad*	*advokat*
manual worker	*ah*-bai-dah	*arbejder*
mechanic	mi-*ka*-ni-gah	*mekaniker*
nurse	*sü*-eh-plai-yah-skeh	*sygeplejerske*
office worker	kon-*tooŕ*-ah-bai-dah	*kontorarbejder*
scientist	*fors*-gah	*forsker*
student	sdoo-*di*-ah-neh	*studerende*
teacher	*lehŕ*-ah	*lærer*
waiter	*cheh*-nah	*tjener*
writer	fo-*fa*-dah	*forfatter*

DANISH

PRETTY PLEASE

Note that there is no equivalent to the word 'please' in
Danish. Politeness is most often expressed by tone of voice
and/or by beginning the sentence with phrases such as
'May I ...' Må jeg ... or 'Could I ...' Kunne jeg ....

DANISH

Religion

What is your religion?
vil-kehn fehlig-*yorn*   *Hvilken religion*
til-her-ah doo?   *tilhører du?*

I'm not religious.
yai ehf ig fehlig-*yers*   *Jeg er ikke religiøs.*

I'm ...	yai ehf ...	Jeg er ...
Buddhist	boo-*deesd*	*buddist*
Catholic	kator-*leeg*	*katolik*
Christian	*kfehs*-dehn	*kristen*
Hindu	*hin*-doo	*hindu*
Jewish	*yer*-theh	*jøde*
Muslim	moos-*leem*	*muslim*

Family

Are you married?   ehf doo geefd?   *Er du gift?*

I'm ...	yai ehf ...	Jeg er ...
married	geefd	*gift*
single	*oo*-geefd	*ugift*

How many children do you have?
vor *mahng*-eh bern hah doo?   *Hvor mange børn har du?*

I don't have any children.
yai hah *ing*-ehn bern   *Jeg har ingen børn.*

I have a daughter/a son.
yai hah in *da*-dah/en sern   *Jeg har en datter/en søn.*

How many brothers/
sisters do you have?
vor *mahng*-eh *bfehrth*-rah/   *Hvor mange brødre/*
sers-dfah hah doo?   *søstre har du?*

Is your husband/wife here?
ehf deen man/*kor*-ne hehf?   *Er din mand/kone her?*

Do you have a boyfriend/girlfriend?
hah doo in *kehfs*-deh?   *Har du en kæreste?*

brother	bŕoŕ	*bror*
children	bern	*børn*
daughter	*da*-dah	*datter*
family	fa-*meel*-yeh	*familie*
father	fah	*far*
grandfather	*behs*-deh-fah	*bedstefar*
grandmother	*behs*-deh-mooŕ	*bedstemor*
grandparents (maternal)	*moŕ*-mooŕ o *moŕ*-fah	*mormor og morfar*
grandparents (paternal)	*fah*-mooŕ o *fah*-fah	*farmor og farfar*
husband	man	*mand*
mother	mooŕ	*mor*
sister	*sers*-dah	*søster*
son	sern	*søn*
wife	*kor*-ne	*kone*

DANISH

Kids' Talk

How old are you?
  vor *gah*-mehl ehŕ doo?   *Hvor gammel er du?*
When's your birthday?
  vo-*nor* hah doo *fer*-sehl-sda?   *Hvornår har du fødselsdag?*
What do you do after school?
  va *la*-wah doo *ehf*-dah skor-leh?   *Hvad laver du efter skole?*
Do you have a pet at home?
  hah doo id *keh*-leh-düŕ?   *Har du et kæledyr?*

I have a ...	yai hah ...	*Jeg har ...*
bird	in fool	*en fugl*
budgerigar	in on-doo-*lad*	*en undulat*
canary	in ka-*nah*-yeh-fool	*en kanariefugl*
cat	in kad	*en kat*
dog	in hoon	*en hund*
frog	in fŕer	*en frø*
guinea pig	id *mah*-sveen	*et marsvin*

DANISH

Feelings

I like ...	yai ka god lee ...	*Jeg kan godt lide ...*
I don't like ...	yai ka ig lee ...	*Jeg kan ikke lide ...*
I'm in a hurry.	yai hah tŕaowld	*Jeg har travlt.*
I'm well.	yai hah di god	*Jeg har det godt.*
I'm sorry.	di ger mai ānd	*Det gør mig ondt*
(condolence)	ad *her*-ah	*at høre.*
I'm grateful.	yai ehŕ	*Jeg er*
	tahg-*nehm*-lee	*taknemlig.*

I'm ...	yai ehŕ ...	*Jeg er ...*
angry	vŕehth	*vred*
happy	glath	*glad*
hungry	*sul*-dehn	*sulten*
sad	tŕeesd	*trist*
sleepy	*serv*-nee	*søvnig*
thirsty	*ters*-dee	*tørstig*
tired (fatigued)	tŕahd	*træt*
worried	be-*kerm*-ŕerth	*bekymret*

I'm cold/hot.	yai fŕü-sah/*svith*-ah	*Jeg fryser/sveder.*
You're right.	doo hah ŕahd	*Du har ret.*

Some Useful Phrases

Sure.
   seh-*fer*-lee/di ehŕ klahd   *Selvfølgelig./Det er klart.*
Just a minute.
   id *oy*-eh-*blig*   *Et øjeblik.*
It's (not) important.
   di ehŕ (ig) *vig*-deed   *Det er (ikke) vigtigt.*
It's (not) possible.
   di ehŕ (ig) *moo*-leed   *Det er (ikke) muligt.*
Wait!
   vehnd!   *Vent!*
Good luck!
   hehl o *ler*-geh!   *Held og lykke!*

BREAKING THE LANGUAGE BARRIER

Do you speak English?
    ta-lah dee *ehng*-ehlsg?   *Taler De engelsk?* (pol)
Does anyone speak English?
    ehŕ dah norn dah   *Er der nogen der*
    ta-lah *ehng*-ehlsg?   *taler engelsk?*
I speak a little ...
    yai *ta*-lah in *smoo*-leh ...   *Jeg taler en smule ...*
I don't speak ...
    yai *ta*-lah ig ...   *Jeg taler ikke ...*
I (don't) understand.
    yai fo-*sdor* (ig)   *Jeg forstår (ikke).*

Could you repeat that?
    koo-neh dee *gehn*-ta di?   *Kunne De gentage det?* (pol)
Could you speak more
slowly please?
    koo-neh dee *ta*-leh   *Kunne De tale*
    lahng-som-ah?   *langsommere?* (pol)
How do you say ...?
    vor-*dan see*-ah man ...?   *Hvordan siger man ...?*
What does ... mean?
    va bi-*tüth*-ah ...?   *Hvad betyder ...?*

I speak ...   yai *ta*-lah ...   *Jeg taler ...*
    English   *ehng*-ehlsg   *engelsk*
    French   fŕahnsg   *fransk*
    German   tüsg   *tysk*
    Italian   ee-tal-*yehnsg*   *italiensk*
    Spanish   sbansg   *spansk*

DANISH

BODY LANGUAGE

The good old handshake is the go in Denmark! The older generation has always used it, and still do, the younger seemed to drop it for a number of years but have reintroduced it. This applies not only to men but also women.

Never shake someone's hand with the other hand in your pocket as this is considered impolite. A single kiss on the cheek (just one) – often accompanied by a hug – is used for closer friends and relatives. And don't forget that men hug in Denmark too!

To express the affirmative, Danes will sometimes pull in air abruptly while making a 'hah' sound accompanied by a slight backward tilt of the head, and a 'no' can be expressed by the usual shaking of the head.

When Danes raise their glasses to toast they will seek brief eye contact with everyone at the table before and after drinking and say Skål!. You shouldn't start eating a meal until everybody is ready and the host(ess) nods to everyone and says Værsgo (please start).

Danes have a tradition of thanking their hosts after a meal or any type of get-together by either ringing up specifically to do so or by saying Tak for sidst (lit. thanks for last) next time they meet.

DANISH

SIGNS	
FORBUDT	PROHIBITED
GRATIS ADGANG	FREE ADMISSION
INDGANG	ENTRANCE
INFORMATION	INFORMATION
INGEN ADGANG	NO ENTRY
NØDUDGANG	EMERGENCY EXIT
RESERVERET	RESERVED
RYGNING FORBUDT	NO SMOKING
TELEFON	TELEPHONE
TOILET	TOILET
UDGANG	EXIT
VARM/KOLD	HOT/COLD
ÅBEN/LUKKET	OPEN/CLOSED

PAPERWORK

address	a-*dŕah*-seh	*adresse*
age	*al*-ah	*alder*
birth certificate	*fer*-sels-a-tehsd/	*fødselsattest/*
	dābs-a-tehsd	*dåbsattest*
border	*gŕahn*-seh	*grænse*
car registration	*in*-feh-gee-sdŕeh-ŕing	*indregistre-ring*
	(s-a-tehsd)	*(sattest)*
customs	tol	*told*
date of birth	*fer*-sehls-da-tor	*fødselsdato*
driver's licence	*ker*-koŕd	*kørekort*
identification	li-gee-tee-ma-*shorn*	*legitimation*
immigration	i-mee-gŕah-*shorn*	*immigration*
marital status	see-*veel*-sdan	*civilstand*
name	naown	*navn*
nationality	na-shor-na-lee-*tid*	*nationalitet*
passport	*pas*	*pas*
passport number	*pas*-nām-mah	*pasnummer*
place of birth	*fer*-theh-*sdehth*	*fødested*
profession	pŕor-feh-*shorn*	*profession*
reason for travel	foŕ-māl meh ŕai-sehn	*formål med rejsen*
religion	ŕeh-leeg-*yorn*	*religion*
sex	kern	*køn*
visa	*vee*-sām	*visum*

GETTING AROUND

What time does	vo-*nor* gor/	*Hvornår går/*
the ... leave/arrive?	*an*-kom-ah ...	*ankommer ...*
(air)plane	*flü*-ehth	*flyet*
boat	*bā*-thehn	*båden*
bus	*boo*-sehn/	*bussen/*
	ŕoo-deh-bee-lehn	*rutebilen*
train	*tā*-wehth	*toget*

DANISH

DANISH

Directions

Where is ...?
vor ehŕ ...?   *Hvor er ...?*

How do I get to ...?
vo-*dan* kom-ah yai ti ...?   *Hvordan kommer jeg til ...?*

Is it far from here?
ehŕ di lahngd hiŕ-fŕah?   *Er det langt herfra?*

Is it near here?
ehŕ di ee *nehŕ*-hi-thehn?   *Er det i nærheden?*

Can I walk there?
ka yai *gā* dah-hehn?   *Kan jeg gå derhen?*

Can you show me (on the map)?
koo-neh dee/doo vee-seh mai di   *Kunne De/du vise mig det*
(pā *koŕd*-ehth)?   *(på kortet)?* (pol/inf)

Are there other means of
getting there?
ehŕ dehŕ *ahn*-dŕah *māth*-ah   *Er der andre måder*
ad *kom*-eh dehŕ-hehn pā?   *at komme derhen på?*

I want to go to ...
yai vi *gehŕ*-neh ti ...   *Jeg vil gerne til ...*

Go straight ahead.
gā *li*-eh ooth   *Gå lige ud.*

It's two streets down.
di ehŕ tor *gath*-ah   *Det er to gader*
lehng-ah *ni*-theh   *længere nede.*

HYGGE!

Hygge is a concept close to Danish hearts. It describes many things, like being cosy and comfortable in a warm bed, or sitting in front of the fireplace with a cup of hot cocoa, or a surprise visitor with whom you stay up all night chatting. So if you're experiencing what you think is hygge, you could always try saying: Det er hyggeligt! and watch the reaction...

Turn left/	d*f*ai ti **vehns**-d*f*ah/	*Drej til venstre/*
right ...	hoy-yah ...	*højre ...*
at the next corner	vi *nehs*-deh yer-neh	*ved næste hjørne*
at the traffic lights	vi t*f*ah-*feeg*-lü-sehth	*ved trafiklyset*

behind	**ba**	*bag*
far	**fyeh***f***n**	*fjern*
near	**neh***f*	*nær*
in front of	*fo*f-an	*foran*
opposite	**pā dehn**	*på den*
	morth-sa-deh	*modsatte*
	see-theh a	*side af*

Booking Tickets

Where can I buy a ticket?
vor ka yai *ker*-beh in bi-*lehd*?   *Hvor kan jeg købe en billet?*

I want to go to ...
yai vi *gehf*-neh ti ...   *Jeg vil gerne til ...*

Do I need to book?
eh*f* di nerth-*vehn*-deed   *Er det nødvendigt*
ad bi-sdi-leh plas?   *at bestille plads?*

I'd like to book a seat to ...
yai vi *gehf*-neh   *Jeg vil gerne*
bi-sdi-leh plas ti ...   *bestille plads til ...*

It's full.
di eh*f* *ful*-d *book*-ehth   *Det er fuldt booket.*

Are there no seats available at all?
eh*f* dah slehd *ing*-ehn   *Er der slet ingen*
***le*-thee plas-ah?**   *ledige pladser?*

Can I get a stand-by ticket?
ka yai mās-gi *ker*-beh   *Kan jeg måske købe*
in stan-*bai* bi-*lehd*?   *en stand-by billet?*

DANISH

I'd like ...	yai vi *gehŕ*-neh ha ...	*Jeg vil gerne have ...*
a one-way ticket	en *ehng*-gild-bi-lehd	*en enkeltbillet*
a return ticket	en *ŕeh-tooŕ*-bi-lehd	*en returbillet*
two tickets	tor bi-*lehd*-ah	*to billetter*
tickets for all of us	bi-*lehd*-ah ti os *al*-eh	*billetter til os alle*
a student discount	sdoo-*dehn*-dah-ŕah-bad	*studenterrabat*
a child's fare	in *ber*-neh-bi-lehd	*en børnebillet*
a pensioner's fare	in pahng-sho-*neesd*-bi-lehd	*en pensionist-billet*
1st class	*fers*-deh *klas*-eh	*første klasse*
2nd class	*an*-ehn *klas*-eh	*anden klasse*

Air

Is there a flight to ...?
  ehŕ dehŕ id flü ti ...?   *Er der et fly til ...?*

When is the next flight to ...?
  vo-*nor* gor *nehs*-deh flü ti ...?   *Hvornår går næste fly til ...?*

How long does the flight take?
  vor lahng tith tah *flüu*-too-ahn?   *Hvor lang tid tager flyveturen?*

What is the flight number?
  va ehŕ *flaid*-näm-mahth?   *Hvad er flight-nummeret?*

You must check in at ... (time)
  doo sga cheh-geh in *klog*-gehn ...   *Du skal checke ind klokken ...*

airport tax	*läfd*-haown-sgad	*lufthavnsskat*
boarding pass	*boŕ*-ding-koŕd	*boardingkort*
customs	tol	*told*

SIGNS

BAGAGE(AFHENTNING)	LUGGAGE PICKUP
BAGAGE(SKRANKE)	BAGGAGE COUNTER
CHECK IN/	CHECKING IN
INDCHEKNING	
CHECK-IN (SKRANKE)	CHECK-IN COUNTER
REGISTRERING	REGISTRATION
TOLD	CUSTOMS

Bus

Where is the bus stop?
   vor eh*f* *boos*-stop-   *Hvor er*
   peh-stehth-ehd?   *busstoppestedet?*
Which bus goes to ...?
   vil-gehn boos gor ti ...?   *Hvilken bus går til ...?*
Does this bus go to ...?
   gor *dehn*-neh boos ti ...?   *Går denne bus til ...?*
How often do buses pass by?
   vor *of*-deh gor *boos*-sen?   *Hvor ofte går bussen?*
Could you let me know
when we get to ...?
   koo-neh dee/doo *see*-eh ti   *Kunne De/du sige til*
   nor vee *kom*-ah ti ...?   *når vi kommer til ...?* (pol/inf)

I want to get off!   yai vi a!   *Jeg vil af!*

What time is the ...	vo-*nor* gor dehn ...	*Hvornår går den ...*
bus?	boos?	*bus?*
next	*nehs*-deh	*næste*
first	*fers*-deh	*første*
last	*sees*-deh	*sidste*

Metro

The first phase of the Copenhagen metro is operational from 2002,
the second from 2003.
(See the Train section, page 32)

DANISH

DANISH

Train

Which line takes me to ...?
vil-gehth tāw gor ti ...? *Hvilket tog går til ...?*
What is the next station?
va ehŕ *nehs*-deh sda-*shorn*? *Hvad er næste station?*
Is this the right platform for ...?
ehŕ *di*-deh dehn *ŕig*-dee *Er dette den rigtige*
pa-*ŕong* nor yai sga *perron når jeg skal*
meh *tā*-wehth ti ...? *med toget til ...?*
The train leaves from platform ...
tā-wehth gor fŕah pa-*ŕong* ... *Toget går fra perron ...*
Passengers must change trains/
platforms.
pa-sa-*shi*-ah-neh sga *Passagererne skal*
sgeef-deh *tāw*/pa-*ŕong* *skifte tog/perron.*

dining car	*sbee*-seh-vown	*spisevogn*
express	ehgs-*pŕahs*	*ekspres*
local	lor-*kal*	*lokal*
sleeping car	sow-eh-vown	*sovevogn*

SIGNS	
AFGANG	DEPARTURES
ANKOMST	ARRIVALS
BILLETKONTOR	TICKET OFFICE
BUSSTOPPESTED	BUS STOP
HOVEDBANEGÅRD	CENTRAL STATION
KØREPLAN	TIMETABLE
MINIMETRO	SUBWAY
PERRONNUMMER	PLATFORM NO.
STATION	STATION
TOGSTATION	TRAIN STATION
UDGANG	WAY OUT
VEKSEL	CHANGE (for coins)

Taxi

Can you take me to ...?
    ka dee/doo ker   *Kan De/du køre*
    mai ti ...?   *mig til ...?* (pol/inf)
How much does it cost to go to ...?
    vor *mah*-eth *kos*-dah   *Hvor meget koster*
    di ad ker ti ...?   *det at køre til ...?*
Here is fine, thank you.
    sdob hehŕ tahg   *Stop her, tak.*
The next corner, please.
    vi *nehs*-deh *yer*-neh tahg   *Ved næste hjørne, tak.*
The next street to the left/right.
    nehs-deh *gath*-eh ti   *Næste gade til*
    vehns-dŕah/*hoy*-yah   *venstre/højre.*
Please slow down.
    vehŕ so *vehn*-lee ad ker   *Vær så venlig at køre*
    lahng-som-ah   *langsommere.*

Continue!	*foŕd*-sehd!	*Fortsæt!*
Stop here!	sdob hehŕ!	*Stop her!*
Please wait here.	vehnd *vehn*-leesd hehŕ	*Vent venligst her.*

Some Useful Phrases

The train is delayed/cancelled.
    tāw-ehth ehŕ fo-*sing*-gehth/   *Toget er forsinket/*
    aw-lüsd   *aflyst.*
How long will it be delayed?
    vor *mah*-ehth ehŕ *tāw*-ehth *Hvor meget er toget*
    fo-*sing*-gehth?   *forsinket?*
Can I reserve a place?
    ehŕ di *moo*-lid ad   *Er det muligt at*
    ŕeh-sehŕ-*vi*-ah plas?   *reservere plads?*
How long does the trip take?
    vor lahng teeth tah *too*-ahn? *Hvor lang tid tager turen?*
Is it a direct route?
    ehŕ di in *dee*-ŕaig-deh   *Er det en direkte*
    fo-*bin*-ehl-seh?   *forbindelse?*

DANISH

Is that seat taken?
    ehŕ dehn plas *ob*-ta-ehth?   *Er den plads optaget?*
I want to get off at ...
    yai vi *gehŕ*-neh a vi ...   *Jeg vil gerne af ved ...*
Where can I hire a bicycle?
    vor ka yai *lai*-eh in *sü*-gehl?   *Hvor kan jeg leje en cykel?*

Car

Where can I rent a car?
    vor ka yai *lai*-eh in beel?   *Hvor kan jeg leje en bil?*
How much is it daily/weekly?
    vor *mah*-eth *kos*-dah di   *Hvor meget koster det*
    pehŕ da/pehŕ *oo*-eh?   *per dag/per uge?*
Does that include insurance/
mileage?
    ing-kloo-*di*-ah di fo-*sig*-ŕing/ *Inkluderer det forsikring/*
    oo-bi-gŕahn-seh-theh   *ubegrænsede*
    kee-lor-*mi*-dah?   *kilometer?*
Where's the next petrol station?
    vor ehŕ *nehs*-deh   *Hvor er næste*
    bin-*seen*-sda-*shorn*?   *benzinstation?*
How long can I park here?
    vor *lehng*-eh mā yai   *Hvor længe må jeg*
    pah-*ki*-ah hiŕ?   *parkere her?*
Does this road lead to ...?
    fer-ah *dehn*-neh vai ti ...? *Fører denne vej til ...?*
I need a mechanic.
    yai hah bŕoo for in   *Jeg har brug for en*
    mi-*ka*-ni-gah   *mekaniker.*
What make is it?
    vil-gehth mehŕ-geh ehŕ di? *Hvilket mærke er det?*
The battery is flat.
    ba-dah-*ŕee*-ehth ehŕ derd   *Batteriet er dødt.*

The radiator is leaking.
 ker-lahn ehŕ *oo*-tehd   *Køleren er utæt.*
I have a flat tyre.
 yai ehŕ pāng-*ti*-ahth   *Jeg er punkteret.*
It's overheating. (engine)
 mor-toŕ-ahn *kā*-wah *ow*-ah   *Motoren koger over.*
It's not working.
 dehn *veeŕ*-gah ig   *Den virker ikke.*

air (for tyres)	lāfd	*luft*
battery	ba-dah-*ŕee*	*batteri*
brakes	*bŕahm*-sah	*bremser*
clutch	*kob*-ling	*kobling*
driver's licence	*ker*-kord	*kørekort*
engine	*mor*-toŕ	*motor*
lights	lüs	*lys*
oil	*orl*-yeh	*olie*
radiator	*ker*-lah	*køler*
road map	*vai*-koŕd	*vejkort*
tyres	dehg	*dæk*
windscreen	for-*ŕoo*-theh	*forrude*

DANISH

SIGNS

BLYFRI	UNLEADED
ENSRETTET	ONE WAY
GARAGE/AUTOVÆRKSTED	GARAGE
INDKØRSEL FORBUDT	NO ENTRY
MEKANIKER	MECHANIC
MOTORVEJ	FREEWAY
OKTAN	OCTANE
OMKØRSEL	DETOUR
PARKERING FORBUDT	NO PARKING
SELVBETJENING	SELF SERVICE
VEJARBEJDE	ROADWORKS
VIGEPLIGT	GIVE WAY

DANISH

ACCOMMODATION

Where is a ...?	vor ehŕ dah id ...?	*Hvor er der et ...?*
cheap hotel	*bee*-leed hor-*tehl*	*billigt hotel*
good hotel	god hor-*tehl*	*godt hotel*
nearby hotel	hor-*tehl* ee *nehŕ*-hith-ehn	*hotel i nærheden*

What's the address?
va ehŕ a-*dŕah*-sehn?   *Hvad er adressen?*
Could you write the address, please?
koo-neh dee *sgŕee*-w a-*dŕah*-sehn nith?   *Kunne De skrive adressen ned? (pol)*

At the Hotel

Do you have any rooms available?
hah ee *lith*-ee *vehŕl*-sah?   *Har I ledige værelser?*

I'd like ...	yai vi *gehŕ*-neh ha ...	*Jeg vil gerne have ...*
a single room	id *ehng*-gild-vehŕl-seh	*et enkeltværelse*
a double room	id *dob*-ehld-vehŕl-seh	*et dobbeltværelse*
to share a dorm	plas ee in *sow*-sahl	*plads i en sovesal*
a bed	in sehng	*en seng*

I want a room with a ...	yai vi *gehŕ*-neh ha id *vehŕl*-seh meh ...	*Jeg vil gerne have et værelse med ...*
bathroom	bath	*bad*
double bed	*do*-behld-sehng	*dobbeltseng*
shower	*bŕoo*-seh-bath	*brusebad*
TV	ti vi	*TV*
window	*vin*-doo	*vindue*

I'm going to stay for ...	yai bleeŕ ...	*Jeg bliver ...*
one day	in nad	*en nat*
two days	tor *nehd*-ah	*to nætter*
one week	in *oo*-eh	*en uge*

Do you have identification?
  hah dee/doo
  li-gee-tee-ma-*shorn*?

*Har De/du
legitimation?* (pol/inf)

Your (pl) membership card, please.
  yehŕs *mehth*-lehms-kord tahg

Jeres medlemskort, tak.

Sorry, we're full.
  bi-*kla*-ah ald ehŕ *ob*-ta-ehth

Beklager, alt er optaget.

How long will you (pl) be staying?
  vor *lehng*-eh bleeŕ ee?

Hvor længe bliver I?

How many nights?
  vor *mahng*-eh *neh*-dah?

Hvor mange nætter?

It's ... per day/per person.
  di *kos*-dah ... pehŕ da/
  pehŕ pehŕ-*sorn*

*Det koster ... per dag/
per person.*

How much is it per night/
per person?
  vor *mah*-eth *kos*-dah
  di pehŕ nad/pehŕ pehŕ-*sorn*?

*Hvor meget koster
det per nat/per person?*

Can I see it?
  mā yai si *vehŕl*-sehth?

Må jeg se værelset?

Are there any others?
  ehŕ dehŕ *ahn*-dŕah *vehŕl*-sah?

Er der andre værelser?

Are there any cheaper rooms?
  fin-ehs dehŕ *bee*-lee-ah
  vehŕl-sah?

*Findes der billigere
værelser?*

DANISH

DANISH

Can I see the bathroom?
   mā yai si *ba*-theh-vehŕl-sehth?   *Må jeg se badeværelset?*
Is there a reduction for
students/children?
   ehŕ dehŕ sdoo-*dehn*-dah-ŕah-bad/   *Er der studenterrabat/*
   ber-neh-ŕah-bad?   *børnerabat?*
Does it include breakfast?
   ehŕ *morn*-math ing-kloo-*di*-ahth?   *Er morgenmad inkluderet?*

It's fine, I'll take it.
   di ehŕ feend yai tah di   *Det er fint, jeg tager det.*
I'm not sure how long I'm staying.
   yai vith ig vo *lehng*-eh   *Jeg ved ikke hvor længe*
   yai bleeŕ   *jeg bliver.*

Where is the bathroom?
   vor ehŕ toy-*lehd*-ehth?   *Hvor er toilettet?*
Is there somewhere to wash clothes?
   ehŕ dehŕ id sdehth yai   *Er der et sted jeg*
   ka vas-geh toy?   *kan vaske tøj?*
Is there a lift?
   ehŕ dehŕ i-leh-*va*-tor?   *Er der elevator?*
Can I use the kitchen?
   mā yai bŕoo *kerg*-nehth?   *Må jeg bruge køkkenet?*
Can I use the telephone?
   mā yai bi-*ner*-deh   *Må jeg benytte*
   ti-leh-*for*-nehn?   *telefonen?*

SIGNS

CAMPINGPLADS	CAMPING GROUND
HOTEL	HOTEL
KRO	INN
MOTEL	MOTEL
PENSIONAT/HOTELPENSION	GUEST HOUSE
VANDREHJEM	YOUTH HOSTEL

Requests & Complaints

Please wake me up at ...
   koo-neh dee *veh*-geh
   mai *klog*-gehn ...?   *Kunne De vække*
                             mig klokken ...? (pol)

The room needs to be cleaned.
   vehŕl-sehth *tŕaing*-ah ti   *Værelset trænger til*
   ad blee gyooŕd ŕehnd   *at blive gjort rent.*

Please change the sheets.
   vi dee *vehn*-leesd *sgeef*-deh   *Vil De venligst skifte*
   sehng-eh-toy-yehth?   *sengetøjet?* (pol)

I can't open/close the window.
   yai ka ig *āb*-neh/   *Jeg kan ikke åbne/*
   lā-geh *vin*-doo-ehth   *lukke vinduet.*

I've locked myself out of my room.
   yai hah lāsd mai *oo*-theh   *Jeg har låst mig ude*
   a *vehŕl*-sehth   *af værelset.*

The toilet won't flush.
   toy-*lehd*-dehth *sger*-lah ig   *Toilettet skyller ikke.*

I don't like this room.
   yai süns ig om *di*-deh   *Jeg synes ikke om dette*
   vehŕl-seh   *værelse.*

It's (too) ...	di ehŕ (fo) ...	*Det er (for) ...*
small	*lee*-leh	*lille*
noisy	*sdoy*-yeh-neh	*støjende*
dark	mergd	*mørkt*
expensive	düŕd	*dyrt*

Some Useful Words & Phrases

I'm/We're leaving now/tomorrow.
   yai/vee *ŕai*-sah noo/i morn   *Jeg/Vi rejser nu/i morgen.*

I'd like to pay the bill.
   yai vi gehŕ-neh bi-*ta*-leh   *Jeg vil gerne betale*
   ŕai-ning-ehn   *regningen.*

DANISH

DANISH

name	naown	*navn*
surname	*ehf*-dah-naown	*efternavn*
address	a-*dŕah*-seh	*adresse*
room number	vehŕl-sehs-nām-mah	*værelsesnummer*
air-conditioning	*ehŕ*-kon-dee-shon	*aircondition*
balcony	bal-*kong*/al-*tan*	*balkon/altan*
bed	sehng	*seng*
bill	*ŕai*-ning	*regning*
blanket	*teh*-beh	*tæppe*
chair	sdorl	*stol*
clean	*ŕehn*	*ren*
dirty	*snaow*-sehth	*snavset*
doona	dü-neh	*dyne*
electricity	i-lehg-tŕee-see-*tid*	*elektricitet*
excluded	*ehgs*-kloo-siw	*ekslusive*
included	ing-kloo-*di*-ahth	*inkluderet*
key	*noy*-leh	*nøgle*
lift (elevator)	i-leh-*va*-tor	*elevator*
light bulb	i-*lehg*-tŕeesg pehŕ	*elektrisk pære*
lock	lās	*lås*
mattress	ma-*dŕahs*	*madras*
mirror	sbail	*spejl*
padlock	*hehng*-eh-lās	*hængelås*
pillow	*hor*-wehth-poo-theh	*hovedpude*
quiet	*sdil*-eh	*stille*
sheet	*la*-yehn	*lagen*
soap	*seh*-beh	*sæbe*
suitcase	*kāf*-ahd	*kuffert*
swimming pool	*sver*-meh-ba-sehng	*svømmebassin*
table	booŕ	*bord*
toilet	toy-*lehd*	*toilet*
toilet paper	toy-*lehd*-pah-peeŕ	*toiletpapir*
towel	*hon*-kleh-theh	*håndklæde*
water	van	*vand*
hot/cold water	vahmd/kold van	*varmt/koldt vand*

AROUND TOWN

I'm looking for ...	yai *li*-thah *ehf*-dah ...	*Jeg leder efter ...*
the art gallery	*kānsd*-moo-sehth	*kunstmuseet*
a bank	in bang-g	*en bank*
the church	*keeŕ*-gehn	*kirken*
the city centre	*sehn*-tŕām	*centrum*
the ...	dehn ...	*den ...*
embassy	ahm-ba-*sa*-theh	*ambassade*
my hotel	meed hor-*tehl*	*mit hotel*
a market	id *mah*-gehth	*et marked*
the museum	moo-*sehth*	*museet*
the police	por-lee-*tee*-ehth	*politiet*
the post office	*posd*-kon-toŕ-ehth	*postkontoret*
a public toilet	id *o*-fehnd-leed toy-*lehd*	*et offentligt toilet*
a telephone centre	in ti-leh-*forn*	*en telefon*
the tourist information office	too-*ŕeesd*-in-for-ma-shor-nehn	*turist-informationen*

DANISH

What time does it open/close?
 vo-*nor* āb-nah/*lā*-gah di?   *Hvornår åbner/lukker det?*

What street/suburb is this?
 vil-gehn *ga*-theh/   *Hvilken gade/*
 for-sdath ehŕ *di*-deh?   *forstad er dette?*

For directions, see the Getting Around section, page 28.

DANISH

At the Post Office

I'd like to send ...	yai vi *gehŕ*-neh sehn-eh ...	*Jeg vil gerne sende ...*
a letter	id *bŕeh*-w	*et brev*
a postcard	id *posd*-kord	*et postkort*
a parcel	in *pah*-geh	*en pakke*
a telegram	id ti-leh-*gŕahm*	*et telegram*

I'd like some stamps.
yai vi *gehŕ*-neh ha *nor*-leh *fŕee*-mehŕ-gah — *Jeg vil gerne have nogle frimærker.*

How much is the postage?
vor *mah*-eth ehŕ *poŕ*-tor-ehn? — *Hvor meget er portoen?*

How much does it cost to send this to ...?
vor *mah*-ehth *kos*-dah di ad *sehn*-eh *di*-deh ti ...? — *Hvor meget koster det at sende dette til ...?*

an aerogram	id eh-ŕor-*gŕahm*	*et aerogram*
air mail	*lāfd*-posd	*luftpost*
envelope	kon-vor-*lood*	*konvolut*
mailbox	*posd*-ka-seh	*postkasse*
parcel	*pah*-geh	*pakke*
registered mail	*ŕeh*-kom-man-di-ahth	*rekommanderet*
surface mail	*ow*-ah-fla-theh-posd	*overfladepost*

Telephone & Internet

I want to ring ...
yai vi *gehŕ*-neh *ŕehng*-eh ti ... — *Jeg vil gerne ringe til ...*

The number is ...
nām-mahth ehŕ ... — *Nummeret er ...*

I want to speak for three minutes.
yai vi *gehŕ*-neh *ta*-leh *tŕeh* mee-*noo*-dah — *Jeg vil gerne tale tre minutter.*

How much does a three-minute call cost?
vo *mah*-ehth *kos*-dah di fo *tŕeh* mee-*noo*-dah? — *Hvor meget koster det for tre minutter?*

How much does each extra
minute cost?
    vo *mah*-ehth *kos*-dah vehfd
    mee-*nood ebgs*-dfah?

*Hvor meget koster hvert
minut ekstra?*

I'd like to speak to (Mr Pedersen).
    yai vi *gehf*-neh *ta*-leh meh
    (hehf *pih*-dah-sehn)

*Jeg vil gerne tale med
(Hr. Pedersen).*

It's engaged.
    dah ehf *ob*-ta-ehth

Der er optaget.

I want to make a reverse-charges
phone call.
    yai *erns*-gah ad *morth*-ta-ahn
    sga bi-*ta*-leh

*Jeg ønsker at modtageren
skal betale.*

I've been cut off.
    yai bli *aow*-bfood

Jeg blev afbrudt.

Where can I get Internet access?
    vor ka yai for *in*-tuh-neht
    ath-guhng?

*Hvor kan jeg få
Internet adgang?*

I'd like to send an email.
    yai vil *gehf*-neh *sehn*-neh
    ehn *ee*-mayl

*Jeg vil gerne
sende en email.*

At the Bank

I want to exchange some money/
travellers cheques.
    yai vi *gehf*-neh *vehgs*-leh
    nor-leh *pehng*-eh/
    fai-seh-shehgs

*Jeg vil gerne veksle
nogle penge/
rejsechecks.*

What is the exchange rate?
    va ehf *koof*-sehn?

Hvad er kursen?

How many kroner per dollar?
    vo *mahng*-eh *kfor*-nah
    pehf *dol*-ah?

*Hvor mange kroner
per dollar?*

Can I have money transferred
here from my bank?
    ka yai få *pehng*-eh *ow*-ah-ferd
    hehf-*til* ffah meen *bahng*-g?

*Kan jeg få penge overført
hertil fra min bank?*

DANISH

How long will it take to arrive?
vo lahng teeth vi di ta
fer dee kom-ah?   *Hvor lang tid vil det tage*
                     før de kommer?

Has my money arrived yet?
ehŕ meen-eh pehng-eh
kom-ehth?   *Er mine penge*
                     kommet?

bank draft	*bahng-g-an-vees-ning*	*bankanvisning*
bank notes	*sehth-lah*	*sedler*
cashier	*ka-si-ah*	*kasserer*
coins	*mern-dah*	*mønter*
credit card	*kŕeh-deed-kord*	*kreditkort*
to exchange	*at vehg-sleh*	*at veksle*
loose change	*smo-pehng-eh*	*småpenge*
signature	*ān-ah-sgŕehfd*	*underskrift*

INTERESTS & ENTERTAINMENT
Sightseeing

Do you (pl) have a guidebook/
local map?
hah ee in ŕai-seh-hon-bāw/
id lor-kal-kord?   *Har I en rejsehåndbog/*
                      et lokalkort?

What are the main attractions?
va ehŕ hor-wehth-
a-tŕahg-shorn-ah-neh? *Hvad er*
                        hovedattraktionerne?

What is that?
va ehŕ di?   *Hvad er det?*

How old is it?
vo gah-mehl ehŕ
dehn/di?   *Hvor gammel er*
                        den/det?

Can I take photographs?
mā yai ta bil-thah?   *Må jeg tage billeder?*

What time does it open/close?
vo-nor āb-nah/
lāg-ah di?   *Hvornår åbner/*
                        lukker det?

ancient	*gah*-mehl/	*gammel*/
	hee-*stor*-feesg	*historisk*
archaeological	ah-keh-or-*lor*-isg	*arkæologisk*
beach	sdráhn	*strand*
building	*büg*-ning	*bygning*
castle	slod	*slot*
cathedral	ka-deh-*dráhl*/	*katedral*/
	dom-keef-geh	*domkirke*
church	*keef*-geh	*kirke*
concert hall	kon-*sehfd*-sal	*koncertsal*
library	beeb-lee-or-*tig*	*bibliotek*
main square	hor-wehth-tofw	*hovedtorv*
market	*mah*-gehth	*marked*
monastery	*klos*-dah	*kloster*
monument	mor-noo-*mehnd*	*monument*
mosque	mor-*sgi*	*moské*
the old city	dehn *gahm*-leh *bü*-dil	*den gamle bydel*
opera house	or-pi-*fah*-hoos	*operahus*
palace	pa-*las*	*palads*
ruins	foo-*een*-ah	*ruiner*
stadium	*sdad*-yon	*stadion*
statues	*sda*-too-ah	*statuer*
synagogue	sü-na-*gor*	*synagoge*
temple	*tehm*-behl	*tempel*
university	oo-nee-vehf-see-*tid*	*universitet*

DANISH

Going Out

What's there to do in the evenings?
va ehŕ dah o *la*-w om *ahfd*-nehn?

Hvad er der at lave om aftenen?

Are there any discos?
ehŕ dah dees-gor-*ti*-gah?

Er der diskoteker?

Are there places where you can hear local folk music?
fin-ehs dah *sdeh*-thah vor man ka *her*-ah *lor*-kal *fol*-geh-moo-seeg?

Findes der steder hvor man kan høre lokal folkemusik?

How much does it cost to get in?	vo *mah*-eth *kos*-dah di ad *kom*-eh in?	*Hvor meget koster det at komme ind?*
cinema	bi-or-*gŕahf*	*biograf*
concert	kon-*sehŕd*	*koncert*
discotheque	dees-gor-*tig*	*diskotek*
theatre	ti-*a*-dah	*teater*

Sports & Interests

What do you do in your spare time?
va *la*-wah doo ee deen *fŕee*-teeth?

Hvad laver du i din fritid? (inf)

What sport do you play?
vil-gehn spord *düŕ*-gah doo?

Hvilken sport dyrker du? (inf)

art	kānsd	*kunst*
basketball	*bah*-sgehd-borl	*basketball*
boxing	*bogs*-ning	*boksning*
cooking	math-la-w-ning	*madlavning*
fishing	fis-gah-*ŕee*	*fiskeri*
going out	gor ee *bü*-ehn	*gå i byen*
going to the cinema	gor ee bee-or-*gŕahf*-ehn	*gå i biografen*
music	moo-*seeg*	*musik*
photography	for-tor-gŕah-*fi*-ŕing	*fotografering*
reading	*leh*-seh	*læse*
rugby	*ŕog*-bee	*rugby*
shopping	*han*-leh	*handle*
soccer	*forth*-bold	*fodbold*
sport	sbord	*sport*
the theatre	ti-*a*-dahth	*teatret*
travelling	*ŕai*-seh	*rejse*
writing	*sgŕee*-weh	*skrive*

DANISH

Festivals

In Denmark the main Christmas celebration takes place on the evening of 24 December, juleaften. The Christmas tree, juletræ, is normally decorated with home-made paper hearts and tinsel. After dinner, which traditionally consists of duck, and and/or roast pork, flæskesteg, followed by ris a l'amande, the family join hands and 'dance' around the tree singing julesalmer (Christmas carols). If you want to exchange Christmas greetings with a Dane, the phrase is god/glædelig jul (merry Christmas).

Fastelavn (Shrovetide) celebrations take place seven weeks before Easter. Children get fastelavnsris, birch rods decorated with sweets and paper cats. During the day they dress up in fancy costumes and walk from door to door singing, for which they receive sweets. A traditional Shrovetide game involves a barrel (fastelavnstønde) full of sweets hanging from a rope, which children take turns to try to break with a bat. During Shrovetide people eat fastelavnsboller (Shrovetide buns).

Påske (Easter) goes from Maundy Thursday (skærtorsdag), including Good Friday (langfredag), until the Monday after Easter Sunday. Traditionally, children look for påskeæg (Easter eggs) hidden by påskeharen (the Easter bunny) on Easter Sunday (påskesøndag), or they paint their own Easter eggs. The Easter greeting in Denmark is god påske (happy Easter).

Pinse (Whitsun) is a Christian holiday on the seventh Sunday after Easter which includes pinsedag (Whit Sunday) and anden pinsedag (Whit Monday). People greet each other with god pinse (Happy Whitsun).

Music festivals play a big role in weekend outdoor entertainment during the Danish summer.

Probably the biggest international music event in Denmark, Roskilde Festival takes place near the town of Roskilde. It attracts as many as 70,000 visitors from all over Europe and spans a huge variety of music, including rock, pop, folk and ethnic music.

Midtfynsfestival, on the island of Funen, is a smaller version of Roskilde, focusing on rock and pop.

Langelandsfestival is a family festival that takes place on the island of Langeland, with a focus on rock, folk and popular music, and lots of fun for kids.

Copenhagen Jazz Festival runs for several weeks over summer. It attracts many brilliant (primarily Danish but also international) jazz, folk and blues artists.

MAD MEAL!

After a meal you should always say Tak for mad (thanks for the meal) before getting up.

IN THE COUNTRY
Weather

What's the weather like?

vo-*dan* ehf *vehf*-ehth?   *Hvordan er vejret?*

It's ... today.	di ehf ... ee da	*Det er ... i dag.*
Will it be ...	bleer di ...	*Bliver det ...*
tomorrow?	ee morn?	*i morgen?*
cloudy	*ow*-ah-sgü-ehth	*overskyet*
cold	kold	*koldt*
foggy	*tä*-wehth	*tåget*
frosty	*ffosd*-vehf	*frostvejr*
hot	vahmd	*varmt*
raining	*fain*-vehf	*regnvejr*
snowing	sni-vehf	*snevejr*
sunny	*sorl*-sgins-vehf	*solskinsvejr*
windy	*bleh*-seh-vehf	*blæsevejr*

Camping

Am I allowed to camp here?

mä yai kahm-*pi*-ah hehf?   *Må jeg campere her?*

Is there a campsite nearby?

fin-ehs dah in *kahm*-ping-plas   *Findes der en campingplads*
ee *nehf*-hith-ehn?   *i nærheden?*

backpack	*ferg*-sehg	*rygsæk*
can opener	*dä*-seh-*äb*-nah	*dåseåbner*
compass	kom-*pas*	*kompas*
crampons	*klad*-fah-yehfn	*klatrejern*
firewood	*bfahn*-eh	*brænde*
gas cartridge	*gas*-bi-hol-ah	*gasbeholder*
hammock	*hehng*-eh-koy-yeh	*hængekøje*
ice axe	*ees*-erg-seh	*isøkse*
mattress	ma-*dfahs*	*madras*
penknife	*lom*-eh-knee-w	*lommekniv*
rope	tow	*tov*
sleeping bag	*sow*-eh-por-seh	*sovepose*

DANISH

DANISH

stove	*kahm*-ping-vown	*campingovn*
tent	tehld	*telt*
tent pegs	*tehld*-peh-leh	*teltpæle*
torch (flashlight)	*lom*-eh-lerg-deh	*lommelygte*
water bottle	*fehld*-flas-geh	*feltflaske*

FOOD

Traditional Danish cooking is dominated by, although not to the same extent as the other Scandinavian countries, smoked, cured, pickled or otherwise preserved food, due to the short growing season and long winters. Regional variations are not strong, although proximity to the ocean flavours menus with seafood.

breakfast	*morn*-math	*morgenmad*
lunch	*frā*-kosd	*frokost*
dinner	mi-da/*ahf*-dehns-math	*middag/aftensmad*

Table for ..., please.
    id boof ti ... tahg   *Et bord til ..., tak.*
Can I see the menu please?
    mā yai si mi-*nü*-ehn?   *Må jeg se menuen?*
I'd like the set menu, please.
    yai tah *dah*-ehns fahd tahg   *Jeg tager dagens ret, tak.*
What does it include?
    va ing-kloo-*di*-ah dehn?   *Hvad inkluderer den?*
Not too spicy please.
    ig fo *kŕerth*-fahth tahg   *Ikke for krydret, tak.*

Vegetarian Meals

I'm a vegetarian.
    yai ehŕ veh-geh-*tah*   *Jeg er vegetar.*
I don't eat meat.
    yai *sbees*-ah ig kerth   *Jeg spiser ikke kød.*
I don't eat chicken, or fish, or pork.
    yai *sbees*-ah ig *kü*-ling eh-lah   *Jeg spiser ikke kylling eller*
    fisg eh-lah *svee*-neh-kerth   *fisk eller svinekød.*

ashtray	*as*-geh-beh-ah	askebæger
the bill	*rai*-ning-ehn	regningen
a cup	in kob	en kop
dessert	di-*sehrd*	dessert
a drink	in *dring*-g	en drink (always alcoholic)
a fork	in *gahf*-ehl	en gaffel
fresh	fehrsg/frehsg	fersk/frisk
a glass	id glas	et glas
a knife	in knee-w	en kniv
a plate	in ta-*lehr*-gehn	en tallerken
spicy	*krerth*-fahth	krydret
a spoon	in sgi	en ske
stale	*gah*-mehl/*dor*-lee	gammel/dårlig
sweet	serth	sød
a teaspoon	in *ti*-sgi	en teske
toothpicks	*tan*-sdi-gah	tandstikker

DANISH

Staple Foods & Condiments

beef	*og*-seh-kerth	oksekød
bread	*brerth	brød
butter	smer	smør
cucumber	a-*goorg*	agurk
garlic	*vith*-loy	hvidløg
meat	kerth	kød
mustard	*seh*-nob	sennep
mutton	lahm	lam
oil	*orl*-yeh	olie
pasta	*pas*-da	pasta
pepper	*pi*-wah	peber
pork	*svee*-neh-kerth	svinekød
potatoes	kah-*tof*-lah	kartofler
rice	*fees	ris
salt	sald	salt
sugar	*sā*-gah	sukker
veal	*kal*-veh-kerth	kalvekød
vegetables	*grern*-sa-ah	grønsager
vinegar	*ith*-geh	eddike

DANISH

MENU DECODER

Breakfast Menu

cheese	*äsd*	ost
coffee	*kaf*-eh	kaffe
corn flakes	*koorn*-flehgs	cornflakes
fried egg	*spail*-ehg	spejlæg
(always sunny side up)		
fruit	frägd	frugt
hardboiled egg	*hor*-kogd ehg	hårdkogt æg
jam	*sül*-deh-toy	syltetøj
milk	mehlg	mælk
oatmeal	*hah*-wah-grün	havregryn
porridge	*hah*-wah-grerth	havregrød
scrambled eggs	*rehr*-ehg	røræg
softboiled egg	*blerth*-kogd ehg	blødkogt æg
tea	ti	te
toast	*rís*-dehht brerth/	ristet brød/
	täwsd	toast
yoghurt	*yoo*-goord	yoghurt

Sandwiches

bøftartar   *berf*-ta-tah
   beef tartar – raw ground beef topped with a raw egg
   yolk, onion and capers

dyrlægens natmad   *dür*-leh-ehns *nad*-math
   'the veterinarian's midnight snack' – liver paté topped
   with a thin slice of salt beef, raw onions and beef jelly

gravad laks   *gráh*-wath lahgs
   cured salmon

leverpostej   *li*-wah-por-sdai
   liver paté

marineret sild   mah-ee-*ni*-ath seel
   pickled herring; served with raw onions

ostemad   äs-deh-math
   cheese – Denmark is famous for its cheeses, and
   produces an enormous variety

rejemad   *rai*-yeh-mahht
   small shrimp served with mayonnaise and lemon slices

røget laks   *róy-*yehth lahgs
   smoked salmon, served with scrambled eggs
røget sild   *róy-*yehth seel
   smoked herring on rye bread with chives and a raw egg yolk
røget ål   *róy-*yehth ål
   smoked eel, a delicacy

baguette	*frahns-*bŕerth	franskbrød
bread	bŕerth	brød
crusty roll	*rän-*sder-geh	rundstykke
Danish pastry	*vee-*nah-bŕerth	wienerbrød
rye bread	*róo-*bŕerth	rugbrød
soft roll	*bol-*eh	bolle

> **Danish Delights**
> Danish open rye bread sandwiches are ornate and tasty
> – a feast for the eye and a delight to the palate!

øllebrød   *er-*leh-bŕerth
   a smooth beer and bread dish, a bit like porridge, served
   hot with milk or whipped cream

Soup
fiskesuppe   *fís-*geh-sä-beh
   fish soup, usually creamy
grønsagssuppe   *gŕern-*sas-sä-beh
   vegetable soup
gule ærter   *goo-*leh *ehŕ-*dah
   split pea soup served with pork
hønsekødssuppe   *hern-*seh-kerth-sä-beh
   chicken soup

Meat
bankekød   *bahng-*geh-kerth
   similar to Wienerschnitzel
boller i karry   *bol-*ah ee kah-ee
   meat balls in a curry sauce, served with rice or potatoes
bøf med løg   berf meh loy
   hamburger served with fried onions, potatoes and
   brown gravy

DANISH

flæskeæggekage (*flehs*-geh)-eh-geh-ka-eh
    egg dish with bacon (a bit like an omelette, but made
    with flour)
flæskesteg   *flehs*-geh-sdai
    pork roast with crispy crackling, served with potatoes,
    brown gravy and pickled cucumbers
frikadeller   fri-ga-*dehl*-ah
    meat patties made of pork, veal and onion served with
    potatoes, brown gravy, and pickled cucumbers
fyldt   füld
hvidkålshoved   *veeth*-käls-hor-wehth
    cabbage leaves wrapped around ground beef
medisterpølse   mi-*dees*-dah-*perl*-seh
    large fried sausage served with potatoes, brown gravy
    and pickled cucumbers
spaghetti med   sba-*gehd*-dee meh
kødsovs   *kerth*-sows
    spaghetti with ground beef in a tomato sauce
stegt flæsk med   sdehgd flehsg meh
persillesovs   pehf-*sil*-eh-sows
    thick slices of fried bacon with potatoes and a white
    parsley sauce

chicken	*kül*-ing	kylling
duck	an	and
hamburger	*hag*-eh-berf	hakkebøf
meat chops	ko-deh-*leh*-dah	koteletter
roast beef	*og*-seh-sdai	oksesteg
roast lamb	*lahm*-meh-sdai	lammesteg
roast pork	*flehs*-geh-sdai	flæskesteg
sausage	*perl*-seh	pølse
sirloin	*mer*-bfah	mørbrad
steak	*ehng*-ehlsg berf	engelsk bøf
turkey	kal-*koon*	kalkun

Denmark is a major meat exporter, and is best known
for its pork, ham and bacon.

Seafood

kogt torsk   kogd torsg
  poached cod in a mustard sauce served with boiled potatoes
stegt sild   sdehgd seel
  fried herring served with potatoes and a white parsley sauce
stegt ål med   sdehgd ål meh
stuvede kartofler   *sdoo*-weh-theh kah-*tof*-lah
  fried eel with boiled potatoes in a white sauce

cod	torsk	torsk
fish	*fis*-g	fisk
haddock	*kool*-ah	kuller
halibut	*hehl*-eh-flün-ah	helleflynder
herring	seel	sild
plaice	*rerth*-sbeh-deh	rødspætte
salmon	lahgs	laks
shrimp	*rai*-yah	rejer
sole	*ser*-täng-eh	søtunge
trout	for-*rahl*	forel

Vegetables

asparagus	a-*sbahs*	asparges
beets	rerth-*bi*-thah	rødbeder
(usually served pickled)		
broccoli	*bro*-kor-lee	broccoli
cabbage	kål	kål
carrots	*goo*-leh-*rerth*-ah	gulerødder
cauliflower	*blom*-kål	blomkål
celery	*blath*-si-lah-*ree*	bladselleri
cucumber	a-*goorg*	agurk
lettuce	*grern* sa-*lad*	grøn salat
mushrooms	*shahm*-pin-yong-ah	champignoner
onions	loy	løg
peas	*ehr*-dah	ærter
pickled	*soord*/	surt/
cucumbers	*sül*-dehth a-*goor*-gah	syltede agurker
potato	kah-*tof*-ehl	kartoffel
rice	*rees*	ris
string beans	*snee*-deh-bern-ah	snittebønner
tomatoes	tor-*ma*-dah	tomater

DANISH

Fruit

apple	*eh*-bleh	æble
banana	ba-*nayn*	banan
grapes	*vin*-droo-ah	vindruver
lemon	sit-*rorn*	citron
orange	ah-behl-*seen*	appelsin
pear	*peh*-rah	pære
strawberry	*yor*-behr	jordbær

Desserts

budding   *boo*-thing
  a kind of pudding flavoured with, for example, rum or
  almonds, served warm
chokoladeis/   shor-gor-*la*-theh-ees/
vanilleis   va-*neel*-yeh-ees
  chocolate ice cream/vanilla ice cream
fromage   fror-*ma*-sheh
  a kind of mousse served cold flavoured with, for example,
  lemon
jordbær   *yor*-behr
med fløde   meh *fler*-theh
  strawberries with cream
kage   *ka*-eh
  cake
konditorkager   kon-*dee*-dah-ka-ah
  French pastries
rødgrød   *rerth*-grerth
med fløde   meh *fler*-theh
  fruit pudding (red currant, raspberry, strawberry) served
  with cream
pandekager   *pa*-neh-ka-ah
  crepes rolled around a jam, sugar, or ice cream filling

Non-Alcoholic Drinks

apple juice	*eh*-bleh-djoos	*æblejuice*
cordial	*sahf*-deh-van	*saftevand*
coffee (with cream)	*kah*-feh (meh *fler*-theh)	*kaffe (med fløde)*
orange juice	ah-behl-*seen*-djoos	*appelsinjuice*
skim milk	*sgā*-mehth-mehlg	*skummetmælk*
soft drink/	*sor*-da-van/	*sodavand/*
carbonated water	*dansg*-van	*danskvand*
tea	ti	*te*
water/ice water	van/*ees*-van	*vand/isvand*
full cream milk	*serth*-mehlg	*sødmælk*

Alcoholic Drinks

øl	erl	beer/lager
hvidvin	*veeth*-veen	white wine
rødvin	*rerth*-veen	red wine

bajer   *bay*-yah
  beer – specifically means a darker beer more like ale, but
  is used colloquially to mean any beer
snaps/akvavit   snahbs/ak-va-*veed*
  various kinds of clear grain alcohol flavoured with different
  herbs, often with caraway. Traditionally consumed with
  pickled herring.
bitter   *bi*-dah
  a darker variant of snaps flavoured with different herbs.
  The most popular kinds are Jägermeister and Gammel
  Dansk. Believed to help settle an uneasy stomach and consumed either at breakfast or with beer.

DANISH

SKÅL OR SKULL?

When Danes raise their glasses to you and say Skål! it
means 'Cheers!', not to be confused with the Australian
concept 'to skull', meaning emptying your drink in one go!
Also, be prepared to say Skål! a lot more than once
during a meal.

DANISH

AT THE MARKET

Basics

bread	bŕerth	brød
butter	smer	smør
cheese	āsd	ost
chocolate	sho-koh-la-theh	chokolade
eggs	ehg	æg
flour	meh-l	mel
jam	sül-deh-toy	syltetøj
margarine	mah-gah-ree-neh	margarine
marmalade	mah-meh-la-theh	marmelade
milk	mehlg	mælk
oil	orl-yeh	olie
pasta	pas-da	pasta
rice	ŕees	ris
sugar	sā-gah	sukker
carbonated water	dansg-van	danskvand
water	van	vand
yoghurt	yoo-gooŕd	yoghurt

Meat & Poultry

beef	og-seh-kerth	oksekød
chicken	kül-ing	kylling
duck	an	and
ham	skin-keh	skinke
meat	kerth	kød
mutton	lahm	lam
pork	svee-neh-kerth	svinekød
sausage	perl-seh	pølse
veal	kal-veh-kerth	kalvekød

Vegetables

beets	ŕerth-bi-thah	rødbeder
broccoli	bŕo-kor-lee	broccoli
cabbage	kāl	kål

AT THE MARKET

carrots	*goo*-leh-ŕerth-ah	gulerødder
cauliflower	*blom*-kål	blomkål
celery	*blath*-si-lah-ŕee	bladselleri
cucumber	a-*goorg*	agurk
lettuce	gŕern sa-*lad*	grøn salat
mushrooms	*shahm*-pin-yong-ah	champignoner
onions	loy	løg
peas	*ehŕ*-dah	ærter
pickled	*soord*/	surt/
cucumbers	*sül*-dehth a-*goor*-gah	syltede agurker
potato	kah-*tof*-ehl	kartoffel
string beans	*snee*-deh-bern-ah	snittebønner
tomatoes	tor-*ma*-dah	tomater
vegetables	*gŕern*-sa-ah	grønsager

DANISH

Seafood
cod	torsk	torsk
fish	*fis*-g	fisk
herring	seel	sild
salmon	lahgs	laks
shrimp	*ŕai*-yah	rejer
sole	*ser*-tãng-eh	søtunge
trout	for-*ŕahl*	forel

Fruit
apple	*eh*-bleh	æble
banana	ba-*nayn*	banan
fruit	fŕägd	frugt
grapes	*vin*-droo-ah	vindruver
lemon	sit-*ŕorn*	citron
orange	ah-behl-*seen*	appelsin
pear	*peh*-ŕah	pære
strawberry	*yoŕ*-behŕ	jordbær

SHOPPING

bookshop	*bāw*-han-ehl	boghandel
camera shop	*for*-tor-han-ehl	fotohandel
clothing store	*toy*-boo-teeg	tøjbutik
delicatessen	de-lee-ka-*teh*-seh-fo-ŕahd-ning	delikatesseforretning
general store/shop	boo-*teeg*	butik
laundry	vas-gah-ŕee	vaskeri
market	*mah*-gehth	marked
newsagency	a-*vees*-kee-yosg	aviskiosk
pharmacy	ah-por-*tig*	apotek
shoeshop	*sgor*-toys-fo-ŕahd-ning	skotøjsforretning
souvenir shop	soo-veh-*neer*-boo-teeg	souvenirbutik
stationers	pah-*peer*-han-ehl	papirhandel
supermarket	*soo*-bah-mah-gehth	supermarked
vegetable shop	*ǵernd*-han-lah	grønthandler

I'd like to buy ...
yai vi *gehŕ*-neh ha ... — *Jeg vil gerne have ...*
How much is it?
vo *mah*-ehth *kos*-dah di? — *Hvor meget koster det?*
Do you (inf) have others?
hah doo *an*-ehth? — *Har du andet?*
I don't like it.
dehn/di ka yai ig li — *Den/Det kan jeg ikke lide.*
Can I look at it?
mā yai si dehn/di? — *Må jeg se den/det?*
I'm just looking.
yai *kee*-gah bah — *Jeg kikker bare.*
Can you write down the price?
ka doo *sgŕee*-w *pŕee*-sehn nith? — *Kan du skrive prisen ned?*
Do you accept credit cards?
tah ee *kŕeh*-*deed*-kord? — *Tager I kreditkort?*

Can I help you?
ka yai *yehl*-beh dehm?   *Kan jeg hjælpe Dem? (pol)*

Will that be all?
ehf di di *hi*-leh?   *Er det det hele?*

Would you like it wrapped?
ern-sgah dee di   *Ønsker De det*
pah-gehth in?   *pakket ind? (pol)*

Sorry, this is the only one.
dis-*vehf di*-deh ehf   *Desværre, dette er*
dehn *i*-nehs-deh   *den eneste.*

How much/many do you want?
vo *mah*-ehth/*mahng*-eh   *Hvor meget/mange*
ern-sgah dee?   *ønsker De? (pol)*

Essential Groceries

bread	b*f*erth	*brød*
butter	smer	*smør*
milk	mehlg	*mælk*
rice	*f*ees	*ris*
salt	sald	*salt*
shampoo	*sham*-por	*shampoo*
sugar	*sä*-gah	*sukker*
toilet paper	toy-*lehd*-pah-pee*f*	*toiletpapir*
toothpaste	*tan*-pas-da	*tandpasta*
vegetables	g*f*ern-sa-ah	*grønsager*

Souvenirs

earrings	er-*f*ing-eh	*øreringe*
handicraft	*känsd*-hon-veh*f*g	*kunsthåndværk*
necklace	*hals*-keh-theh	*halskæde*
pottery	ki-ah-*meeg*	*keramik*
ring	*f*ing	*ring*
rug	*teh*-beh	*tæppe*

DANISH

DANISH

Clothing

clothing	toy	tøj
coat	*frah*-geh	frakke
dress	*kyor*-leh	kjole
jacket	*yah*-geh	jakke
jumper (sweater)	*sweh*-dah	sweater
shirt	*sgyor*-deh	skjorte
shoes	sgor	sko
skirt	*nith*-ah-dil	nederdel
trousers	*bāg*-sah	bukser
It doesn't fit.	dehn *pas*-ah ig	Den passer ikke.
It's too ...	dehn ehí fo ...	Den er for ...
big	sdoor	stor
small	*lee*-leh	lille
short	kord	kort
long	lahng	lang
tight	sdrahm	stram
loose	lers	løs

Materials

cotton	*bom*-ool	bomuld
handmade	*hon*-la-wehth	håndlavet
leather	*lehth*-ah	læder
brass	*mehs*-sing	messing
gold	gool	guld
silver	serl	sølv
silk	*sil*-geh	silke
wool	ool	uld

Colours

black	sord	sort
blue	blā	blå
brown	broon	brun
green	grern	grøn

orange	or-*rang*-sheh	*orange*
pink	*ror*-sa	*rosa*
purple	*li*-la	*lilla*
red	*rerth*	*rød*
white	veeth	*hvid*
yellow	gool	*gul*

Toiletries

comb	kahm	*kam*
condoms	kon-*dorm*-ah	*kondomer*
deodorant	di-or-dor-*rahnd*	*deodorant*
hairbrush	*hor*-bers-deh	*hårbørste*
moisturising cream	*fåg*-dee-hiths-krehm	*fugtighedscreme*
razor	bah-*bir*-knee-w	*barberkniv*
sanitary napkins	bin	*bind*
shampoo	shahm-poo	*shampoo*
shaving cream	bah-*bir*-krehm	*barbercreme*
soap	*seh*-beh	*sæbe*
sunblock cream	*sorl*-krehm	*solcreme*
tampons	tahm-*pong*-ah	*tamponer*
tissues	*rahn*-seh-sehr-vee-ehd	*renseserviet*
toilet paper	toy-*lehd*-pah-peer	*toiletpapir*
toothbrush	*tan*-bers-deh	*tandbørste*
toothpaste	*tan*-pas-da	*tandpasta*

Stationery & Publications

map	kord	*kort*
newspaper	a-*vees*	*avis*
newspaper in English	a-*vees* på *ehng*-ehlsg	*avis på engelsk*
novels in English	*ro-man*-ah	*romaner*
	på *ehng*-ehlsg	*på engelsk*
paper	pa-*peer*	*papir*
pen (ballpoint)	*koo*-leh-pehn	*kuglepen*
scissors	sahgs	*saks*

DANISH

DANISH

Photography

How much is it to process this film?
vo *mah*-ehth *kos*-dah
di ad *frahm*-ka-leh
dehn-neh feelm?

*Hvor meget koster det
at fremkalde
denne film?*

When will it be ready?
vo-*nor* ehr dehn *fehr*-dee?

Hvornår er den færdig?

I'd like a film for this camera.
yai vi *gerh*-neh ha in feelm
ti *deh*-deh ka-meh-*rah*

*Jeg vil gerne have en film
til dette kamera.*

B&W (film)	*sord*-veeth	*sort-hvid*
camera	*ka*-meh-*rah*	*kamera*
colour (film)	*fah*-weh	*farve*
film	feelm	*film*
flash	bleeds	*blitz*
lens	ob-yehg-*tee*-w	*objektiv*
light meter	*lüs*-mā-lah	*lysmåler*

Smoking

A packet of cigarettes, please.
in *pah*-geh
see-gah-*rah*-dah tahg

*En pakke
cigaretter, tak.*

Are these cigarettes strong/mild?
ehr *dees*-eh see-gah-*rah*-dah
sdehr-geh/*meel*-eh?

*Er disse cigaretter
stærke/milde?*

Do you have a light?
hah doo il?

Har du ild? (inf)

cigarette papers	see-gah-*rahd*-pah-peer	*cigaretpapir*
cigarettes	see-gah-*rah*-dah	*cigaretter*
filtered	meh *feel*-dah	*med filter*
lighter	*lai*-dah	*lighter*
matches	*tehn*-sdig-ah	*tændstikker*
menthol	mehn-*torl*	*mentol*
pipe	*pee*-beh	*pibe*
tobacco (pipe)	*pee*-be-tor-bahg	*pibetobak*

Sizes & Comparisons

small	*lee*-leh	*lille*
big	*sdoor*	*stor*
heavy	tāng	*tung*
light	lehd	*let*
more	*mi*-ah	*mere*
less	min-*drah*	*mindre*
too much/many	fo *mah*-ehth/	*for meget/*
	mahng-eh	*mange*
many	mahng-eh	*mange*
enough	nog	*nok*
also	os-eh	*også*
a little bit	in *lee*-leh *smoo*-leh	*en lille smule*

DANISH

HEALTH

Where is the ...?	*vor* ehr ...?	*Hvor er ...?*
hospital	hors-bi-*ta*-lehth	*hospitalet*
chemist	ah-por-*tig*-ehth	*apoteket*
the casualty ward	sga-theh-sdoo-ehn	*skadestuen*

Where is a ...?	*vor* ehr dehr in ...?	*Hvor er der en ...?*
doctor	*leh*-eh	*læge*
dentist	*tan*-leh-eh	*tandlæge*

I'm sick.
  yai ehr sü   *Jeg er syg.*
My friend is sick.
  meen vehn ehr sü   *Min ven er syg.*
Could I see a female doctor?
  mā yai fā in *kvin*-lee *leh*-eh?   *Må jeg få en kvindelig læge?*
What's the matter?
  va ehr dah ee *vai*-yehn?   *Hvad er der i vejen?*

DANISH

Where does it hurt?   *Hvor gør det ondt?*
  vof ger di ānd?
It hurts here.   *Det gør ondt her.*
  di ger ānd heef
My ... hurts.   *Min/mit ... gør ondt.*
  meen/meed ... ger ānd

Parts of the Body

ankle	*ahng*-gehl	*ankel*
arm	ahm	*arm*
back	ferg	*ryg*
chest	bfersd	*bryst*
ear	*er*-ah	*øre*
eye	*oy*-yeh	*øje*
finger	*fing*-ah	*finger*
foot	forth	*fod*
hand	hon	*hånd*
head	*hor*-wehth	*hoved*
heart	*yehf*-deh	*hjerte*
leg	bin	*ben*
mouth	mān	*mund*
ribs	*ree*-bin	*ribben*
skin	hooth	*hud*
stomach	*ma*-weh	*mave*
teeth	*tehn*-ah	*tænder*
throat	hals	*hals*

Ailments

I have (a/an) ...	yai hah ...	*Jeg har ...*
allergy	a-lah-*gee*	*allergi*
anaemia	a-neh-*mee*	*anæmi*
blister	in *va*-behl	*en vabel*
burn	id *bŕahn*-sor	*et brandsår*
cold	in fo-*kerl*-seh	*en forkølelse*
constipation	fo-*sdob*-ehl-seh	*forstoppelse*
cough	*hors*-deh	*hoste*
diarrhoea	dee-a-*ŕeh*	*diarré*
fever	*fi*-bah	*feber*
headache	*hor*-wehth-pee-neh	*hovedpine*
hepatitis	hi-pa-*tee*-tees	*hepatitis*
indigestion	*ma*-weh-bi-svehŕ	*mavebesvær*
infection	in in-fehg-*shorn*	*en infektion*
influenza	in-floo-*ehn*-sa	*influenza*
lice	loos	*lus*
low/high	*la*-wd/hoyd	*lavt/højt*
blood pressure	*blorth*-tŕerg	*blodtryk*
sore throat	ānd ee *hal*-sehn	*ondt i halsen*
sprain	in fo-*sdoo*-ning	*en forstuvning*
stomachache	ānd ee *ma*-wehn	*ondt i maven*
temperature	*fi*-bah	*feber*
venereal disease	in *kerns*-sü-dom	*en kønssygdom*
worms	oofm	*orm*

DANISH

Some Useful Words & Phrases

I'm ...	yai hah ...	*Jeg har ...*
asthmatic	*asd*-ma	*astma*
diabetic	dee-a-*bi*-tehs	*diabetes*
epileptic	eh-pee-lehb-*see*	*epilepsi*

I'm allergic to antibiotics/penicillin.
  yai ehŕ a-*lehŕ*-geesg *ow*-ah   *Jeg er allergisk over*
  fo an-tee-bee-*or*-tee-ka/   *for antibiotika/*
  pin-ee-see-*leen*   *penicillin.*

DANISH

I'm pregnant.
    yai ehŕ gŕah-*veeth*   *Jeg er gravid.*
I'm on the pill.
    yai *bŕoo*-ah *pi*-pil-lah   *Jeg bruger p-piller.*
I haven't had my period for ... months.
    yai hah ig hahfd   *Jeg har ikke haft*
    mins-dŕoo-ah-*shorn* ee ... *menstruation i ...*
    mā-neh-thah   *måneder.*
I have been vaccinated.
    yai ehŕ *bli*-wehth   *Jeg er blevet*
    vahg-see-*ni*-ahth   *vaccineret.*
I have my own syringe.
    yai hah meen *ai*-yehn ka-*nü*-leh   *Jeg har min egen kanyle.*
I feel better/worse.
    yai hah di *behht*-ah/*vehŕ*-ah   *Jeg har det bedre/værre.*

At the Chemist

I need medication for ...
    yai sga *bŕoo*-eh nā-ehth   *Jeg skal bruge noget*
    mi-dee-*seen* morth ...   *medicin mod ...*
I have a prescription.
    yai hah in ŕeh-*sehbd*   *Jeg har en recept.*

At the Dentist

I have a toothache.
    yai hah *tan*-pee-neh   *Jeg har tandpine.*
I've lost a filling.
    yai hah tahbd en *plām*-beh *Jeg har tabt en plombe.*
I've broken a tooth.
    yai hah *kneh*-gehth in tan *Jeg har knækket en tand.*
My gums hurt.
    meed *tan*-kerth ger ānd   *Mit tandkød gør ondt.*
I don't want it extracted.
    yai vi ig ha dehn   *Jeg vil ikke have den*
    tŕā-gehth ooth   *trukket ud.*
Please give me an anaesthetic.
    yai vi *gehŕ*-neh bi-*der*-wehs   *Jeg vil gerne bedøves.*

Some Useful Words

accident	*oo*-ler-geh	*ulykke*
addiction	ahw-*hehng*-ee-hith	*afhængighed*
aspirin	as-bee-*reen*	*aspirin*
a bandage	in ban-*da*-sheh	*en bandage*
blood test	*blorth*-pfer-veh	*blodprøve*
contraception	*pfeh*-vehn-*shorn*	*prævention*
medicine	mi-dee-*seen*	*medicin*
menstruation	mins-*dfo*-oah-*shorn*	*menstruation*
nausea	*kval*-meh	*kvalme*
oxygen	og-sü-*gin*/eeld	*oxygen/ilt*
vitamins	vee-ta-*meen*-ah	*vitaminer*

DANISH

TIME & DATES

What date is it today?
    vil-gehn *da*-tor ehf di ee da?   *Hvilken dato er det i dag?*
What time is it?
    va ehf *klog*-gehn?   *Hvad er klokken?*
It's ... am/pm.
    klog-gehn ehf ...   *Klokken er ...*
    om *morn*-n/*ahfd*-nehn   *om morgenen/aftenen.*

in the morning	om *morn*	*om morgenen*
in the afternoon	om *ehf*-dah-mi-da-ehn	*om eftermiddagen*
in the evening	om *ahfd*-nehn	*om aftenen*

Days of the Week

Monday	*man*-da	*mandag*
Tuesday	*teefs*-da	*tirsdag*
Wednesday	*āns*-da	*onsdag*
Thursday	*tofs*-da	*torsdag*
Friday	*ffeh*-da	*fredag*
Saturday	*ler*-da	*lørdag*
Sunday	*sern*-da	*søndag*

DANISH

Months

January	*yan*-oo-ah	*januar*
February	*feb*-foo-ah	*februar*
March	mahds	*marts*
April	a-*preel*	*april*
May	mai	*maj*
June	*yoo*-nee	*juni*
July	*yoo*-lee	*juli*
August	ahw-*gāsd*	*august*
September	sib-*tehm*-bah	*september*
October	org-*tor*-bah	*oktober*
November	nor-*vehm*-bah	*november*
December	di-*sehm*-bah	*december*

Seasons

summer	*som*-ah	*sommer*
autumn	*ehf*-dah-or	*efterår*
winter	*vin*-dah	*vinter*
spring	*for*-or	*forår*

Present

today	ee da	*i dag*
this morning	ee mo*f*-seh	*i morges*
tonight	ee nad	*i nat*
this week	*dehn*-neh *oo*-eh	*denne uge*
this year	ee or	*i år*
now	noo	*nu*

Past

yesterday	ee gor	*i går*
day before yesterday	ee *for*-gors	*i forgårs*
yesterday morning	ee gor mor-seh	*i går morges*
last night	ee (gor) nad;	*i (går) nat;*
	ee (gor) *ahf*-dehs	*i (går) aftes*
last week	*for*-ee *oo*-eh	*forrige uge*
last year	*sees*-deh or	*sidste år*

Future

tomorrow	ee morn	*i morgen*
day after tomorrow	ee *ow*-ah-morn	*i overmorgen*
tomorrow morning	ee morn *teeth*-lee	*i morgen tidlig*
tomorrow afternoon/ evening	ee morn *ehf*-dah-mi-da/ *ahf*-dehn	*i morgen eftermiddag/ aften*
next week	*nehs*-deh *oo*-eh	*næste uge*
next year	*nehs*-deh or	*næste år*

During the Day

afternoon	*ehf*-dah-mi-da	*eftermiddag*
dawn	*daow*-gŕü	*daggry*
day	da	*dag*
early	*teeth*-lee	*tidlig*
midnight	*meeth*-nad	*midnat*
morning	morn	*morgen*
night	nad	*nat*
noon	*mi*-das-teeth	*middagstid*
sundown	*sorl*-nith-gahng	*solnedgang*
sunrise	*sorl*-ob-gahng	*solopgang*

NUMBERS & AMOUNTS

0	nāl	*nul*
1	in	*en*
2	tor	*to*
3	tŕeh	*tre*
4	feeŕ	*fire*
5	feh	*fem*
6	sehgs	*seks*
7	sü-w	*syv*
8	*ā*-deh	*otte*
9	nee	*ni*
10	tee	*ti*
11	*ehl*-veh	*elve*

DANISH

12	tol	*tolv*
13	*tŕah*-dehn	*tretten*
14	*fyor*-dehn	*fjorten*
15	*fehm*-dehn	*femten*
16	*sais*-dehn	*seksten*
17	*ser*-dehn	*sytten*
18	*a*-dehn	*atten*
19	*ni*-dehn	*nitten*
20	*tü*-weh	*tyve*
21	*in*-o-tü-weh	*enogtyve*
30	*tŕahth*-veh	*tredive*
40	*feŕ*-eh	*fyrre*
50	hal-*tŕehs*	*halvtreds*
60	*tŕehs*	*tres*
70	hal-*fyehŕs*	*halvfjerds*
80	*feeŕs*	*firs*
90	hal-*fehms*	*halvfems*
100	*hoon*-ahth	*hundrede*
1000	*too*-sehn	*tusind*
one million	in mee-lee-*orn*	*en million*

1st	*fers*-deh	*første*
2nd	*an*-ehn	*anden*
3rd	*tŕehth*-yeh	*tredje*
1/4	in *fyi*-ah-dil	*en fjerdedel*
1/3	in *tŕehth*-yeh-dil	*en tredjedel*
1/2	in hal	*en halv*
3/4	tŕeh *fyi*-ah-di-leh	*tre fjerdedele*

Some Useful Words

a little (amount)	en *lee*-leh *smoo*-leh	*en lille smule*
double	*dob*-ehld	*dobbelt*
a dozen	id doo-*seen*	*et dusin*
enough	nog	*nok*
few	fã	*fã*
less	*min*-dřah	*mindre*
many	*mahng*-eh	*mange*
more	*mi*-ah	*mere*
once	*in* gahng	*en gang*
a pair	id pah	*et par*
percent	přor-*sehnd*	*procent*
some	*nor*-leh	*nogle*
too much	fo *mah*-ehth	*for meget*
twice	tor *gahng*-eh	*to gange*

ABBREVIATIONS

0800/2000	am/pm
a/s – aktieselskab	Ltd/Inc.
BZ – besættere	squatters
DSB – de Danske Statsbaner	the Danish National Railways
DUH – de Danske Ungdomsherberger	Danish Youth Hostel Association
DVH – de Danske Vandrehjem	Danish Youth Hostel Association
dagl. – dagligt	daily (Monday to Saturday)
EF – det Europæiske Fællesmarked	EEC, the Common Market
ekskl. – eksklusive	excluded, except
EU – den Europæiske Union	the European Union
FN – de Forenede Nationer	UN
f.kr/e.kr.	BC/AD
frk. – frøken	Miss
fr – fredag	Friday
fru	Mrs
Gd/V	St/Rd

DANISH

DANISH

hel. – hellig	holy (as in holiday)
hlp. – holdeplads	bus stop
Hr. – herr	Mr/Sir
inkl. – inklusive	including
jb – jernbane	railway
jrbst – jernbanestation	station/railway station
Kbh – København	Copenhagen
KDAK	the Royal Danish Automobile Association
kgl. – kongelig	royal
kl. – klasse	class (on trains and aeroplanes)
kl. – klokken	o'clock
km/t – kilometer i timen	kilometres per hour
kr – krone	crown (Danish monetary unit)
lø – lørdag	Saturday
m. – med	with
ma – mandag	Monday
moms	VAT, sales tax (included in the price on all goods and services)
ndf. – nedenfor	below (used in notices, timetables, etc)
Ndr. – nordre	to the north (pertaining to place names)
on – onsdag	Wednesday
SAS	Scandinavian Airline System
Sdr. – søndre	to the south (pertaining to place names)
sø – søndag	Sunday
t.h. – til højre	to the right (used in addresses)
ti – tirsdag	Tuesday
tlf. – telefon	telephone
to – torsdag	Thursday
t.v. – til venstre	to the left (used in addresses)

EMERGENCIES

Go away!	fo-*svin*!	*Forsvind!*
Help!	yehlb!	*Hjælp!*
Thief!	tüw!	*Tyv!*

It's an emergency!
   deh-deh ehf en
   nerth-si-too-a-shorn!

Dette er en nødsituation!

There's been an accident!
   dah ehf skid in *oo*-ler-geh!

Der er sket en ulykke!

Call a doctor!
   fing *ehf*-dah in *leh*-eh!

Ring efter en læge!

Call an ambulance!
   fing *ehf*-dah in
   ahm-boo-*lahng*-seh!

Ring efter en ambulance!

I've been raped.
   yai ehf *bli*-wehth *vol*-ta-ehth

Jeg er blevet voldtaget.

I've been robbed.
   yai ehf *bli*-wehth bi-*sdyā*-lehth!

Jeg er blevet bestjålet!

Call the police!
   fing ehf-dah por-li-*tee*-ehth!

Ring efter politiet!

Where is the police station?
   vor ehf por-li-*tee*-sda-shor-nehn?

Hvor er politistationen?

I'll call the police!
   yai *fing*-ah ti por-li-*tee*-ehth!

Jeg ringer til politiet!

I'm/My friend is ill.
   yai ehr/meen vehn ehf sü

Jeg er/Min ven er syg.

I'm lost.
   yai ehf *fah*-ehth vil

Jeg er faret vild.

Where are the toilets?
   vor ehf toy-*lehd*-dah-neh?

Hvor er toiletterne?

Could you help me please?
   ka dee *yehl*-beh mai?

Kan De hjælpe mig? (pol)

Could I please use the telephone?
   mā yai *lā*-neh ti-leh-*for*-nehn?

Må jeg låne telefonen?

DANISH

DANISH

I'm sorry. I apologise.
　bi-*kla*-ah. *ān*-sgül　　　　*Beklager. Undskyld.*

I didn't realise I was doing
anything wrong.
　yai *vis*-deh *ig* ad yai　　　*Jeg vidste ikke at jeg*
　gyo*ŕ nā*-ehth gald　　　　*gjorde noget galt.*

I didn't do it.
　di vah ig *mai* dah *gyoŕ* di　*Det var ikke mig der gjorde det.*

I wish to contact my embassy/
consulate.
　yai vi *gehŕ*-neh kon-*tahg*-deh　*Jeg vil gerne kontakte*
　meen ah-mba-*sa*-theh/　　　*min ambassade/*
　meed kon-soo-*lad*　　　　*mit konsulat.*

I speak English.
　yai *ta*-lah *ehng*-elhsg　　　*Jeg taler engelsk.*

I have medical insurance.
　yai hah *sü*-eh-fo-sig-*ŕing*　　*Jeg har sygeforsikring.*

My possessions are insured.
　mee-neh *ai*-ehn-*di*-leh ehŕ　*Mine ejendele er*
　fo-*sig*-fahth　　　　　　*forsikret.*

My ... was stolen.　meed/meen ... ehŕ　*Mit/min... er*
　　　　　　　　　bli-wehth *sdyā*-lehth　*blevet stjålet.*

I've lost my...　yai hah *mis*-dehth ...　*Jeg har mistet ...*
　bags　　　　　meen ba-*ga*-sheh　　*min bagage*
　handbag　　　meen *hon*-tas-geh　*min håndtaske*
　money　　　　mee-neh *pehng*-eh　*mine penge*
　passport　　　meed pas　　　　*mit pas*
　travellers cheques　mee-neh *ŕai*-seh-shehgs　*mine rejsechecks*

FAROESE

QUICK REFERENCE

Hello.	huh-lloh!/huhy!	Halló!/Hey!
Goodbye.	for-vael	Farvæl.
Yes./No.	yae/nai	Ja./Nei.
Excuse me.	or-sae-kuh!	Orsaka!
Sorry.	um-shil-duh/	Umskylda/
	or-saek-i-meh	Orsakið meg.
Please.	djehr-i so vael	Gerið so væl.
Thank you.	tuhk	Takk.
That's fine./	on-chi uh	Onki at
You're welcome.	tuhk-kuh fi-ri	takka fyri.
I'd like ...	kun-di ehg fin-dji ...	Kundi eg fingið ...
a one-way	ain-veh-yis	einvegis
ticket	fehr-uh-seh-yil	ferðaseðil
a return	fehr-uh-seh-yil	ferðaseðil
ticket	uht-tur o fruhm	aftur og fram

I (don't) understand.
   eh shil-yi (ich-i)   Eg skilji (ikki).
Do you speak English?
   du-vir too ain-gilst?   Dugir tú eingilskt?
Where is ...?
   kvaer ehr ...?   Hvar er ...?
Go straight ahead.
   faer baint fruhm   Far beint fram.
Turn left/right.
   faer teel vin-stru/herg-ru.   Fær til vinstru/høgru.
Do you have any rooms
available?
   ehr-u nerk-ur luhys   Eru nøkur leys
   kerm-ur?   kømur?
I'm looking for a public toilet.
   eh lait-eh eht-tir   Eg leiti eftir
   uhl-mehn-nun vehs-eh   almennum vesi.

1	aitt	eitt	6	sehks	seks
2	tvuhy	tvey	7	shuhy	sjey
3	trooi	trý	8	ot-tuh	átta
4	fooir-uh	fíra	9	nooi-djeh	níggju
5	fim	fimm	10	tooi-djeh	tíggju

Faroese (often spelled Faeroese) is a twig of the North Germanic branch of the Indo-European tree, which includes Icelandic, Danish, Norwegian and Swedish.

The population of the Faroe Islands, or Faroes, is about 46,000, which means that Faroese is the mother tongue of only a very small number of people.

The Norwegian settlers (about 900 AD) brought their own language to the places they colonised, among them the Faroes, and over the centuries a distinct language developed in the Faroe Islands. The most important factor in the preservation of the language was the oral literature, particularly the kvæði, long epic ballads dealing with ancient legendary characters and events, which are a unique cultural heritage.

Historically the Faroe Islands have been under Norwegian and Danish rule. For several centuries Danish was the dominating language in all administration and in public institutions like schools and the church, and Faroese was degraded to the privacy of the home. In 1846 a Faroese scholar set out to recreate a written norm for Faroese. Today books and newspapers are in Faroese, as are church services and school lessons.

Modern Faroese is under the constant influence of the surrounding world, particularly through the mass media, and there is an ongoing struggle to promote and nourish Faroese in the face of the massive influence of Danish and American English.

PRONUNCIATION

The written norm, created in 1846 and still in use, is based on etymology and thus reflects an older stage of Faroese than does the pronunciation.

STRESS

Stress is normally on the first syllable of the word.

Pronunciation is given in the pronunciation guide at the front of this book, with the following exceptions:

Vowels

In front of two or more consonants, vowels are short and have a more open quality than their long equivalents.

Semivowels

FAROESE	GUIDE	SOUND
á long	wah	as the 'oi' in French *moi*
í, ý long	ooi	as in Spanish *muy*

Consonants

FAROESE	GUIDE	SOUND
ð		silent in a final position; otherwise taking on the value of surrounding vowels
ðr	gr	as the 'gr' in 'grab'
dj, ge, gi, gy, gey, gj, ggj	dj	as the 'j' in 'jaw'
ft	tt	as the 'tt' in 'bitter'
g		silent in a final position; otherwise taking on the value of surrounding vowels
hj	y	as the 'y' in 'yet'
ke, ki, ky, key, kj	ch	as the 'ch' 'chew'
r	r	as the 'r' in 'grab'
rn	dn	as the 'dn' in 'hadn't'
ll	dl	as the 'dl' in 'saddle'
sj, sk, ske, ski, sky, skey, skj	sh	as in 'ship'

FAROESE

GREETINGS & CIVILITIES
Top Useful Phrases

Hello.	huh-lloh!/huhy!	*Halló!/Hey!*
How do you do?	goh-uhn dae(-yin)	*Góðan dag(in).*
Goodbye.	for-vael	*Farvæl.*
See you later.	veet sooi-djuhst	*Vit síggjast.*
Yes/No.	yae/nai	*Ja./Nei.*
Excuse me.	or-sae-kuh!	*Orsaka!*
Maybe.	kuhn-skuh	*Kanska.*
Please.	djehr-i so vael	*Gerið so væl.*
Thank you.	tuhk	*Takk.*

May I? Do you mind?
    kuhn eh? slehp-pi eh?   *Kann eg? Sleppi eg?*
Sorry. (excuse me, forgive me)
    um-shil-duh/or-saek-i-meh   *Umskylda/Orsakið meg.*
Many thanks.
    too-sun tuhk   *Túsund takk.*
    (lit. thousand thanks)

You too!
    sholv/-ur tuhk!   *Sjálv/-ur takk!* (f/m)
    (lit. self thanks)

That's fine. You're welcome.
    on-chi uh tuhk-kuh fi-ri   *Onki at takka fyri.*
That's all right.
    tae ehr ooi lae-yee   *Tað er í lagi.*

FAROESE

THANKS FOR THE MEMORIES

Takk fyri seinast.   tuhk fi-ri sain-uhst
    Thanks for the last time I saw you – used when you
    meet someone again after a party or a social event
Manga takk!   muhn-guh tuhk!
    Many thanks – used to your hostess after a meal
Væl gagnist!   vael guhg-nist
    May the food do you good – answer to the above

Greetings

Good morning.	goh-uhn mor-gun	*Góðan morgun.*
Good afternoon.	goh-uhn dae(-yin)	*Góðan dag(in).*
Good evening.	gott kverld	*Gott kvøld.*
Good night.	goh-uh nott	*Góa nátt.*
How are you?	kvus-seh	*Hvussu*
	heh-vur too tae?	*hevur tú tað?*
Well, thanks.	gott tuhk	*Gott takk.*

Forms of Address

Madam/Mrs	froo	*frú*
Sir/Mr	huhr-ruh	*harra*
Miss	frer-kun	*frøkun*
companion/friend	vin-kon-uh/vee-nur	*vinkona/vinur* (f/m)

FAROESE

PRONOUNS		
SG		
I	eh	*eg*
you	too	*tú*
she/he/it	hon/huhn/tae	*hon/hann/tað*
PL		
we	veed	*vit*
you (pl)	teed	*tit*
they	taer/tair/tuhy	*tær/teir/tey* (f/m/n)

SMALL TALK
Meeting People

What is your name?   kvus-seh ai-tuh ti-yun?   *Hvussu eita tygum?*
My name is ...   eh ai-ti ...   *Eg eiti ...*

I'd like to introduce you to ...
    chehn-nir too ...?   *Kennir tú ...?*
                                                 (lit. know you ...?)

I'm pleased to meet you.
    stutt-litt aet hitt-uh teh   *Stuttligt at hitta teg.*

Nationalities

Where are you from?
    kvae-uhn-i ehr-u tiy-un?   *Hvaðani eru tygum?*

I'm from ...	eh ehr-i oor ...	*Eg eri úr ...*
Australia	uhu-strah-li-uh	*Avstralia*
Canada	kah-nuh-duh	*Kanada*
Denmark	duhm-muhrsk	*Danmark*
England	ong-luhn-di	*Onglandi*
Iceland	ooish-luhn-di	*Íslandi*
Ireland	ur-luhn-di	*Írlandi*
New Zealand	nooi-sae-luhn-di	*Ný Sælandi*
Norway	nor-ruh	*Noregi*
Scotland	sgot-luhn-di	*Skotlandi*
Sweden	sverr-ooi-chi	*Svøríki*
the USA	uh-mehr-i-kuh/	*Amerika/*
	u-ehs-ah	*USA*

FAROESE

Age

How old are you?
    kvus-seh go-mul/   *Hvussu gomul/*
    gae-muhl ehrs-too?   *gamal ert tú?* (f/m)
I'm ... years old.
    eh ehr-i ... wah-ruh go-mul/   *Eg eri ... ára gomul/*
    gae-muhl   *gamal.* (f/m)

Occupations

What do you do?

    kvaet djeh-ruh ti-yun?   *Hvat gera tygum?* (pol)

I work as ...	eh uhr-buh-yi sum ...	*Eg arbeiði sum ...*
artist	lis-tuh-ferlk	*listafólk*
business person	huhn-dils-kvin-nuh/	*handilskvinna/*
	huhn-dil-mae-vur	*handilsmaður* (f/m)
doctor	luhk-ni/dok-tuhr-i	*lækni/doktari*
engineer	muh-sheen-mai-stuhr-i	*maskinmeistari*
farmer	bern-di	*bóndi*
journalist	tooin-duh-ferlk	*tíðindafólk*
lawyer	saek-ferr-uhr-i	*sakførari*
manual worker	uhr-bais-kvin-nuh/	*arbeiðskvinna/*
	uhr-bais-mae-vur	*arbeiðsmaður* (f/m)
mechanic	meh-kahn-i-kuhr-i	*mekanikari*
nurse	shook-ruh-sis-tir	*sjúkrasystir*
office worker	skriv-sto-vu-ferlk	*skrivstovufólk*
sailor/seaman	shoh-mae-vur	*sjómaður*
scientist	voois-in-duh-ferlk	*vísindafólk*
student	stu-dehn-tur	*studentur*
teacher	lae-ruhr-i	*lærari*
waiter	tae-nuhr-i	*tænari*
writer	rit-her-vun-dur	*rithøvundur*

Religion

What is your religion?

    kverr-yuh trigv heh-vur too?   *Hvørja trúgv hevur tú?*

I'm not religious.

    eh ehr-i ich-i reh-li-gi-ers/-ur   *Eg eri ikki religiøs/-ur.* (f/m)

I'm (a) ...	eh ehr-i ...	*Eg eri ...*
Buddhist	budd-is-tur	*buddistur*
Catholic	kuh-to-lik-kur	*katolikkur*
Christian	kris-tin	*kristin*
Hindu	hin-du	*hindu*
Jewish	yer-di	*jødi*
Muslim	mus-lee-mur	*muslimur*

FAROESE

Family

Are you married?	ehrs-too djift/-ur	*Ert tú gift/-ur?* (f/m)
I'm ...	eh ehr-i ...	*Eg eri ...*
single	oh-djift/-ur	*ógift/-ur* (f/m)
married	djift/-ur	*gift/-ur* (f/m)
divorced	shild/-ur	*skild/-ur* (f/m)
a widow/er	ain-chuh/	*einkja/*
	ain-chu-mae-vur	*einkjumaður* (f/m)
available	luhys/-ur	*leys/-ur* (f/m)

How many children do you have?
    kvus-su nehgv   *Hvussu nógv*
    berdn heh-vur too?   *børn hevur tú?*

I don't have any children.
    eh hae-vi on-dji berdn   *Eg havi ongi børn.*

I have a daughter/a son.
    eh hae-vi ain-uh der-ttur/   *Eg havi eina dóttur/*
    ain son   *ein son.*

How many brothers/
sisters do you have?
    kvus-su nehgv sish-in   *Hvussu nógv systkin*
    heh-vur too?   *hevur tüu?*

Do you have a boyfriend/girlfriend?
    Heh-vur too shaik/dah-mu?   *Hevur tú sjeik/damu?*

brother	brohir/bai-dji	*bróðir/beiggi*
children	berdn	*børn*
daughter	der-ttir	*dóttir*
family	fuhm-il-yuh/shil-ferlk	*familja/skyldfólk*
father	fae-yir/pwah-pi	*faðir/pápi*
grandfather	uhb-i	*abbi*
grandmother	om-uh	*omma*
husband	mae-vur	*maður*
mother	moh-ir/muhm-uh	*móðir/mamma*
sister	sis-tir	*systir*
son	son-ur	*sonur*
wife	ko-nuh	*kona*

FAROESE

Kids' Talk

How old are you?

kvu-su nehgv wahr ehrs-too? *Hvussu nógv ár ert tú?*

When's your birthday?

naer fidl-ir too? *Nær fyllir tú?*

What do you do after school?

kvaet gehrs-too ehtt-ir *Hvat gert tú eftir*
skoo-luh-tooi? *skúlatíð?*

Do you have a pet at home?

Heh-vur too nae-kuh *Hevur tú nakað*
chehl-i-dooir? *kelidýr?*

I have/own a ...	eh hae-vi/ai-yi ...	*eg havi/eigi ...*
bird	ain fugl	*ein fugl*
budgerigar	un-du-laht	*undulat*
canary	kuhn-ahr-i-u-fugl	*kanariufugl*
cat	cheht-u	*kettu*
dog	hund	*hund*

Feelings

I (don't) like ...

maer dwah-muhr (ich-i) ... *Mær dámar (ikki)...*

I love/hate ...

eh ehl-shi/hae-ti ... *Eg elski/hati ...*

I'm in a hurry.

eh mwah skund-uh maer *Eg má skunda mær.*
(lit. I must hurry me)

I'm well.

eh hae-vi tae got *Eg havi tað gott.*

I'm sorry. (condolence)

tae vaer sind ooi taer/ *Tað var synd í tær/*
tik-un *tykkum.* (sg/pl)

I'm grateful.

eh si-yi stohr-uh tuhk *Eg sigi stóra takk.*
(lit. I say great thank-you)

You're right.	too heh-vur ruhtt	*Tú hevur rætt.*
I'm ...	eh ehr-i ...	*Eg eri ...*
angry	idl/-ur	*ill/-ur* (f/m)
cold	kerld/kuhld-ur	*køld/kaldur* (f/m)
full/satisfied	mehtt/-ur	*mett/-ur* (f/m)
happy	glae/-vur	*glað/-vur* (f/m)
hot	hait/-ur	*heit/-ur* (f/m)
hungry	svong/svehng-ur	*svong/svangur* (f/m)
sad	chehdd/-ur	*kedd/-ur* (f/m)
thirsty	tist/-ur	*tyst/-ur* (f/m)
tired (fatigued)	moh/-ur	*móð/-ur* (f/m)
worried	stoor-in	*stúrin*

FAROESE

Some Useful Phrases

Just a minute.
    booi-yuh aitt sin-dur   *Bíða eitt sindur.*
It's (not) important.
    tae ehr (ich-i) um-rwahn-di   *Tað er (ikki) umráðandi.*
It's (not) possible.
    tae ehr (ich-i) mer-vi-litt   *Tað er (ikki) møguligt.*
Wait!
    booi-yuh!/booi-yi!   *Bíða!/Bíðið!* (sg/pol & pl)
Good luck!
    goh-uh ehd-nu!   *Góða eydnu!*

BODY LANGUAGE

The Faroese are rather shy or wary when it comes to expressing their feelings, be it in words or in physical manifestation.

Shaking hands is the usual form of greeting when you meet someone for the first time. Friends and family who meet after having been apart for some time may hug each other, and good friends also kiss each other. Women tend to hug and kiss more than men, who mostly prefer to slap each other's back. When you meet people who you see often, you don't shake hands every time, nor do you shake hands every time you leave.

Gesticulation is not a characteristic of the Faroese, more typically they keep their hands and arms still, and some – particularly men – keep one or both hands in their pockets.

BREAKING THE LANGUAGE BARRIER

Do you speak English?
    du-vir too ain-gilst?   *Dugir tú eingilskt?*
Does anyone speak English?
    du-vir nae-gar ain-gilst?   *Dugir nakar eingilskt?*
I speak a little ...
    eh du-vi aitt sin-dur ...   *Eg dugi eitt sindur ...*
I don't speak ...
    eh du-vi ich-i ...   *Eg dugi ikki ...*
I (don't) understand.
    eh shil-yi (ich-i)   *Eg skilji (ikki).*
Could you repeat that?
    kuhnst too tae-kuh
    huhtt-uh up-uhtt-ur?   *Kanst tú taka*
                        hatta uppaftur?
Could you speak more
slowly please?
    kuhns-too djehr-uh so   *Kanst tú gera so*
    vael uht tos-uh saint?   *væl at tosa seint?*
How do you say ...?
    kvus-u si-yuh teet ...?   *Hvussu siga tit ...?*

I speak ...	eh du-vi ...	*Eg dugi ...*
English	ain-gilst	*eingilskt*
French	fruhnkst	*franskt*
German	tooikst	*týskt*
Italian	i-tuhlst	*italskt*
Spanish	spuhnkst	*spanskt*

PAPERWORK

address	boos-tae-vur	*bústaður*
age	uhld-ur	*aldur*
birth certificate	fer-yi-braev	*føðibræv*
car owner's title	beel-skrwah-seht-ing-uhr-vott-uhn	*bilskrásetingarváttan*
car registration	vot-tuhn	*váttan*
customs	to-dlur	*tollur*
date of birth	fer-ying-uhr-dae-vur	*føðingardagur*
driver's licence	koy-ri-korst	*koyrikort*
identification	suhm-lai-kuh-prehgv	*samleikaprógv*
immigration	in-fleet-ing	*innflyting*
marital status	choon-uh-ster-vuh	*hjúnastøða*
name	nuhun	*navn*
nationality	choh-skae-pur	*tjóðskapur*
passport (number)	puhs(-num-uhr)	*pass(nummar)*
place of birth	fer-ying-uhr-stae-vur	*føðingarstaður*
profession	uhr-bai-yi	*arbeiði*
reason for travel	ehn-duh-mwahl	*endamál*
	vee fehr-in-i	*við ferðini*
religion	trigv	*trúgv*
sex	cheen	*kyn*
visa	vee-suh	*visa*

FAROESE

PREPOSITIONS

English 'at' corresponds to a number of Faroese prepositions (*í ooi, á wah, við vee*).

GETTING AROUND

What time does the ... leave/arrive?	naer fehr/ chehm-ur ...?	*Nær fer/ kemur ...?*
(air)plane	flog-faer-i	*flogfarið*
boat	bwaht-ur-in	*báturin*
bus (city)	(booi)bus-ur-in	*(bý)bussurin*
bus (intercity)	bus-ur-in	*bussurin*
car ferry	beel-fehr-yuhn	*bilferjan*

Directions

Where is ...?
kvaer ehr ...?   *Hvar er ...?*

How do I get to ...?
kvus-seh slehp-i eh teel ...?   *Hvussu sleppi eg til ...?*

Is it far from here?
ehr tae lehnkt hee-yuhn-i?   *Er tað langt hiðani?*

Can I walk there?
kuhn eh faer-uh til gong-u hae-uhr?   *Kann eg fara til gongu hagar?*

Can you show me (on the map)?
kun-nu tiy-um vooi-suh maer (wah korst-in-um)?   *Kunnu tygum vísa mær (á kortinum)?*

Are there other means of getting there?
kvus-seh kuhn ain uhn-uhrs faer-uh hae-uhr?   *Hvussu kann ein annars fara hagar?*

I want to go to ...
ehg uht-li maer uht faer-uh teel ...   *Eg ætli mær at fara til ...*

Go straight ahead.
faer baint fruhm   *Far beint fram.*

It's two streets down.
tae ehr tvaer gert-ur o-muhn-ehtt-ir   *Tað er tvær gøtur omaneftir.*

FAROESE

Turn left/ right at the ...	faer teel vin-stru/ herg-ru ...	*Fær til vinstru/ høgru ...*
next corner	wah nuhst-uh hod-ni	*á næsta horni*
traffic lights	vee fehrs-leh-lyohs-in-i	*við ferðsluljósini*

behind	uht-tuhn-feer-i	*aftanfyri*
far	lehnkt	*langt*
in front of	fruhm-muhn-feer-i	*frammanfyri*
near	naer	*nær*
opposite	ee-vir-aev	*yvirav*

FAROESE

SIGNS

ATGONGD BANNAÐ/ EINGIN ATGONGD	ENTRANCE PROHIBITED
BUSSUR	BUS
EINVEGIS	ONE WAY
FARSTØÐIN	TERMINAL
FERÐASEÐLAR	TICKETS
FLOGVØLLUR	AIRPORT
FRÁFERÐ	DEPARTURE
HÝRUVOGNUR	TAXI
KOMA	ARRIVAL
NEYÐÚTGONGD	EMERGENCY EXIT
ROYKING BANNAÐ	NO SMOKING
TOLLUR	CUSTOMS
UPPLÝSINGAR	INFORMATION

Booking Tickets

Where can I buy a ticket?		
	kvaer fwah-yi ehg chuhypt fehr-uh-seh-yil?	*Hvar fái eg keypt ferðaseðil?*
I want to go to ...		
	eh veel feh-yin faer-uh teel ...	*Eg vil fegin fara til ...*
Do I need to book?		
	mwah eh booi-leh-djuh?	*Má eg bíleggja?*
I'd like to book a seat to ...		
	eh sgael bi-yuh um aitt plos teel ...	*Eg skal biðja um eitt pláss til ...*
Is it completely full?		
	ehr tae hailt ootsehlt?	*Er tað heilt útselt?*
Can I get a stand-by ticket?		
	kuhn eh fwah ain fehr-uh-seh-yil ooi sooist-u lert-u?/kuhn eh slehp-uh wah booi-yeh-list-uh?	*Kann eg fái ein ferðaseðil í síðstu løtu?/Kann eg sleppa á biðilista?*

I'd like ...	kun-di ehg fin-dji ...	*Kundi eg fingið ...*
a one-way ticket	ain-veh-yis fehr-uh-seh-yil	*einvegis ferðaseðil*
a return ticket	fehr-uh-seh-yil uht-tur o fruhm	*ferðaseðil aftur og fram* (lit. ticket back and forth)
two tickets	tvair fehr-uh-sehl-uhr	*tveir ferðaseðlar*
a student's fare	ain fehr-uh-seh-yil teel leh-suhn-di	*ein ferðaseðil til lesandi*
a child's fare	ain buhd-nuh-fehr-uh-seh-yil	*ein barnaferðaseðil*
a pensioner's fare	fehr-uh-seh-yil teel pehn-sion-ist	*ein ferðaseðil til pensionist*
1st class	fis-ti kluhs-si	*fyrsti klassi*
2nd class	uhn-nuhr kluhs-si	*annar klassi*

FAROESE

Air

Is there a flight to ...?
ehr naek-uh flo-faer teel ...?   *Er nakað flogfar til ...?*
How long does the flight take?
kvus-seh long ehr   *Hvussu long er*
flig-vi-tooi-yin?   *flúgvitíðin?*

airport tax	flo-vuhdl-uhr-skuht-tur	flogvallarskattur
boarding pass	bor-ding puhs	boarding pass

Bus

Where is the bus stop?
kvaer ehr bus-steh-dji-plos-si?   *Hvar er bussteðgiplássið?*
Which bus goes to ...?
kverr bus-sur fehr teel ...?   *Hvør bussur fer til ...?*
Could you let me know
when we get to ...?
kun-nuh ti-yun si-yuh maer   *Kunna tygum siga mær*
frwah twah ooi veet   *frá tá ið vit*
ko-muh teel ...?   *koma til ...?*
I want to get off!
eh veel slehp-puh aev!   *Eg vil sleppa av!*
Must I change buses?
sgael eh shif-tuh bus?   *Skal eg skifta buss?*

What time is	naer fehr ...	*Nær fer ...*
the ... bus?	bus-sur-in?	*bussurin?*
next	nuhs-ti	*næsti*
first	fis-ti	*fyrsti*
last	sain-uhs-ti	*seinasti*

FAROESE

DID YOU KNOW ...	There are no trains in the Faroe Islands.

Boat

Which harbour is next?
  kverr ehr nuhs-tuh huhvn?   *Hvør er næsta havn?*

Is this the ferry for ...?
  ehr heht-tuh fehr-yuhn teel ...?   *Er hetta ferjan til ...?*

cafeteria	kuhff-eh-teh-ri-uh	*kafeteria*
car deck	beel-dehk	*bildekk*
smoking saloon	roy-chi-suh-long	*roykisalon*
sun deck	sohl-dehk	*sóldekk*
ticket including a bunk	koy-dju-plos	*koyggjupláss*

Taxi

Can you take me to ...?
  kun-nuh ty-djun koy-ruh   *Kunna tygum koyra*
  meh teel ...?   *meg til ...?*

How much does it cost to go to ...?
  kvus-seh nehgv kos-tuhr   *Hvussu nógv kostar*
  tae teel ...?   *tað til ...?*

Here is fine, thank you.
  hehr ehr fooint tuhk   *Her er fint, takk.*

Continue!
  koyr long-ur!   *Koyr longur!*

The next street to the left/right.
  nuhs-tuh ger-tuh teel   *Næsta gøta til*
  vin-stru/herg-ru   *vinstru/høgru.*

Stop here!
  stehg-guh hehr!   *Steðga her!*

Please slow down.
  djehr-i so vael uht min-kuh   *Gerið so væl at minka*
  fehr-in-uh   *ferðina.*

Please wait here.
  djehr-i so vael uht   *Gerið so væl at*
  booi-yuh hehr!   *bíða her!*

FAROESE

Some Useful Phrases

The ... is delayed/cancelled.
    ... ehr sain-kuh-vur/
    aev-loois-tur

... er seinkaður/
avlýstur.

How long will it be delayed?
    kvus-seh nehgv ehr huhn
    sain-kuh-vur?

Hvussu nógv er hann
seinkaður?

There is a delay of ... hours.
    sain-chin-djin ehr ...
    tooi-muhr

Seinkingin er ...
tímar.

Can I reserve a place?
    kuhn eh booi-leh-djuh
    plos?

Kann eg bíleggja
pláss?

How long does the trip take?
    kvus-su lehng-uh tooi
    tehk-ur toor-ur-in?

Hvussu langa tíð
tekur túrurin?

Is it a direct route?
    ehr tae ain bain-lai-yis
    rut-uh?

Er tað ein beinleiðis
ruta?

Is that seat taken?
    ehr huht-tuh plos-si
    up-teech-i?

Er hatta plássið
upptikið?

I want to get off at ...
    eh sgael aev ooi ...

Eg skal av í ...

Where can I hire a bicycle?
    kvaer fwah-yi eh lai-yuh
    ain-uh sük-klu?

Hvar fái eg leigað
eina súkklu?

FAROESE

Car

Where can I rent a car?
  kvaer fwah-yi eh
  lai-yuh ain beel?

*Hvar fái eg
leigað ein bil?*

How much is it daily/weekly?
  kvus-seh nehgv kos-tuhr
  huhn um dae-yin/vee-ku-nuh?

*Hvussu nógv kostar
hann um dagin/vikuna?*

Does that include insurance/
mileage?
  ehr tri-djing/keel-o-meh-truh-
  tael rok-nuh up-ooi?

*Er trygging/
kilometratal roknað uppi?*

Where's the next petrol station?
  kvaer ehr nuhst-uh
  behns-een-ster?

*Hvar er næsta
bensinstøð?*

How long can I park here?
  kvus-su lain-dji ehr lov aet
  puhr-kehr-uh hehr?

*Hvussu leingi er lov at
parkera her?*

Does this road lead to ...?
  ehr heht-tuh veh-vur-in
  teel ...?

*Er hetta vegurin
til ...?*

air (for tyres)	luft (teel dehk)	*luft (til dekk)*
battery	uhk-ku-mo-lah-tor-ur	*akkumolatorur*
brakes	brehm-sir	*bremsur*
clutch	kob-ling	*kobling*
driver's licence	koy-ri-korst	*koyrikort*
engine	mo-tor-ur	*motorur*
lights	lyohs	*ljós*
oil	ol-yuh	*olja*
puncture	punk-tehr-ing	*punktering*
radiator	ker-luhr-i	*kølari*
road map	veh-korst	*vegkort*
tyres	dehk	*dekk*
windscreen	fruhm-roo-tur	*framrútur*

FAROESE

I need a mechanic.
eh haev-i brook fir-i ain-un   *Eg havi brúk fyri einum*
meh-kahn-i-kuhr-uh   *mekanikara.*
The battery is flat.
buht-tuhr-ooi-yi er fluhtt   *Battaríið er flatt.*
The radiator is leaking.
kerl-uhr-in lehk-ur   *Kølarin lekur.*
I have a flat tyre.
ehg ehr-i punk-tehr-uh-vur   *Eg eri punkteraður.*
It's overheating. (engine)
huhn gong-ur hait-ur   *Hann gongur heitur.*
It's not working.
huhn rig-guhr i-chi   *Hann riggar ikki.*

ACCOMMODATION

Where is a ...?   kvaer ehr aitt ...?   *Hvar er eitt ...?*
  cheap hotel   booil-itt ho-tehll   *bíligt hotell*
  good hotel   gott ho-tehll   *gott hotell*
  nearby hotel   ho-tehll ooi nond   *hotell í nánd*

What is the address?
kvus-seh ait-ur gert-uhn?   *Hvussu eitur gøtan?*
Could you write the address,
please?
kun-nu ti-yun djehr-uh so vael   *Kunnu tygum gera so væl*
aet sgree-vuh ger-tu-nuhv-ni?   *at skriva gøtunavnið?* (pol)

FAROESE

+---+
| SIGNS |
+---+
| *GISTINGARHÚS*   GUESTHOUSE |
| *HOTELL*   HOTEL |
| *VALLARAHEIM*   YOUTH HOSTEL |
+---+

At the Hotel

Do you have any rooms available?
    ehr-u nerk-ur luhys kerm-ur?   *Eru nøkur leys kømur?*

Sorry, we're full.
    tooi-vehr-ri hehr ehr fult   *Tíverri, her er fult.*

How many nights?
    kvus-seh nehg-vuhr naet-ur?   *Hvussu nógvar nætur?*

It's ... per day/per person.
    tae kos-tuhr ...   *Tað kostar ...*
    um dae-yin fyr-i kvern   *um dagin fyri hvønn.*

How much is it per night/per person?
    kvus-seh nehgv kos-tuhr   *Hvussu nógv kostar tað*
    tae fir-i kvern ain-uh nott?   *fyri hvønn eina nátt?*

I'd like ...	ehg veel feh-yin	*Eg vil fegin*
	haev-uh ...	*hava ...*
a single room	aitt	*eitt*
	ain-kult-kaem-uhr	*einkultkamar*
a double room	aitt	*eitt*
	du-bult-kaem-uhr	*dupultkamar*
to share a dorm	aitt	*eitt*
	feh-luhks-kaem-uhr	*felagskamar*
a bed	ain-uh song	*eina song*

I want a room	eh veel haev-uh aitt	*Eg vil hava eitt*
with a ...	kaem-uhr vee ...	*kamar við ...*
bathroom	bae	*bað*
shower	broos-u	*brúsu*
TV	shohn-vuhrs-pi	*sjónvarpi*
window	vin-dae	*vindeyga*

I'm going to	eh steh-dji ooi ...	*Eg steðgi í ...*
stay for ...		
one day	ain dae	*ein dag*
two days	tvair dehahr	*tveir dagar*
one week	ain-uh veek-u	*eina viku*

FAROESE

Requests & Complaints

Can I see it?
    kuhn eh slehp-puh aet   *Kann eg sleppa at*
    sooi-djuh tae?   *síggja tað?*

Are there any other/cheaper rooms?
    ehr-u nerk-ur on-nur/   *Eru nøkur onnur/*
    booi-li-yuhr-i kerm-ur?   *bíligari kømur?*

Is there a reduction for students/
children?
    ehr aev-slot-tur fir-i   *Er avsláttur fyri*
    stu-dehnt-uhr/berdn?   *studentar/børn?*

Does it include breakfast?
    ehr mor-gun-maet-ur   *Er morgunmatur*
    up-pi ooi?   *uppi í?*

It's fine, I'll take it.
    tae ehr fooint eh tae-chi tae *Tað er fínt, eg taki tað.*

I'm not sure how long I'm staying.
    eh vait i-chi kvus-seh   *Eg veit ikki hvussu*
    lain-dji eh steh-dji   *leingi eg steðgi.*

Where is the bathroom?
    kvaer ehr bae-yi-room-i?   *Hvar er baðirúmið?*

Is there somewhere to wash clothes?
    behr teel aet vuhs-kuh klae-yi? *Ber til at vaska klæði?*

Can I use the kitchen?
    kuhn eh broo-kuh ker-chin? *Kann eg brúka køkin?*

Can I use the telephone?
    kuhn eh broo-kuh   *Kann eg brúka*
    tehl-eh-fon-in-uh?   *telefonina?*

Some Useful Words & Phrases

I'm/We're leaving now/tomorrow.
    eh faer-i/veet faer-uh noo/ *Eg fari/Vit fara nú/*
    ooi mor-djin   *í morgin.*

I'd like to pay the bill.
    kuhn eh fwah rok-nin-djin-uh? *Kann eg fáa rokningina?*

FAROESE

FAROESE

name	nuhun	*navn*
surname	eht-tir-nuhun	*eftirnavn*
address	boo-stae-vur	*bústaður*
room number	kaem-uhr-num-muhr	*kamarnummar*
bathroom	bae-yi-room	*baðirúm*
bed	song	*song*
blanket	tehp-peh	*teppi*
chair	sdohl-ur	*stólur*
clean	raint	*reint*
dirty	shee-ti	*skitið*
double bed	dub-ilt-song	*dupultsong*
electricity	ruhu-muhgn	*ravmagn*
excluded	i-chi ooi-rok-nuh	*ikki írokna*
included	ooi-rok-nuh	*íroknað*
key	lee-chil	*lykil*
lift (elevator)	lif-tuh	*lyfta*
light bulb	lyohs-pehr-uh	*ljóspera*
a lock	lwahs	*lás*
mattress	muh-druhs-suh	*madrassa*
mirror	spehgl	*spegl*
padlock	hon-dji-lwahs	*heingilás*
pillow	kod-di	*koddi*
room (in hotel)	kaem-uhr	*kamar*
quiet	free-yuhr-litt	*friðarligt*
sheet	laek	*lak*
shower	broos-uh	*brúsa*
soap	swahb-uh	*sápa*
suitcase	kuf-fehrst	*kuffert*
swimming pool	svim-yeh-heel-ur	*svimjihylur*
table	bor	*borð*
toilet (paper)	veh-seh(-puhp-pooir)	*vesi(pappír)*
towel	huhn-klae	*handklæði*
(hot/cold) water	(haitt/kuhlt) vuhtn	*(heitt/kalt) vatn*
window	vin-dae	*vindeyga*

AROUND TOWN

I'm looking	eh lait-eh	*Eg leiti*
for the/a ...	eht-tir ...	*eftir ...*
art gallery	list-uh-suhun-in-un	*listasavninum*
bank	ain-un buhn-kuh	*einum banka*
church	ain-uhr-eh chir-cheh	*einari kirkju*
city centre	mib-booi-nun	*miðbýnum*
... embassy	... uhm-buhs-sah-dun-eh	*... ambassaduni*
hotel	ain-un ho-tehll-i	*einum hotelli*
market street	huhn-dils-gert-ehn-eh	*handilsgøtuni*
museum	fon-min-ni-su-hun-in-un	*fornminnis-savninum*
police	lerg-rehg-lun-eh	*løgregluni*
post office	post-hoos-in-un	*posthúsinum*
public toilet	uhl-mehn-nun vehs-eh	*almennum vesi*
telephone centre	teh-leh-fon-ster-yin-eh	*telefonstøðini*
tourist information office	fehr-uh-skreev-sto-vun-eh/ tu-rist-kon-tohr-in-un	*ferða-skrivstovuni/ turistkontórinum*

What time does it open/close?
naer klok-kuhn leht-ur	*Nær klokkan letur*
tae up/uht-tur?	*tað upp/aftur?*

What ... is this? kvus-seh ait-ur ...? *hvussu eitur ...?*
street	hehn-duh gert-uhn	*henda gøtan*
suburb	hehs-in	*hesin*
	booi-uhr-puhrs-tur-in	*býarparturin*

For directions, see the Getting Around section, page 90.

FAROESE

At the Post Office

I'd like to send ...	eh sgael sehn-duh ...	*Eg skal senda ...*
a letter	aitt braev	*eitt bræv*
a postcard	aitt post-korst	*eitt postkort*
a parcel	ain puhk-kuh	*ein pakka*
a telegram	aitt teh-leh-gruhm	*eitt telegramm*

I'd like some stamps.
    kuhn eh fwah nerg-ur   *Kann eg fáa nøkur*
    frooi-mehr-cheh?   *frímerki?*
How much does it cost
to send this to ...?
    kvus-seh nehgv kos-tuhr tae   *Hvussu nógv kostar tað*
    aet sehn-duh heht-tuh teel ...?   *at senda hetta til ...?*

an aerogram	aitt luft-braev	*eitt luftbræv*
air mail	luft-post-ur	*luftpostur*
e-mail	tehl-deh-post-ur	*teldupostur*
envelope	braev-bdjolv-eh/	*brævbjálvi/*
	kon-vo-lut-tur	*konvoluttur*
mailbox	post-kuhs-seh	*postkassi*
registered mail	in-sgree-vuh braev	*innskrivað bræv*
surface mail	ships-post-ur	*skipspostur*
		(lit. ship post)

Telephone & Internet

I want to ring ...
    eh sgael rin-djuh teel ...   *Eg skal ringja til ...*
The number is ...
    num-muhr-eh ehr ...   *Nummarið er ...*
How much does a three-minute
call cost?
    kvus-seh nehgv kos-tuhr aet   *Hvussu nógv kostar at*
    tos-uh ooi trooi-djuhr min-ut-tir?   *tosa í tríggjar minuttir?*
How much does each extra minute cost?
    kvus-seh nehgv kos-tuhr   *Hvussu nógv kostar*
    kverr uhy-kuh min-ut-tur?   *hvør eyka minuttur?*
I'd like to speak to (Mr Pedersen).
    kuhn eh slehp-puh aet tos-uh   *Kann eg sleppa at tosa*
    vee (huhr-ruh peh-dehr-sehn)?   *við (harra Pedersen)?*

It's engaged.
    tae ehr bun-deh   *Tað er bundið.*
I want to make a reverse-charges
phone call.
    eh sgael rin-djuh   *Eg skal ringja*
    moh-tae-kuhr-in beh-tae-lir   *móttakarin betalir.*
I've been cut off.
    eh bluhyv aev-brot-in   *Eg bleiv avbrotin.*

Where can I get Internet access?
    kvaer fwah-yeh eh brookt   *Hvar fái eg brúkt*
    in-tehr-neh-ti?   *internetið?*
I'd like to send an email.
    eh veel feh-yin sehn-duh   *Eg vil fegin senda*
    ain ee-mayl   *ein e-mail.*

FAROESE

At the Bank

I want to exchange some money/
travellers cheques.

eh sgael vehk-sluh aitt sin-dur
aev pehng-um/fehr-uh-chehk-kum

*Eg skal veksla eitt sindur
av pengum/ferðakekkum.*

What is the exchange rate?

kvaet ehr kurs-ur-in

Hvat er kursurin?

How many kroner per dollar?

kvus-seh nehg-vuhr krohn-ur
fir-i doll-uhr-uhn?

*Hvussu nógvar krónur
fyri dollaran?*

bank draft	pehng-uh-wah-vooi-sing	*pengaávísing*
bank notes	pehng-uh-sehl-uhr	*pengaseðlar*
cashier	kuhs-suh-dahm-uhn	*kassadaman*
coins	min-tir	*myntir*
credit card	kreh-ditt-korst	*kredittkort*
exchange	vehk-sling	*veksling*
loose change	smwah-pehng-uhr	*smápengar*
signature	un-dir-skrift	*undirskrift*

FAROESE

INTERESTS & ENTERTAINMENT
Sightseeing

Do you have a guidebook/local map?

haev-uh tee-yun naek-ruh
fehr-uh-huhnd-bohk/
naek-uh korst?

*Hava tygum nakra
ferðahandbók/
nakað kort?* (pol)

What are the main attractions?

kvaet ehr vehrst aet sooi-djuh?

Hvat er vert at síggja?
(lit. what is worth to see?)

What is that?

kvaet ehr huht-tuh?

Hvat er hatta?

How old is it?

kvus-seh gaem-uhlt ehr tae?

Hvussu gamalt er tað?

Can I take photographs?

kuhn eh taek-uh min-dir

Kann eg taka myndir?

What time does it open/close?

naer leht-ur tae up/uhtt-ur? *Nær letur tað upp/aftur?*

ancient	fod-nur	*fornur*
archaeological	fon-frer-yi-lee-yur	*fornfrøðiligur*
beach	suhn-dur/strond	*sandur/strond*
building	big-ning-ur	*bygningur*
castle	slott	*slott*
cathedral	dohm-chir-chuh	*dómkirkja*
church	chir-chuh	*kirkja*
concert hall	kon-sehrt-herdl	*konserthøll*
library	boh-kuhs-uhun	*bókasavn*
main square	mib-booi-yur	*miðbýur*
market	huhn-dils-chuhd-neh	*handilskjarni*
monastery	klos-tur	*klostur*
monument	min-nis-vaer-eh	*minnisvarði*
old city	gaem-uhl	*gamal*
	booi-uhr-puhrst-ur	*býarpartur*
opera house	op-ehr-uh-hoos	*opera hús*
palace	kongs-borg	*kongsborg*
ruins	hoos-uh-laiv-dir	*húsaleivdir*
stadium	ooi-trot-uhr-verdl-ur	*itróttarvøllur*
statues	stuhnd-min-dir	*standmyndir*
temple	tehm-pil	*tempul*
university	froh-sgae-buhr-seh-dur	*fróðskaparsetur*

Going Out

What's there to do in the evenings?

kvaet kuhn muhn djehr-uh *Hvat kann mann gera*
um kverl-deh? *um kvøldið?*

Are there places where you can
hear local folk music?

behr teel uh hoy-ruh *Ber til at hoyra*
ferr-is-guhn tohn-laig? *føroyskan tónleik?*

Can one see Faroese dancing anywhere?

behr teel uh sooi-djuh ferr-is-guhn *Ber til at síggja føroyskan*
duhns nae-gruh-staen-i? *dans nakra staðni?*

FAROESE

How much does it cost to get in?
kvus-seh nehgv kos-tuhr *Hvussu nógv kostar*
tae uh slehp-puh in? *tað at sleppa inn?*

cinema	bi-o-gruhf-ur	*biografur*
concert	kon-sehrst	*konsert*
discotheque	dis-ko-tehk	*diskotek*
theatre	shohn-laig-uhr-hoos	*sjónleikarhús*

UNDER AGE?		
aldursmark	uhl-durs-muhrsk	age limit

Sports & Interests

What do you do in your spare time?
kvaet djehr-stoo ooi *Hvat gert tú í*
frooi-tooi-yin-eh? *frítíðini?*

What sport do you play?
kvern ooi-trott ooik-kuhr too? *Hvønn ítrótt iðkar tüu?*

art	list	*list*
basketball	kurv-uh-berlt	*kurvabólt*
boxing	bok-sing	*boksing*
cooking	muh-djehr	*matgerð*
fishing trout	uh fis-kuh sooil	*at fiska síl*
football/soccer	foht-berlt	*fótbólt*
going/out	uh faer-uh/ooi booi-yin	*at fara/í býiin*
to the cinema	ooi bi-o-gruhf	*í biograf*
music	tohn-laig	*tónleik*
photography	fo-to-gruh-fehr-ing	*fotografering*
reading	leh-sing	*lesing*
shopping	uh faer-uh teel huhn-dils	*at fara til handils*
sport	ooi-trott	*ítrótt*
the theatre	shohn-laig	*sjónleik*
travelling	uh fehr-uhst	*at ferðast*
writing	uh sgreev-uh	*at skriva*

FAROESE

Festivals

During the summer months, June and July, almost every weekend offers a village festival. The first one is Norðoyastehvna in Klaksvík, and the last one is Ólavsøka in Tórshavn. There are sports events, music and dancing, and many people wear their national costume. The traditional rowing competition features the ancient Faroese rowing boat – a descendant from the Viking ship. Participants are boys and girls from the competing villages.

Grækarismessa 12 March – celebrated as the arrival day of the national bird tjaldur. Boy- and girlscouts march in procession and speeches are delivered.

Flag Day 25 April – celebrated in memory of the sanctioning of the Faroese flag by the British during WWII.

Ólavsøka 29 July – celebration in the capital Tórshavn lasting at least two days. In ancient times the celebration was for the Holy King Olav of Norway who died in 1030 AD.

A relatively new custom is having a bonfire on the small beach in Tórshavn on the shortest night of the year, 21 June.

IN THE COUNTRY
Weather

What's the weather like?
kvus-seh ehr vehg-reh?	*Hvussu er veðrið?*

It's ... today.
vehg-reh ehr ... ooi dae	*Veðrið er ... í dag.*

Will it be ...	Vehr-ur tae ...	Verður tað ...
tomorrow?	ooi mor-djin?	*í morgin?*
cloudy	sgooi-djuh	*skýggjað*
cold	kuhlt	*kalt*
foggy	myerr-cheh	*mjørki*
frosty	frost	*frost*
hot	haitt	*heitt*
raining	rehgn	*regn*
snowing	kaev-eh	*kavi*
sunny	serl-shin	*sólskin*
windy	vin-dur	*vindur*

FAROESE

Camping

Am I allowed to camp here?
ehr loyft uh chuhl-duh hehr?   *Er loyvt at tjalda her?*
Is there a campsite nearby?
ehr naeg-uh chuhld-plos   *Er nakað tjaldpláss*
ooi nond?   *í nánd?*

backpack	rigg-sehk-kur	*ryggsekkur*
can opener	dohs-uh-op-nuhr-eh	*dósaopnari*
compass	kum-puhs	*kumpass*
firewood	brehn-neh	*brenni*
gas cartridge	guhs-puh-trohn	*gass patrón*
mattress	muh-druhs-suh	*madrassa*
penknife	fehd-leh-knooi-vur	*felliknívur*
rope	buhnd	*band*
sleeping bag	so-veh-pos-eh	*soviposi*
stove	ohn-ur	*ovnur*
tent (pegs)	chuhld (hael-ir)	*tjald (hælir)*
torch/flashlight	ligt	*lykt*
water bottle	vuhn-flers-guh	*vatnfløska*

FAROESE

SIGNS

TJÁLDPLASS	CAMPING GROUND

FOOD

Traditional Faroese food includes fish, mutton, whalemeat and birds from the steep cliffs. Not many vegetables are cultivated in the Faroes, but potatoes and rhubarb are popular.

A Faroese specialty is skerpikjøt, mutton which has been wind dried, eaten mostly with bread. Another dish is ræst kjøt, the same meat only half dried and then cooked or roasted. The same drying methods are used with fish and whalemeat.

Some Useful Words & Phrases

breakfast	mor-gun-drehk-kuh	*morgundrekka*
lunch	mor-gun-maet-ur	*morgunmatur*
dinner	derv-reh	*døgurði*

Table for ..., please.	bor teel ... tuhk	*Borð til ... takk.*

Can I see the menu please?
    kuhn eh fwah maet-seh-yil-in?   *Kann eg fáa matseðilin?*
What does it include?
    kvaet hoy-rir teel?   *Hvat hoyrir til?*

ashtray	ers-keh-beek-uhr	*øskubikar*
the bill	rok-nin-djin	*rokningin*
a cup	ain kop-pur	*ein koppur*
dessert	deh-sehrst/ o-muhn-wah	*dessert/ omaná*
a drink	ok-kurst uh drehk-kuh	*okkurt at drekka*
a fork	ain guhf-fil	*ein gaffil*
fresh	nooi-djur/fehs-kur	*nýggjur/feskur*
a glass	aitt glaes	*eitt glas*
a knife	ain knooi-vur	*ein knívur*
a plate	ain bor-isk-ur	*ein borðiskur*
spicy	krid-duh	*kryddað*
a spoon	ain sgai	*ein skeið*
stale	sbil-tur	*spiltur*
sweet	sert-ur	*søtur*
a teaspoon	ain teh-sgai	*ein teskeið*
toothpicks	tuhn-nuhs-tuhy-tuhr-uhr	*tannasteytarar*

Vegetarian Meals

I'm a vegetarian.

eh eht-i baer-uh grern-meht-eh;	*Eg eti bara grønmeti;*
eh ehr-eh veh-geh-tuhr-ur	*Eg eri vegetarur.*

I don't eat meat.

eh eht-i i-chi chert	*Eg eti ikki kjøt.*

I don't eat chicken, or fish, or pork.

eh eht-i ich-i hers-nuhr-ung-uh	*Eg eti ikki høsnarunga*
edl-uh fisk edl-uh grwees-uh-chert	*ella fisk ella grísakjøt.*

Staple Foods & Condiments

bread	bruhy	*breyð*
butter	smerr	*smør*
garlic	kvooit-luhy-gur	*hvítleykur*
meat	chert	*kjøt*
mustard	sin-nop-pur	*sinoppur*
oil	ol-yuh	*olja*
pepper	pee-puhr	*pipar*
pickled cucumbers	sült-uh-yuhr	*súltaðar*
	uh-gursk-ir	*agurkir*
rice	roois	*rís*
salt	suhlt	*salt*
string beans	bern-ir	*bønir*
sugar	suk-ur	*sukur*
vinegar	eh-dik-kur	*edikur*

Vegetables

beets (usually served pickled)	ruhy-rert-ur	reyðrøtur
cabbage	kwahl	kál
carrots	gu-luh-rert-ur	gularøtur
cauliflower	blom-kwahl	blomkál
celery	sehl-luh-rooi	sellarí
cucumber	uh-gursk	agurk
mashed potatoes	eh-pluh-morl	eplamorl
mushrooms	hun-duh-luhnd	hundaland
onions	luhy-kur	leykur
peas	ehrs-truhr	ertrar
pickled cucumbers	sült-uh-yuhr uh-gursk-ir	súltaðar agurkir
potato (boiled/baked)	eh-pli (kohg-uh/baeg-uh)	epli (kókað/bakað)
rice	roois	rís
string beans	bern-ir	bønir

Fruit

apple	süur-eh-pleh	súrepli
banana	buh-nahn	banan
grapes	vooin-drüu-vir	víndrúvur
lemon	si-trohn	sitrón
orange	uh-pil-seen	appilsin
pear	peh-ruh	pera
strawberry	jar-ber	jarðber

FAROESE

MENU DECODER

Breakfast Menu

toast	rist-uh bruhy	*ristað breyð*
bacon	buhy-kon	*bacon*
cheese	ost-ur	*ostur*
eggs	ehgg	*egg*
jam	sül-teh-toy	*súltutoy*
milk	myerlk	*mjólk*
rye bread	rub-bruhy	*rugbreyð*
white bread	fruhns-bruhy	*fransbreyð*

Main Meals

chicken	hers-nuhr-un-djeh	*høsnarungi*
lamb chops	luhms-chert	*lambskjøt*
roast beef	nuhy-tuh-staik	*neytasteik*
roast lamb	luhms-staik	*lambssteik*
roast pork	groois-uh-staik	*grísasteik*
sausage	pil-suh	*pylsa*
steak	büf-fur	*búffur*
whale meat with blubber	grind o speek	*grind og spik*
wind-dried meat (boiled or roasted)	ruhst chert	*ræst kjøt*
wind-dried meat	turt chert/ shehr-peh-chert	*turt kjøt/ skerpikjøt*
wind-dried fish (boiled)	ruhst-ur fis-kur	*ræstur fiskur*
wind-dried fish	tur-rur fis-kur	*turrur fiskur*

Seafood

fish	fis-kur	*fiskur*
haddock	hoois-uh	*hýsa*
halibut	kuhlv-i	*kalvi*
herring	sild	*sild*
plaice	rehs-prerk-uh	*reyðsprøka*
salmon	luhk-sur	*laksur*
shrimp	raech-ur	*rækjur*
sole	tung-uh	*tunga*
trout	sooil	*síl*

Soups

fesk súpan fehsk soop-uhn
  broth from boiled meat with vegetables
røst súpan rerst soop-uhn
  broth from boiled *ræst kjøt* with vegetables and rice
breyðsúpan bruhy-soop-uhn
  soup made from bread, sugar and non-alcoholic beer

fiskasúpan	fis-kuh-soop-uhn	fish soup
asparssúpan	uhs-puhrs-soop-uhn	asparagus soup
blábersúpan	blwah-behr-soop-uhn	blueberry soup

Desserts

ice cream	oois-ur	*ísur*
cake	kaek-uh	*kaka*
rhubarb cake	ruh-buhr-beh-kaek-uh	*rabarbukaka*
rhubarb jelly	ruh-buhr-beh-gruhyt-ur	*rabarbugreytur*
pancakes	puhn-neh-kaek-ur	*pannukakur*

Drinks

coffee(with cream)	kuhf-fi (vee roh-muh)	*kaffi (við róma)*
orange juice	uhp-pil-seen-djoos	*appelsindjús*
skim/	skoo-muh/	*skúmað/*
full cream milk	vuhn-li myerlk	*vanlig mjólk*
soft drink,	suhft, so-duh-vuhtn	*saft,sodavatn*
carbonated water		
tea	teh	*te*
(ice) water	(oois-)vuhtn	*(ís)vatn*

snapsur snuhp-sur
  small glass 2-4 cl of (particularly) akvavit
flúgvari flig-vuhr-i
  mixture of coke and akvavit (lit. flyer)
svartideyð svuhr-steh-duhy-yeh
  Icelandic brand of alcohol (lit. the black death)
durasnapsur dur-uh-snuhp-sur
  snaps offered at the door as you enter (lit. door *snaps*)
bjóða ein lítlan byoh-uh ain looitl-uhn
  also *snaps* (lit. offer a 'small one')

FAROESE

SHOPPING

How much is it?

kvus-seh nehgv kos-tuhr tae?   *Hvussu nógv kostar tað?*

bookshop	bohk-huhnd-il	*bókhandil*
camera shop	foto huhnd-il	*foto handil*
clothing store	kluhd-nuh-huhnd-il	*klædnahandil*
general store/shop	huhnd-il	*handil*
laundry	vuhs-kuhr-ooi	*vaskarí*
market	muhrk-nuh-vur	*marknaður*
newsagency	ki-osk	*kiosk*
pharmacy	uh-po-tehk	*apotek*
shoeshop	skoh-huhnd-il	*skóhandil*
souvenir shop	su-vehn-eer huhnd-il	*souvenir handil*
stationers	puhp-pooirs-huhnd-il	*pappírshandil*
supermarket	sholvt-erk-eh-huhnd-il	*sjálvtøkuhandil*
vegetable shop	grern-meht-is-huhnd-il	*grønmetishandil*

I'd like to buy ...

eh sgael chuhy-puh ...   *Eg skal keypa ...*

Do you have others?

haev-uh teet aer-uhr?   *Hava tit aðrar?* (inf)

I don't like it.

maer dwahm-uhr haen-uh/   *Mær dámar hana/*
huhn/tae i-chi   *hann/tað ikki.* (f/m/n)

Can I look at it?

kuhn eh sooi-djuh haen-uh/   *Kann eg síggja hana/*
huhn/tae?   *hann/tað?* (f/m/n)

I'm just looking.

eh baer-uh hi-djeh   *Eg bara hyggi.*

Can you write down the price?

kuhns-too sgreev-uh   *Kannst tú skriva*
proois-in nee-yur?   *prísin niður?*

Do you accept credit cards?
    taek-uh teet kreh-ditt-korst?   *Taka tit kredittkort?*
Can I help you?
    fwah-yeh eh yolt tee-yuhn?   *Fái eg hjálpt tygum?* (pol)
Will that be all?
    naeg-uh uhn-nuh?   *Nakað annað?*

Essential Groceries

bread	bruhy	*breyð*
butter	smerr	*smør*
milk	myerlk	*mjólk*
rice	roois	*rís*
salt	suhlt	*salt*
shampoo	shuhm-po	*shampo*
sugar	suk-ur	*sukur*
toilet paper	veh-seh-puhp-pooir	*vesipappír*
toothbrush	tuhn-bust	*tannbust*
vegetables	grern-meht-i	*grønmeti*

Souvenirs

earrings	oyr-nuhr-ing-uhr	*oyrnaringar*
handicraft	hond-uhr-bai-yeh	*handarbeiði*
necklace	hols-buhnd	*hálsband*
pottery	stain-toy	*steintoy*
ring	ring-ur	*ringur*
rug	tehp-pi	*teppi*

Clothing

coat	fruh-chi	*frakki*
dress	chohl-eh	*kjóli*
jacket	yuh-cheh	*jakki*
jumper (sweater)	troy-djuh	*troyggja*
shirt	shür-tuh	*skjúrta*
shoes	skehg-vuhr	*skógvar*
skirt	shürt	*skjúrt*
trousers	buk-sir	*buksur*

FAROESE

It doesn't fit.

    tae puhs-suhr i-chi   *Tað passar ikki.*

It's too ...	tae ehr o ...	*Tað er ov ...*
big	sterrst	*stórt*
small	looit-i	*lítið*
short	stutt	*stutt*
long	lehnkt	*langt*
tight	tronkt	*trongt*
loose	vooit	*vítt*

Materials

cotton	bum-udl	*bumull*
handmade	hond-djerrt	*hondgjørt*
leather	leh-vur	*leður*
brass	mehs-sing	*messing*
gold	gudl	*gull*
silver	sil-vur	*silvur*
silk	sil-chi	*silki*
wool	udl	*ull*
of wool	ud-lint	*ullint*

Colours

black	svuhrt	*svart*
blue	blott	*blátt*
brown	brünt	*brúnt*
green	grernt	*grønt*
orange	uhp-pil-seen-gult	*appelsingult*
pink	lyohs-uh-rehtt	*ljósareytt*
purple	lil-luh	*lilla*
red	rehtt	*reytt*
white	kvooitt	*hvítt*
yellow	gult	*gult*

Toiletries

comb	kuhm-bur	*kambur*
condoms	hooit-ir	*hítir*
deodorant	deh-o-do-ruhnt	*deodorant*
hairbrush	ho-uhr-bust	*hárbust*
moisturising cream	vae-teh-krehm	*vætukrem*
razor	rae-cheh-muh-sheen-uh	*rakimaskina*
sanitary napkins	(duh-meh)bind	*(damu)bind*
shampoo	shuhm-po	*shampo*
shaving cream	rae-cheh-swah-puh	*rakisápa*
soap	swah-puh	*sápa*
sunblock cream	sohl-krehm	*sólkrem*
tampons	tuhm-pon-djir	*tampongir*
tissues	sehr-vi-eht-tuhr	*serviettar*
toilet paper	veh-seh-puhp-pooir	*vesipappír*
toothpaste	tuhn-krehm	*tannkrem*

FAROESE

Stationery & Publications

map	korst	*kort*
newspaper	(ain-gilst)	*(eingilskt)*
(in English)	duhg-blae	*dagblað*
novels in English	ain-gils-guhr	*eingilskar*
	skuhld-ser-vur	*skaldsøgur*
paper	puhp-pooir	*pappír*
pen (ballpoint)	koo-lu-pehn-nur	*kúlupennur*
scissors	suhk-sur	*saksur*

Photography

How much is it to process this film?

| kvus-seh nehgv kos-tuhr duh uh fruhm-kuhd-luh hehn-duh film-in? | *Hvussu nógv kostar tað at framkalla henda filmin?* |

When will it be ready?

| naer vehr-ur huhn li-yu-vur? | *Nær verður hann liðugur?* |

I'd like a film for this camera.

| eh sgael haev-uh ain film teel heht-tuh fo-to-toh-leh | *Eg skal hava ein film til hetta fototólið.* |

B&W (film)	svuhrt kvooit-ur film-ur	*svart hvítur filmur*
camera	fo-to-tohl	*fototól*
colour (film)	leet-film-ur	*litfilmur*
film	fil-mur	*filmur*
flash	blits	*blits*
lens	lin-suh	*linsa*
light meter	lyohs-mwah-tuhr-eh	*ljósmátari*

Smoking

A packet of cigarettes, please.

| ain si-guh-rehtt-puhk-kuh tuhk | *Ein sigarettpakka, takk.* |

Are these cigarettes strong/mild?

| ehr-u hehs-uhr si-guh-rehtt-ir-nuhr stehr-kuhr/mil-duhr? | *Eru hesar sigarettirnar sterkar/mildar?* |

Do you have a light?

| heh-vur too ehld? | *Hevur tú eld?* |

cigarette papers	si-guh-rehtt-puhp-pooir	*sigarettpappír*
cigarettes	si-guh-reht-tir	*sigarettir*
filtered	vee fil-tri	*við filtri*
lighter	tehn-druh-ri	*tendrari*
matches	svwah-vul-pin-nuhr	*svávulpinnar*
menthol	mehn-tol	*mentol*
pipe	pooi-puh	*pípa*
tobacco (pipe)	tub-buhk	*tubbakk*

FAROESE

Sizes & Comparisons

big	sterrt	*stórt*
small	looiti	*lítið*
heavy	tunkt	*tungt*
light	luhtt	*lætt*
more	mai-ri/flai-ri	*meiri/fleiri*
less	min-ni	*minni*
too much/many	o mic-hi/o nehgv	*ov mikið/ov nógv*
many	nehgv	*nógv*
enough	noh mi-chi/noh nehgv	*nóg mikið/nónógv*
also	ai-sin-i	*eisini*
a little bit	aitt sin-dur	*eitt sindur*

HEALTH

Where is ...?	kvaer ehr ...?	*Hvar er ...?*
the chemist	uh-po-teh-cheh	*apotekið*
a doctor	ain luhk-neh	*ein lækni*
a dentist	ain tuhn-luhk-neh	*ein tannlækni*
the hospital	shook-ruh-hoos-eh	*sjúkrahúsið*

I'm sick.
  eh ehr-i shook/-ur   *Eg eri sjúk/-ur. (f/m)*
My friend is sick.
  veen-ur mooin ehr shook-ur *Vinur mín er sjúkur.*
Could I see a female doctor?
  kuhn eh slehp-puh uh tos-uh *Kann eg sleppa at tosa*
  vee ain kvin-neh-li-yuhn   *við ein kvinnuligan*
  luhk-nuh?   *lækna?*
What's the matter?
  kvaet bae-yir?   *Hvat bagir ?*
Where does it hurt?
  kvaer heh-vur too ilt?   *Hvar hevur tú ilt?*
It hurts here.
  eh haev-i ilt hehr   *Eg havi ilt her.*

FAROESE

Ailments

I have (a/an) ...	eh haev-i ...	Eg havi ...
allergy	o-vee-kvae-meh	*ovviðkvæmi*
anaemia	bloh-muhng-ul	*blóðmangul*
blister	bler-ru	*bløðru*
burn	bruhnd-swahr	*brandsár*
cold	krooim	*krím*
constipation	haer-uhn book	*harðan búk*
cough	hos-tuh	*hosta*
diarrhoea	lehst looiv	*leyst lív*
fever	fehb-ur	*fepur*
headache	her-vu-pooin-eh	*høvuðpínu*
hepatitis	liv-ruh-brun-uh	*livrabruna*
indigestion	ilt ooi boo-chin-un	*ilt í búkinum*
infection	brun-uh	*bruna*
influenza	in-flu-ehn-suh	*influensa*
lice	loois	*lýs*
low/high	logt/herkt	*lágt/høgt*
blood pressure	bloh-trooist	*blóðtrýst*
sore throat	ilt ooi hol-sin-un	*ilt í hálsinum*
a sprained foot	kok-tuhn foht	*keiktan fót*
stomachache	boo-kil-sku	*búkilsku*
temperature	fehb-ur	*fepur*
venereal disease	cheen-shoo-ku	*kynssjúku*
worms	orm	*orm*

Parts of the Body

ankle	er-kul	*økul*
arm	uhrm-ur	*armur*
back	baek	*bak*
chest	bring-uh/brerst	*bringa/bróst*
ear	oy-ruh	*oyra*
eye	uhy-yuh	*eyga*
finger	fing-ur	*fingur*
foot	foht-ur	*fótur*
hand	hond	*hond*
head	herdd	*høvd*

FAROESE

heart	yuhrt-uh	*hjarta*
leg	bain	*bein*
mouth	mun-nur	*munnur*
ribs	riv-yuh-bain	*rivjabein*
skin	hoo	*húð*
stomach	book-ur	*búkur*
teeth	tehn	*tenn*
throat	hols-ur	*hálsur*

Some Useful Words & Phrases

I'm ...

	eh ehr-i ...	*Eg eri ...*
diabetic	su-kur-shook/-ur	*sukursjúk/-ur* (f/m)
epileptic	eh-pi-lehp-ti-kuhr-eh	*epileptikari*
asthmatic	uhs-muh-shook/-ur	*astmasjúk/-ur* (f/m)

I'm allergic to antibiotics/penicillin.
    eh tol-i i-cheh uhn-ti-bi-o-tik-uh/   *Eg toli ikki antibiotika/*
    pehn-i-sill-een   *penisillin.*
I'm pregnant.
    eh ehr-i up wah veh-yin   *Eg eri upp á vegin.*
I haven't had my period for ... months.
    eh haevi- i-cheh huhft   *Eg havi ikki havt*
    mwah-nuh-shook-un-uh ooi ...   *mánasjúkuna í ...*
    mwahn-uhr   *mánaðar.*
I have been vaccinated.
    eh ehr-i vuhk-si-nehr-uh/-vur   *Eg eri vaksineraðl/-ur.* (f/m)

accident	oh-luk-kuh	*ólukka*
addiction	trongd	*trongd*
aspirin	pooin-eh-tuhb-leht-tir	*pínutablettir*
a bandage	for-bind-ing	*forbinding*
blood test	bloh-roynd	*blóðroynd*
contraceptive	fi-ri-bir-djing	*fyribyrging*
medicine	hai-li-vwah-vur	*heilivágur*
nausea	vuhml	*vaml*
oxygen	soo-rehv-ni	*súrevni*
vitamins	vi-tuh-meen-ir	*vitaminir*

At the Chemist

I need medication for ...
kuhn eh fwah hail-i-vwah
fi-ri ...?

*Kann eg fáa heilivág
fyri ...?*

I have a prescription.
eh haev-i reh-sehpt

Eg havi resept.

At the Dentist

I have a toothache.
eh haev-i tuhn-nuh-pooin-eh

Eg havi tannapínu.

I've lost a filling.
eh haev-i mist ain-uh plom-beh

Eg havi mist eina plombu.

I've broken a tooth.
eh haev-i brot-i ain-uh ton

Eg havi brotið eina tonn.

My gums hurt.
tae pooin-ir ooi
tuhn-huhl-din-un

*Tað pínir í
tannhaldinum.*

Please give me an anaesthetic.
kuhn eh fwah doy-ving?

Kann eg fáa doyving?

TIME & DATES

What date is it today?
kverr dae-vur ehr ooi dae?

Hvør dagur er í dag?

What time is it?
kvaet ehr klok-kuhn?

Hvat er klokkan?

It's ... am/pm.
hon ehr ...

Hon er ...

in the morning	um mor-gun-in	*um morgunin*
in the afternoon	said-nuh-puhrst-in	*seinnapartin*
in the evening	um kverl-deh	*um kvøldið*

FAROESE

Days of the Week

Monday	mwah-nuh-dae-vur	*Mánadagur*
Tuesday	toois-dae-vur	*Týsdagur*
Wednesday	mee-ku-dae-vur	*Mikudagur*
Thursday	hers-dae-vur	*Hósdagur*
Friday	frooi-djuh-dae-vur	*Fríggjadagur*
Saturday	luhy-yuhr-dae-vur	*Leygardagur*
Sunday	sun-nu-dae-vur	*Sunnudagur*

Months

January	djuhn-vwahr	*Januar*
February	feh-bruv-uhr	*Februar*
March	muhrs	*Mars*
April	uhp-rooil	*Apríl*
May	mai	*Mai*
June	dju-ni	*Juni*
July	dju-li	*Juli*
August	uhu-gust	*August*
September	sehp-tehm-bir	*September*
October	ok-to-bir	*Oktober*
November	no-vehm-bir	*November*
December	dehs-ehm-bir	*Desember*

Seasons

summer	sumuhr	*summar*
autumn	hehst	*heyst*
winter	veh-tur	*vetur*
spring	vwahr	*vár*

Present

today	ooi dae	*í dag*
this morning	ooi mor-gun	*í morgun*
tonight	ooi kverld/ooi nott	*í kvøld/í nátt*
this week/	heh-suh vee-ku-nuh/	*hesa vikuna/*
this year	ooi wahr	*í ár*
now	noo	*nú*

FAROESE

Past

yesterday	ooi djwahr	*í gjár*
day before yesterday	ooi fir-ruh-dae-yin	*í fyrradagin*
yesterday morning	ooi djwahr-uh-mor-gun-in	*í gjáramorgunin*
last night	djwahr-kverl-di	*í gjárkvøldið*
last week/last year	ooi soois-tu vee-ku/ soois-tuh wahr	*í síðstu viku/ síðsta ár*

Future

tomorrow	ooi mor-djin	*í morgin*
day after tomorrow	o-vur-mor-djin	*ovurmorgin*
tomorrow morning	ooi mor-djin-wahr-i	*í morginári*
tomorrow afternoon	said-nuh-puhrs-tin	*seinnapartin*
	ooi mor-djin	*í morgin*
tomorrow evening	ooi uhn-nuh-kverld	*í annaðkvøld*
next week	nuhs-tu vee-ku	*næstu viku*
next year	nuhs-uh wahr	*næsta ár*

During the Day

afternoon	said-nuh-puhrs-tur	*seinnapartur*
dawn	ooi loois-in-djin-i	*í lýsingini*
day	dae-vur	*dagur*
early	tooil-yuh	*tíðliga*
midnight	mid-nott	*midnátt*
morning	mor-gun	*morgun*
night	nottt	*nátt*
noon	wah mid-deh-yi	*á miðdegi*

FAROESE

NUMBERS & AMOUNTS

0	null	*null*
1	aitt	*eitt*
2	tvuhy	*tvey*
3	trooi	*trý*
4	fooir-uh	*fíra*
5	fim	*fimm*
6	sehks	*seks*
7	shuhy	*sjey*
8	ot-tuh	*átta*
9	nooi-djeh	*níggju*
10	tooi-djeh	*tíggju*
11	ehd-lehv-eh	*ellivu*
12	terlv	*tólv*
13	treht-tuhn	*trettan*
14	fdjürs-tuhn	*fjúrtan*
15	fim-tuhn	*fimtan*
16	sehks-tuhn	*sekstan*
17	suhy-chuhn	*seytjan*
18	wah-chuhn	*átjan*
19	nooi-chuhn	*nítjan*
20	choo-vu	*tjúgu*
21	ain-o-choo-vu	*einogtjúgu*
30	treh-di-veh	*tretivu*
40	fyerr-it-eh	*fjøruti*
50	fim-ti	*fimti*
60	sehks-ti	*seksti*
70	shoo-ti	*sjúti*
80	waht-tuh-ti	*áttati*
90	nooi-ti	*níti*
100	hun-druh	*hundrað*
1000	too-sin	*túsund*
one million	ain mil-liohn	*ein millión*

1st	fis-teh	*fyrsti*
2nd	uhn-nuhr	*annar*
3rd	tree-yi	*triðji*

1/4	ain fyoh-ring-ur	*ein fjórðingur*
1/3	ain tree-ying-ur	*ein triðjingur*
1/2	aitt holt	*eitt hálvt*
3/4	trooi-djir fyoh-ring-uhr	*tríggir fjórðingar*

Some Useful Words

a little (amount)	aitt sin-dur	*eitt sindur*
double	du-bult	*dupult*
enough	noh mi-chi/noh nehgv	*nóg mikið/nógv*
few	fwahr/fwah-yir/fwah	*fáar/fáir/fá* (f/m/n)
less	min-ni	*minni*
many	nehg-vuhr/nehg-vir/nehgv	*nógvar/nógvir/nógv* (f/m/n)
more	mai-ri/flai-ri	*meiri/fleiri*
once	ain-uh-fehr	*einaferð*
a pair	aitt paer/tvuhy	*eitt par/tvey*
percent	pro-sehnt	*procent*
some	naek-ruhr/naek-rir/nerk-ur	*nakrar/nakrir/nøku* (f/m/n)
too much	o nehgv	*ov nógv*
twice	tvaer fehr-ir	*tvær ferðir*

ABBREVIATIONS

SLS	*trandfaraskip Landsins*	Faroese national ferry company
ES	*Evropasamveldið*	European Community
ST	*Sameindu tjóðir*	United Nations
AA	*Atlantic Airways*	Faroese national airlines
km		kilometres
FO		Faroe Islands (letters used on cars/computer adresses, etc.)

FAROESE

EMERGENCIES

I'm lost.	eh ehr-i vilst/-ur	*Eg eri vilst/-ur.* (f/m)
I've been raped.	eh ehr-i nuhy-ti-chin	*Eg eri neyðtikin.*
Go away!	faer burs-tur!	*Far burtur!*
Help!	djolp!	*Hjálp!*
Thief!	choh-vur!	*Tjóvur!*

SIGNS	
LØGREGLA	POLICE

It's an emergency!
  heht-tuh ehr ain nuhy-ster-vuh! *Hetta er ein neyðstøða!*
There's been an accident!
  ain oh-luk-kuh ehr hehnd! *Ein ólukka er hend!*
Call a doctor/an ambulance!
  rin-ji eht-tir luhk-uht/ *Ringið eftir lækna/*
  shook-ruh-bee-li! *sjúkrabili!*
Call the police!
  rin-dji eht-tir lerg-rehg-lu-neh! *Ringið eftir løgregluni!*
Where is the police station?
  kvaer ehr lerg-rehg-lus-ter-yin? *Hvar er løgreglustøðin?*
I'll call the police!
  eh rin-dji eht-tir lerg-rehg-lu-neh! *Eg ringi eftir løgregluni!*
I'm/My friend is ill.
  eh ehr-i/veen-ur mooin *Eg eri/vinur mín*
  ehr shook-ur *er sjúkur.*
Where are the toilets?
  kvaer ehr-u veh-seh-ni? *Hvar eru vesini?*
Could you (pol) help me please?
  kun-nu ti-yun djeh-ruh so *Kunnu tygum gera so*
  vael uh djol-puh maer? *væl at hjálpa mær?*
Could I please use the telephone?
  kuhn eh lae-nuh *Kann eg læna*
  teh-leh-fon-in-uh? *telefonina?*
I didn't do it.
  eh hae-vi i-chi djerrt duh *Eg havi ikki gjørt tað.*

FAROESE

FAROESE

I'm sorry. I apologise.
um-shil-duh. eh bi-yeh um fi-ri-djehv-ing — *Umskylda. Eg biði um fyrigeving.*

I didn't realise I was doing anything wrong.
eh vis-ti i-chi aet eh djerr-di nae-guh sgaift — *Eg visti ikki, at eg gjørdi nakað skeivt.*

I wish to contact my embassy/consulate.
eh veel to-suh vee mooi-nuh uhm-buhs-suh-du/mooitt kon-su-lwaht — *Eg vil tosa við mína ambassadu/mítt konsulát.*

I speak English.
eh to-si ain-djilst — *Eg tosi eingilskt.*

I have medical insurance.
eh hae-vi shook-ruh-tri-djing — *Eg havi sjúkratrygging.*

My possessions are insured.
Mooi-nuhr og-nir ehr-u tri-djuh-yuhr — *Mínar ognir eru tryggjaðar.*

| My ... | mooin/mooitt ... | *Mín/Mítt ...* |
| was stolen. | ehr sto-lin/sto-li | *er stolin/stolið.* |

I've lost my ...	eh hae-vi mist ...	*Eg havi mist ...*
bags	mooi-nuhr tuhs-kur	*mínar taskur*
handbag	mooi-nuh hond-tuhs-ku	*mína hondtasku*
money	mooi-nuhr pehng-uhr	*mínar pengar*
passport	mooitt puhs	*mítt pass*
travellers cheques	mooi-nuhr feh-ruh-chehk-kuhr	*mínar ferðakekkar*

FINNISH

QUICK REFERENCE

Hello.	*hay/ tehrr*-veh	Hei/Terve.
Goodbye.	*na*-keh-meen	Näkemiin.
Yes.	*kül*-lah/yoo	Kyllä/Joo.
No.	ay	Ei.
Excuse me.	*uhn*-teehk-si	Anteeksi.
Sorry.	*o*-lehn	Olen
	puh-hoyl-luh-ni;	pahoillani;
	so-rri	Sori.
Thank you.	*kee*-toss	Kiitos.
You're welcome.	*o*-leh *hü*-va	Ole hyvä.
I understand.	*üm*-marr-rran	Ymmärrän.
I don't understand.	*ehn üm*-marr-rra	En ymmärrä.
Where is ...?	*mis*-sa on ...?	Missä on ...?
Go straight ahead.	*kul*-yeh *su-o*-rrahn	Kulje suoraan.

Turn left/right.
kaan-nü *vuh*-sehm-pahn/   Käänny vasempaan/
oy-keh-ahn.   oikeaan.

Do you speak English?
pu-hut-ko   Puhutko
ehng-luhn-ti-uh?   englantia?

Do you have any rooms available?
on-ko *tayl*-la *vuh*-pah-tuh   Onko teillä vapaata
hu-o-neht-tuh?   huonetta?

Where is a public toilet?
mis-sa on *ü*-lays-ta *vehs*-sah/   Missä on yleistä vessaa/
ü-lay-nehn *vehs*-suh?   yleinen vessa?

I'd like ...	*sahn*-ko ...	Saanko ...
a one-way ticket	meh-no-*li*-pun	menolipun
a return ticket	meh-no-pa-	meno-pa
	loo-*li*-pun	luulipun

1	*ük*-si	yksi	6	*koo*-si	kuusi
2	*kuhk*-si	kaksi	7	*sayt*-seh-man	seitsemän
3	*kol*-meh	kolme	8	*kuhkh*-dehk-suhn	kahdeksan
4	*nehl*-ya	neljä	9	*ükh*-dehk-san	yhdeksän
5	*vee*-si	viisi	10	*küm*-meh-nehn	kymmenen

FINNISH

FINNISH

Finnish, or suomi as it's called in Finland, is almost unique. It's not closely related to any language other than Estonian and Karelian and a handful of other rare languages. Linguistically, Finnish belongs to the Finnic (or more widely, Finno-Ugric) group of languages. Hungarian is the most widely spoken of the Finno-Ugric languages, but similarities with Finnish are extremely few.

Finnish is spoken by some five million people. It isn't related to any Indo-European languages. There are, however, many loan words from Baltic, Slavonic and Germanic languages, and many words deriving from French and, especially, English.

The main difficulties with Finnish are the suffixes (endings) added to noun and verb roots, which often alter in this process, and the habit of constructing long words by putting several small words together.

Outside the large towns, few people speak fluent English, so it's advisable to learn some phrases in Finnish to make your visit more rewarding. Finns appreciate any effort made by a non-native speaker and are eager to help further. Finnish is by no means an easy language to master, but it's easy to read out loud and the phonetics are not difficult – and mistakes made by foreigners are usually disregarded. There is also a notable Swedish-speaking minority in Finland, and all Finns learn Swedish in school, so you may need your Swedish vocabulary in Finland from time to time.

FINNISH

PRONUNCIATION

Pronunciation is given in the pronunciation guide at the front of this book, with the following exceptions:

Vowels

Finnish has eight vowels and the alphabet also includes Swedish å (see page 308).

FINNISH	GUIDE	SOUNDS
u	u	as in 'pull'

WHAT COMES AFTER Z?

The last three letters of the alphabet are å, ä and ö. So, while Aatami would be one of the first entries in a telephone book, Äänekoski would be one of the last.

Vowel Harmony

Finnish divides vowels into two groups: those formed 'in the front of the mouth' (e, i, y, ä, ö) and those formed 'in the back of the mouth' (a, o, u). This distinction is very important when forming words with suffixes, because the vowels in the suffixes must be of the same type as the vowels in the root word. For example, koulussa, 'in school', is formed by adding -ssa, not -ssä, to the root.

Double Vowels

Double vowels are tricky to pronounce, so follow the pronunciation guide carefully. You will find that some double vowels are pronounced as one sound within one syllable, others as diphthongs, and some as separate syllables.

FINNISH	GUIDE	SOUNDS
ää	aa	as the 'a' in American 'fast', but even longer

FINNISH

Consonants

There are only 13 consonants in Finnish, although the alphabet includes English consonants. The letter x can be written as ks, and z can be written, and is pronounced, as ts. Finns consider v and w more or less as the same letter, and in phone books you will find both under 'V'. In literature of a certain type, w makes a word look 'older.' Vanha is 'old', but wanha is 'definitely old'.

FINNISH	GUIDE	SOUNDS
p	p	soft, as in 'spirit'
b	b	explosive, as the 'b' in 'bug'
t	t	soft, as in 'steak'
k	k	soft, as in 'skate'
g	g	explosive, as the 'g' in 'gutter'
s	s	as in 'sun', but weaker
h	h	as in 'horse'
	kh	almost as strong as the 'ch' in Scottish 'loch'

PRONOUNS

SG		
I	mi-na	minä
you	si-na	sinä
he/she/it	han/han/seh	hän/hän/se
PL		
we	meh	me
you (pl & pol)	teh	te
they	heh/neh	he/ne (inf)

Double Consonants

Double consonants like kk in viikko, 'week', or mm in summa, 'sum', are held longer and they always split the word into two syllables. Note that ng and nk both make two syllables, and are pronounced as -ng-ng- and -ng-k-. For example, vangit, 'prisons', is vuhng-ngit. Note also that np is pronounced as mp, as in olenpa, o-lehm-puh, 'I am'.

FINNISH

SIGNS

AUKI/SULJETTU	OPEN/CLOSED
KIELLETTY	PROHIBITED
KUUMA/KYLMÄ	HOT/COLD
LÄHTÖSELVITYS	CHECK-IN COUNTER
MATKATAVARAT	BAGGAGE COUNTER
OPASTUS/NEUVONTA	INFORMATION
PUHELIN	TELEPHONE
PÄÄSY KIELLETTY	NO ENTRY
SISÄÄN	ENTRANCE
TULLI	CUSTOMS
TUPAKOINTI KIELLETTY	NO SMOKING
ULOS	EXIT
VAPAA PÄÄSY	FREE ADMISSION
VARATTU	RESERVED
VARAULOSKÄYNTI	EMERGENCY EXIT
WC	TOILETS

GREETINGS & CIVILITIES
Top Useful Phrases

Hello.	hay/tehrr-veh/moy	Hei/Terve/Moi. (pol/inf)
Goodbye.	na-keh-meen/moy	Näkemiin/Moi. (pol/inf)
Yes.	kül-lah/yoo	Kyllä/Joo. (pol/inf)
No.	ay	Ei.
Excuse me.	uhn-teehk-si	Anteeksi.
Thank you.	kee-toss/keet-ti	Kiitos/Kiitti. (inf)
Many thanks.	puhl-yon kee-tok-si-uh	Paljon kiitoksia.

May I? Do you mind?
  sai-sin-ko?   *Saisinko?*

Sorry.
  o-lehn *puh*-hoyl-luh-ni; *so*-rri   *Olen pahoillani; Sori.* (inf)

That's fine. You're welcome.
  o-leh *hü*-va; *ay*-pa *kehs*-ta   *Ole hyvä; Eipä kestä.* (inf)

FINNISH

There's no frequently used word for 'please' in Finnish. Often kiitos (thank you) is used. Another useful expression is 'could you', voisitteko, plus a verb. If you assume equality, or generally deal with informal situations, you are free to use less formal expressions. Speaking to a young clerk at a ticket booth or in a bank, you can say voitko, or even voitsä, 'are you able to', whereas an elderly lady would like to hear voisitteko, 'could you'.

Greetings

Good morning.
    (*hü*-vaa) *hu*-o-mehn-tuh   *(Hyvää) huomenta.*

Good afternoon.
    hü-vaa *pa*-i-vaa/*pa*-i-vaa   *Hyvää päivää./Päivää.* (inf)

Good evening/night.	*hü*-vaa *il*-tah/*ü-er*-ta	*Hyvää iltaa/yötä.*
How are you?	*mi-ta koo*-loo?	*Mitä kuuluu?*
Well, thanks.	*kee*-toss *hü*-vaa	*Kiitos hyvää.*

Forms of Address

Madam/Mrs	*rrohv*-vuh	*Rouva*
Sir/Mr	*hehrr*-rruh	*Herra*
Miss	*nay*-ti	*Neiti*
companion/friend	*üs*-ta-va/*kuh*-veh-rri	*ystävä/kaveri* (inf)

SMALL TALK

When you ask for a favour, use the most polite word: Te ('you' in the plural).

Minä means 'I', sinä is 'you'. Not everyone uses these words, however. In southern Finland, especially in Helsinki, most people say mä and sä. In Turku, Tampere and Oulu it's mää, for 'I', and sää for 'you' (nää in Oulu). In southern Savo they say mie and sie. In Helsinki it would be better to use mä instead of minä, to express that you don't place yourself above the other person. In northern Savo and places in Karelia, people still use minä – elsewhere you may sound rather egoistic if you use it. An asterisk (*) indicates where you could consider using some other form as you tour Finland.

Meeting People

What's your name?
mi-ka *tay*-dan *ni*-mehn-neh *on*?;   *Mikä teidän nimenne on?*;
mi-ka *sun* ni-mi *on*?   *Mikä sun nimi on?* (inf)

My name is ...
mi-nun *ni*-mehn-ni *on* ...;   *Minun nimeni on ...*;
mun ni-mi *on* ...   *Mun nimi on ...* (inf)

I'd like to introduce you to ...
huh-lu-ai-sin   *Haluaisin*
eh-si-tehl-la *si*-nut ...   *esitellä sinut ...-lle.*

I'm pleased to meet you.
hows-kuh *tuh*-vuh-tuh   *Hauska tavata.*

Nationalities

Where are you from?
mis-ta *si*-na *o*-let *ko*-toy-sin?   *Mistä sinä* olet kotoisin?*

I'm from ...	*o*-lehn ...	*Olen ...*
Australia	*owst*-rruh-li-uhs-tuh	*Australiasta*
Canada	*kuh*-nuh-duhs-tuh	*Kanadasta*
England	*ehng*-luhn-nis-tuh	*Englannista*
Finland	su-*o*-mehs-tuh	*Suomesta*
Ireland	*irr*-luhn-nis-tuh	*Irlannista*
New Zealand	oo-dehs-tuh	*Uudesta-*
	seeh-luhn-nis-tuh	*Seelannista*
Scotland	*scot*-luhn-nis-tuh	*Skotlannista*
the USA	*ükh*-düs-vuhl-loys-tuh/	*Yhdysvalloista/*
	uh-*meh*-rri-kuhs-tuh	*Amerikasta*
Wales	*wayl*-sis-ta	*Walesistä*

DID YOU KNOW ... In Finnish, the word for Finland is Suomi and the word for Finnish (the language) is suomi.

FINNISH

Age

How old are you?
*ku-in-*kuh *vuhn-*huh *si-*na *o-*leht?   *Kuinka vanha sinä* olet?*

I'm ... years old.
*o-*lehn ... *vu-o-*ti-uhs   *Olen ...-vuotias.*

Occupations

What work do you do?
*mi-*ta *si-*na *teeht tüh-erk-*seh-si?   *Mitä sinä* teet työksesi?*

I'm (a/an) ...	*o-*lehn ...	*Olen ...*
artist	*tai-*tay-li-yuh	*taiteilija*
businessperson	*lee-*keh-mi-ehs	*liikemies*
engineer	*in-*si-ner-rri	*insinööri*
farmer	*mahn-vil-*yeh-li-ya	*maanviljelijä*
journalist	*yohrr-*nuh-lis-ti/ *lekh-*ti-mi-ehs	*journalisti/ lehtimies*
lawyer	*yu-*rris-ti/ *luh-*ki-mi-ehs	*juristi/ lakimies*
mechanic	*meh-*kaa-nik-ko	*mekaanikko*
doctor	*laa-*ka-rri	*lääkäri*
nurse	*sai-*rrahn-*hoy-*tuh-yuh	*sairaanhoitaja*
office worker	*toy-*mis-to-*tü-ern-teh-*ki-ya	*toimistotyöntekijä*
scientist	*tut-*ki-yuh/ *ti-eh-*deh-*mi-ehs	*tutkija/ tiedemies*
student	*o-*pis-keh-li-yuh	*opiskelija*
teacher	*o-*peht-tuh-yuh	*opettaja*
waiter	*tuhrr-*yoy-li-yuh	*tarjoilija*
writer	*kihrr-*yai-li-yuh	*kirjailija*

FINNISH

Religion

What is your religion?
mi-ka *on si*-nun *us*-kon-to-si?   *Mikä on sinun uskontosi?*
I'm not religious.
ehn o-leh *us*-kon-nol-li-nehn/   *En ole uskonnollinen/*
us-ko-vai-nehn   *uskovainen.*

I'm (a) ...	*o*-lehn ...	*Olen ...*
Buddhist	*bud*-huh-lai-nehn	*buddhalainen*
Catholic	*kuh*-to-li-nehn	*katolinen*
Christian	*krris*-tit-tü	*kristitty*
Hindu	*hin*-du-lai-nehn	*hindulainen*
Jewish	*yoo*-tuh-lai-nehn	*juutalainen*
Lutheran	*lu*-teh-rri-lai-nehn	*luterilainen*
Muslim	*mus*-li-mi	*muslimi*

Family

Are you married?   *o*-leht-ko *nai*-mi-sis-suh?   *Oletko naimisissa?*

I'm ...	*o*-lehn ...	*Olen ...*
single	*nai*-muh-ton	*naimaton*
married	*nai*-mi-sis-suh	*naimisissa*
in a relationship	uhvo-lee-tos-suh	*avoliitossa*

How many children do you have?
ku-in-kuh *mon*-tuh   *Kuinka monta*
luhs-tuh *sul*-luh *on*?   *lasta sinulla on?*
I don't have any children.
mul-luh *ay o*-leh *luhp*-si-uh   *Minulla ei ole lapsia.*
I have a daughter/a son.
mul-luh *on tü*-tarr/*poy*-kuh   *Minulla on tytär/poika.*
How many brothers/sisters
do you have?
ku-in-kuh *mon*-tuh *vehl*-yeh-a/   *Kuinka monta veljeä/*
sis-uhrr-tuh *si*-nul-luh *on*?   *sisarta sinulla on?*
Do you have a boyfriend/girlfriend?
on-ko *sul*-luh *poy*-kuh-*üs*-ta-vaa/   *Onko sinulla poikaystävää/*
tüt-ter-*üs*-ta-vaa?   *tyttöystävää?*

FINNISH

brother	*veh*-li	*veli*
children	*luhp*-set	*lapset*
daughter	*tü*-tarr	*tytär*
family	*pehrr*-heh	*perhe*
father	*i*-sa	*isä*
grandfather	*i*-so-*i*-sa/ *vah*-rri/ *uk*-ki	*isoisä/vaari/ukki*
grandmother	*i*-so-*a*-*i*-ti/ *mum*-mi	*isoäiti/mummi*
husband	*uh*-vi-o *mi*-ehs	*aviomies*
mother	*a*-*i*-ti	*äiti*
partner	*e*-lam-an-*kump*-puh-ni	*elämänkumppani*
sister	*sis*-ko	*sisko*
son	*poy*-kuh	*poika*
wife	*vai*-mo	*vaimo*

Kids' Talk

How old are you?
  ku-in-kuh *vuhn*-huh
  si-na *o*-let?

Kuinka vanha sinä olet?

When's your birthday?
  kos-kuh *sun sünt*-ta-rrit *on?*

Koska sun synttärit on?

What do you do after school?
  mi-ta *si*-na *te*-eht *koh*-lun *jal*-keehn?

Mitä sinä teet koulun jälkeen?

Do you have a pet at home?
  on-ko *si*-nul-luh *lehm*-mik-ki-*eh*-la-in-ta *ko*-to-nuh?

Onko sinulla lemmikki-eläintä kotona?

I have a ...	*mi*-nul-luh *on* ...	*Minulla on* ...
bird	*lin*-tu	*lintu*
budgerigar	*un*-du-laht-ti	*undulaatti*
canary	*kuh*-nuhrr-i-*uhn*-*lin*-tu	*kanarianlintu*
cat	*kis*-suh	*kissa*
dog	*koy*-rruh	*koira*
goldfish	*kul*-tuh-*kuh*-luh	*kultakala*

FINNISH

Feelings

I like ...	*pi*-dan ...-sta/stuh	Pidän ...-sta/stä.
I don't like ...	*ehn pi*-da ...-sta/stuh	En pidä ...-sta/stä.
I'm well.	*voyn hü*-vin	Voin hyvin.

I'm ...	*mi*-nul-luh on ...	Minulla on ...
cold	*kiül*-ma	kylmä
hot	*koo*-muh	kuuma
in a hurry	*kee*-rreh	kiire

I'm ...	*o*-lehn ...	Olen ...
angry	*vi*-hai-nehn	vihainen
grateful	*kee*-tol-li-nehn	kiitollinen
happy	*i*-loy-nehn	iloinen
right	*oy*-keh-uhs-suh	oikeassa
sad	*su*-rrul-li-nehn	surullinen
sleepy	*u*-ni-nehn	uninen
tired	*va*-sü-nüt	väsynyt
worried	*hu*-o-lis-suh-ni	huolissani

I'm sorry. (condolence)
    o-tuhn *o*-sah *o*-lehn   Otan osaa, olen
    puh-hoyl-luh-ni   pahoillani.

BREAKING THE LANGUAGE BARRIER

Do you speak English?
    pu-hut-ko *ehng*-luhn-ti-uh?   Puhutko englantia?
Does anyone speak English?
    pu-hoo-ko ku-kahn   Puhuuko kukaan
    ehng-luhn-ti-uh?   englantia?

I speak a little ...	*pu*-hun va-han ...	Puhun vähän ...
I don't speak ...	*ehn pu*-hu ...	En puhu ...
I understand.	*üm*-marr-rran	Ymmärrän.
I don't understand.	*ehn üm*-marr-rra	En ymmärrä.

Could you speak more slowly please? | | |
voy-sit-ko *pu*-hu-uh *hi*-tahm-min? | | *Voisitko puhua hitaammin?* |
Could you repeat that? | | |
voyt-ko *toys*-tah? | | *Voitko toistaa?* |
How do you say ...? | | |
mi-tehn *suh*-no-tahn ...? | | *Miten sanotaan ...?* |
What does ... mean? | | |
mi-ta ... *tuhrr*-koyt-tah? | | *Mitä ... tarkoittaa?* |

I speak ...	*pu*-hun ...	*Puhun ...*
English	*ehng*-luhn-ti-uh	*englantia*
French	*rruhns*-kah	*ranskaa*
German	*suhk*-sah	*saksaa*
Swedish	*rru*-ot-si-uh	*ruotsia*

Some Useful Phrases

Just a minute.	*heht*-ki-nehn	*Hetkinen.*
Wait!	*o*-do-tuh!	*Odota!*

Good luck!
on-neh-uh! (*lükh*-kü-a *tüh*-ker!) *Onnea! (Lykkyä tykö!)*
It's (not) important.
seh on (*ay* o-leh) *tarr*-keh-aa *Se on (ei ole) tärkeää.*
It's (not) possible.
seh on (*ay* o-leh) *muhkh*-dol-lis-tuh *Se on (ei ole) mahdollista.*

BODY LANGUAGE

You are in the country of the 'silent Finn': it's not felt necessary to make small talk all the time, and lack of eye contact doesn't indicate shiftiness or rudeness. If there are empty seats on a bus or in the cinema (and there always are), it's not usual to sit down right next to a stranger – leave a 'buffer zone.'

Shake hands when you meet someone for the first time.

FINNISH

PAPERWORK

address	*o*-soy-teh	*osoite*
age	*i*-ka	*ikä*
birth certificate	*sün*-tü-ma-*to*-dis-tus	*syntymätodistus*
border	*rruh*-yuh	*raja*
car registration	*rreh*-kis-teh-rri *nu*-meh-rro	*rekister inumero*
customs	*tul*-li	*tulli*
date of birth	*sün*-tü-ma *ai*-kuh/	*syntymäaika/*
	hen-ki-ler-*tun*-nus	*henkilötunnus*
driver's licence	*uh*-yo-korrt-ti	*ajokortti*
identification	*hehn*-ki-ler-*puh*-peh-rrit	*henkilöpaperit*
make of car	*ow*-ton *mehrrk*-ki	*auton merkki*
marital status	*si*-vee-li-*saa*-tü	*siviilisääty*
name	*ni*-mi	*nimi*
nationality	*kuhn*-suh-lai-soos	*kansalaisuus*
passport	*puhs*-si	*passi*
passport number	*puhs*-sin *nu*-meh-rro	*passin numero*
place of birth	*sün*-tü-ma-*paik*-kuh	*syntymäpaikka*
profession	*uhm*-muht-ti	*ammatti*
reason for travel	*muht*-kuhn *tuhrr*-koy-tus	*matkan tarkoitus*
religion	*us*-kon-to	*uskonto*
sex	*su*-ku-*pu*-*o*-li	*sukupuoli*
visa	*vee*-su-mi	*viisumi*

SIGNS

AIKATAULU	TIMETABLE
ALIKULKUKÄYTÄVÄ	SUBWAY (pedestrian)
ASEMA	STATION
BUSSI/RATSIKKA PYSÄKKI	BUS/TRAM STOP
LIPPUTOIMISTO	TICKET OFFICE
LÄHTEVÄT	DEPARTURES
METRO	SUBWAY (train)
RAUTATIEASEMA	TRAIN STATION
SAAPUVAT	ARRIVALS

FINNISH

GETTING AROUND

As you look for places, visit them and leave them, you'll use different words in each case, and a little grammar is needed to gain an understanding of how words are constructed. Finnish grammar is extremely complicated. With all the possible suffixes and meanings, you can construct over 450 different words from any noun root.

-ssa or -ssä, 'in something': koulu-ssa, 'in school'
-sta or -stä, 'from something': koulu-sta, 'from school'
-double vowel plus n, 'to something': koulu-un, 'to school'
-lla or -llä, 'on', 'at' or 'in something' or 'somebody': koulu-lla, 'at school'
-lta or -ltä, 'from something' or 'somebody': koulu-lta, 'from school'
-lle, 'to something' or 'somebody': koulu-lle, 'to school'

Consider the following examples of expressing 'in ...', and 'to ...' (a town):

Helsinki:	Helsingi-ssä	Helsinki-in
Turku:	Turku-ssa	Turku-un
Varkaus:	Varkaude-ssa	Varkaute-en
Tampere:	Tamperee-lla	Tamperee-lle
Rovaniemi: (and others ending -niemi)	Rovaniemе-llä	Rovaniemе-lle
Seinäjoki: (and others ending -joki)	Seinäjoe-lla	Seinäjoe-lle
Kemijärvi: (and others ending -järvi)	Kemijärve-llä	Kemijärve-lle

To express being inside a vehicle, hotel etc, the -ssa suffix is used for 'in', and a double vowel plus -n for 'to': juna-ssa/juna-an, hotelli-ssa/hotelli-in. When you use a vehicle, you use the -lla suffix, as matkustaa juna-lla, 'to travel by train'.

What time does ...	mi-hin ai-kahn ...	Mihin aikaan ...
leave/arrive?	lakh-teeh/sah-poo?	lähtee/saapuu?
the (aero)plane	lehn-to-ko-neh	lentokone
the boat	lai-vuh	laiva
the bus (city)	bus-si	bussi
the bus (intercity)	bus-si/lin-yuh-ow-to	bussi/linja-auto
the train	yu-nuh	juna
the tram	rrai-ti-o-vow-nu/	raitiovaunu/
	rruh-tik-kuh	ratikka (inf)

Directions

Where is ...?	mis-sa on ...?	Missä on ...?

How do I get to ...?
    mi-ten mi-na paa-sen ...?   *Miten minä* pääsen ...?*

Is it far from/near here?
    on-ko seh kow-kuh-nuh/   *Onko se kaukana/*
    la-hehl-la?   *lähellä?*

Can I walk there?
    voy-ko sin-neh ka-vehl-la?   *Voiko sinne kävellä?*

Can you show me (on the map)?
    voyt-ko na-üt-taa mul-leh   *Voitko näyttää minulle*
    (kuhrr-tuhs-tuh)?   *(kartasta)?*

Are there other means of getting there?
    paa-seeh-ker sin-neh yol-luh-kin   *Pääseekö sinne jollakin*
    mool-luh tuh-vuhl-luh?   *muulla tavalla?*

I want to go to ...
    huh-lu-uhn men-na ...   *Haluan mennä ...*

Go straight ahead.
    kul-yeh su-o-rrahn   *Kulje suoraan.*

It's two blocks down.
    seh on kuhkh-den   *Se on kahden*
    korrt-teh-lin paas-sa   *korttelin päässä.*

FINNISH

Turn left/right ...	*kaan*-nü *vuh*-sehm-pahn/	*Käänny vasempaan/*
	oy-keh-ahn ...	*oikeaan ...*
at the next corner	seh-u-rrah-vuhs-tuh	*seuraavasta*
	kuh-dun-*kul*-muhs-tuh	*kadunkulmasta*
at the traffic lights	lee-kehn-neh-	*liikenne valoissa*
	vuh-loys-suh	

behind	...-n *tuh*-kuh-nuh	*...-n takana*
far	kow-kuh-nuh	*kaukana*
near	la-hehl-la	*lähellä*
in front of	eh-dehs-sa	*edessä*
opposite	*vuhs*-tuh *paa*-ta ...	*vastapäätä ...*
	-ta/-tuh	*-ta/-tä*

Booking Tickets

Where can I buy a ticket?
| *mis*-ta *voy os*-tah *li*-pun? | *Mistä voi ostaa lipun?* |

I want to go to ...
| *ha*-lu-uhn *men*-na ... | *Haluan mennä ...-lle/ ...vowel + n* |

Do I need to book?
| *ta-ü*-tüü-ker *vuh*-rruh-tuh? | *Täytyykö varata?* |

I'd like to book a seat to ...
| *ha*-lu-ai-sin *vuh*-rruh-tuh | *Haluaisin varata* |
| is-tu-muh-*pai*-kuhn ... | *istumapaikan ...lle/...vowel + n* |

I'd like ...	*sahn*-ko ...	*Saanko ...*
a one-way ticket	meh-no-*li*-pun	*menolipun*
a return ticket	meh-no-*pa*-loo-*li*-pun	*menopaluulipun*
two tickets	*kuhk*-si *lip*-pu-uh	*kaksi lippua*
a student's fare	o-pis-keh-li-ya-*li*-pun	*opiskelijalipun*
a child's fare	*luhs*-tehn-*li*-pun	*lastenlipun*
a pensioner's fare	*eh*-la-keh-la-is-tehn	*eläkeläisten*
	li-pun	*lipun*

1st class	*en*-sim-ma-i-nehn	*ensimmäinen*
	lu-ok-kuh	*luokka*
2nd class	*toy*-nehn *lu-ok*-kuh	*toinen luokka*

FINNISH

Is it completely full?

    on-ko *se ai*-vuhn *ta-ün*-na?   *Onko se aivan täynnä?*

Can I get a stand-by ticket?

    voyn-ko sah-duh

    li-pun *il*-muhn   *Voinko saada*

    paik-kuh-*vuh*-rrows-tuh?   *lipun ilman*

     paikkavarausta?

Air

Is there a flight to ...?

    on-ko ... *len*-to-uh?   *Onko ...-lle/ (vowel + n) lentoa?*

How long does the flight take?

    kow-uhn-ko *len*-to *kehs*-taa?   *Kauanko lento kestää?*

What is the flight number?

    mi-ka on *len*-non

    nu-meh-rro?   *Mikä on lennon*

     numero?

You must check in at ...

    tay-dan (*sun*) taü-tüü   *Teidän (sun) täytyy*

    kheh-kuh-tuh ... -la   *tsekata ...-lla*

airport tax	*lehn*-to-*kehnt*-ta *veh*-rro	*lentokenttävero*
boarding pass	*tuhrr*-kuhs-tus-*korrt*-ti	*tarkastuskortti*
customs	*tul*-li/ *tul*-li-*tuhrr*-kuhs-tus	*tulli/tullitarkastus*

Bus

Does this bus go to ...?

    meh-neeh-ker *ta*-ma

    bus-si ...?   *Meneekö tämä*

     bussi ... vowel + n/...lle?

Could you let me know
when we get to ...?

    voyt-ko suh-no-uh, *mil*-loyn

    tul-ehm-meh ...-n *lu*-o-nuh?   *Voitko sanoa, milloin*

     tulemme ...-n luona?

I want to get off!

    mi-na *huh*-lu-uhn

    jaa-da *poys*!   *Minä* haluan*

     jäädä pois!

What time is	*mi*-hin *ai*-kahn	*Mihin aikaan*
the ... bus?	on ... bus-si?	*on ... bussi?*
next	*seh-u*-rrah-vuh	*seuraava*
first	*ehn*-sim-ma-i-nehn	*ensimmäinen*
last	*vee*-may-nehn	*viimeinen*

Train

Is this the right platform for ...?
on-ko *ta*-ma *oy*-keh-uh *Onko tämä oikea*
rrai-deh ...? *raide ... vowel + n/...lle?*

Passengers must change trains.
muht-kus-tuh-*yi*-ehn on *Matkustajien on*
vaikh-deht-tuh-vuh *yu*-nah *vaihdettava junaa*

The train leaves from platform ...
yu-nuh *lakh*-teeh rrai-teehl-tuh ... *Juna lähtee raiteelta ...*

dining car	*rruh*-vin-to-luh-*vow*-nu	*ravintolavaunu*
express	*pi*-kuh-*yu*-nuh	*pikajuna*
local	*pai*-kuhl-lis-*yu*-nuh	*paikallisjuna*
sleeping car	*muh*-koo-*vow*-nu	*makuuvaunu*

Metro

Which direction takes me to ...?
kum-pahn *soon*-tahn *Kumpaan suuntaan*
paa-seeh ...? *pääsee ...lle/...vowel + n?*

What is the next station?
mi-ka on *seh-u*-rrah-vuh *Mikä on seuraava asema?*
uh-seh-muh?

SIGNS

KAUKOLIIKENNE	LONG-DISTANCE TRAFFIC
KOLIKOT	CHANGE (for coins)
LAITURIALUE	PLATFORM AREA (for ticket check)
LÄHILIIKENNELIPPUJA	LOCAL TRAIN TICKETS
LÖYTÖTAVARAT	LOST AND FOUND
RAIDE	PLATFORM NO
VR MATKAPALVELU	TRAVEL SERVICE

FINNISH

Taxi

How much does it
cost to go to ...?
puhl-yon-ko *muhk*-sah
muht-kuh ...?
Paljonko maksaa
matka ...vowel + n/...lle?

Here is fine, thank you!
tas-sa *on hü*-va *kee*-toss!   *Tässä on hyvä, kiitos!*

Continue!
yuht-kuh *vi*-eh-la!   *Jatka vielä!*

Stop here!
pü-sa-ü-ta *tas*-sa!   *Pysäytä tässä!*

The next street to the left/right.
seh-u-rrah-vah *kuh*-tu-uh   *Seuraavaa katua*
vuh-sehm-muhl-leh/   *vasemmalle/oikealle.*
oy-keh-uhl-leh

Please slow down.
hi-das-tuh *va*-han   *Hidasta vähän.*

Please wait here.
voyt-ko *o*-dot-tah *tas*-sa *va*-han   *Voitko odottaa tässä vähän.*

Some Useful Phrases

The train is delayed/cancelled.
yu-nuh *on* mü-*er*-has-sa/   *Juna on myöhässä/*
peh-rroo-teht-tu   *peruutettu.*

How long will it be delayed?
kow-uhn-ko *seh* onmu-*er*-has-sa?   *Kauanko se on myöhässä?*

There is a delay of ... hours.
seh on ... *tun*-ti-uh mu-*er*-has-sa   *Se on ... tuntia myöhässä.*

How long does the trip take?
kow-uhn-ko *muht*-kuh *kehs*-taa?   *Kauanko matka kestää?*

Is it a direct route?
on-ko *se* su-*o*-rruh *rrayt*-ti?   *Onko se suora reitti?*

Is that seat taken?
on-ko *toy paik*-kuh *vuh*-rruht-tu?   *Onko tuo paikka varattu?*

I want to get off at ...
   mi-na *jaan poys* ...-ssa/lla   *Minä* jään pois ...-ssa/-lla.*
Where can I hire a bicycle?
   mis-ta *mi*-na *voyn vu-ok*-rruh-tuh   *Mistä minä* voin vuokrata*
   pol-ku-*pü-er*-rran?   *polkupyörän?*
Is there room for the bicycle?
   makh-too-ko *tan*-neh   *Mahtuuko tänne*
   pol-ku-*pü-er*-rra?   *polkupyörä?*

Car

Where can I rent a car?
   mis-ta *mi*-na *voy*-sin   *Mistä minä* voisin*
   vu-ok-rruh-tuh *ow*-ton?   *vuokrata auton?*
daily/weekly
   *pehrr pa-i-*va/*pehrr veek*-ko   *per päivä/per viikko*
Does that include insurance/
unlimited mileage?
   koo-loo-ko *see*-hen *vuh*-koo-tus/   *Kuuluuko siihen vakuutus/*
   rruh-yoyt-tuh-muh-ton   *rajoittamaton*
   ki-lo-meht-rri *maa*-rra?   *kilometrimäärä?*
Where's the next petrol station?
   mis-sa *on la*-hin *ben*-suh   *Missä on lähin bensa*
   uh-seh-muh?   *-asema?*
How long can I park here?
   kow-uhn-ko *tas*-sa *sah*   *Kauanko tässä saa*
   parrk-keeh-rruh-tuh?   *parkkeerata?*
Does this road lead to ...?
   meh-neeh-ker *ta*-ma *ti-eh* ...?   *Meneekö tämä tie*
        ...vowel + n/...lle?

I need a mechanic.
   mi-na *tarr*-vit-sehn *korr*-yah-yah   *Minä* tarvitsen korjaajaa.*
The battery is flat.
   uhk-ku *on tükh*-ya   *Akku on tyhjä.*
The radiator is leaking.
   yaakh-dü-tin *vu-o*-tah   *Jäähdytin vuotaa.*
I have a flat tyre.
   rrehng-nguhs *on tükh*-ja   *Rengas on tyhjä.*

FINNISH

It's overheating.
   seh koo-meh-neeh *lee*-kah   *Se kuumenee liikaa.*
It's not working.
   seh ay toy-mi   *Se ei toimi.*

air (for tyres)	*il*-muh	*ilma*
battery	*uhk*-ku	*akku*
brakes	*yuhrr*-rrut	*jarrut*
clutch	*küt*-kin	*kytkin*
driver's licence	*uh*-yo-*korr*-tih	*ajokortti*
engine	*morrt*-to-rri/*ko*-neh	*moottori/kone*
lights	*vuh*-lot	*valot*
oil	*erl*-yü	*öljy*
puncture	*rrehng*-nguhs-*rrik*-ko	*rengasrikko*
radiator	*yaakh*-dü-tin	*jäähdytin*
road map	*ti-eh*-kuhrrt-tuh	*tiekartta*
tyres	*rrehn*-kaht	*renkaat*
windscreen	*too*-li-*luh*-si	*tuulilasi*

SIGNS

BENSA-ASEMA	FILLING STATION
HUOLTOASEMA	GARAGE
ITSEPALVELU	SELF SERVICE
JÄINEN TIE	ICE ON ROAD
KELIRIKKO	BAD ROAD
KIELLETTY AJOSUUNTA	NO ENTRY
KIERTOTIE	DETOUR
KORJAAMO	MECHANIC
LYIJYTÖN 95E	UNLEADED
MOOTTORITIE	FREEWAY
PYSÄKÖINTI KIELLETTY	NO PARKING
STOP	STOP
TIETYÖ	ROADWORKS
YKSISUUNTAINEN AJOTIE	ONE WAY
97 OKTAANIA	NORMAL LEADED
99 OKTAANIA	SUPER LEADED

FINNISH

ACCOMMODATION

Where is ...?	*mis*-sa o-li-si ...?	*Missä olisi ...?*
a cheap hotel	*huhl*-puh ho-tehl-li	*halpa hotelli*
a good hotel	*hü*-va ho-tehl-li	*hyvä hotelli*
a nearby hotel	*la*-hin ho-tehl-li	*lähin hotelli*

What is the address?
mi-ka on o-soy-teh?　　*Mikä on osoite?*

Could you write the address, please?
voy-sit-teh-ko *kirr*-yoyt-tah　　*Voisitteko kirjoittaa*
o-soyt-teen　　*osoitteen.*

At the Hotel

Do you have any rooms available?
on-ko *tayl*-la *vuh*-pah-tuh　　*Onko teillä vapaata*
hu-o-neht-tuh?　　*huonetta?*

I'd like ...	*ha*-lu-ai-sin ...	*Haluaisin ...*
a single room	*ükh*-dehn *hehng*-ngehn hu-o-neehn	*yhden hengen huoneen*
a double room	*kuhkh*-dehn *hehng*-ngehn hu-o-neehn	*kahden hengen huoneen*
to share a dorm	muh-koo-*suh*-lin san-kü-*pai*-kuhn	*makuusalin sänkypaikan*
a bed	sang-ngün	*sängyn*

I want a room	*mi*-na *huh*-lu-uhn	*Minä* haluan*
with a ...	hu-o-neehn ...	*huoneen ...*
bathroom	*kül*-pü-*hu*-o-neehl-luh	*kylpyhuoneella*
shower	su-ih-kul-luh	*suihkulla*
television	yos-suh on teh-leh-vi-si-o	*jossa on televisio*
window	yos-suh on ik-ku-nuh	*jossa on ikkuna*

I'm going to stay for ...	*mi*-na *ai*-on vee-pü-a ...	*Minä* aion viipyä ...*
one day	*ükh*-dehn *pai*-van	*yhden päivän*
two days	*kuhk*-si *pai*-vaa	*kaksi päivää*
one week	vee-kon	*viikon*

FINNISH

Do you have identification?
    on-ko *tayl*-la/*sul*-luh
    hehn-ki-ler-*puh*-peh-rray-tuh?   *Onko teillä/sulla*
        henkilöpapereita? (pol/inf)
Your membership card, please.
    sahn-ko *ya*-sehn-*korrt*-tin   *Saanko jäsenkortin.*
Sorry, we're full.
    vuh-li-teht-tuh-vuhs-ti *mayl*-la
    on *ta-üt*-ta   *Valitettavasti meillä*
        on täyttä.
How many nights?
    ku-in-kuh *mon*-tuh *u-er*-ta?   *Kuinka monta yötä?*
How much is it per night/per person?
    puhl-yon-ko *seh* on *ü-erl*-ta/
    hehng-ngehl-ta?   *Paljonko se on yöltä/*
        hengeltä?

Can I see it?
    voyn-ko *mi*-na *nakh*-da *sehn*?   *Voinko minä* nähdä sen?*
Are there any others?
    on-ko *mi*-taan *mu-i*-tuh?   *Onko mitään muita?*
Are there any cheaper rooms?
    on-ko *huhl*-vehm-pah
    hu-o-neht-tuh?   *Onko halvempaa*
        huonetta?
Can I see the bathroom?
    voyn-ko *mi*-na *nakh*-da
    kül-pü-*hu-o*-neehn?   *Voinko minä**
        nähdä kylpyhuoneen?
Is there a reduction for
students/children?
    sah-ko *o*-pis-keh-li-yuh/*luhp*-si
    uh-lehn-nus-tuh?   *Saako opiskelija/lapsi*
        alennusta?
Does it include breakfast?
    koo-loo-ko *ah*-mi-ai-nehn
    hin-tahn?   *Kuuluuko aamiainen*
        hintaan?

FINNISH

It's fine, I'll take it.
   se on hü-va *mi*-na *o*-tuhn *sen*   *Se on hyvä, minä* otan sen.*
I'm not sure how long I'm staying.
   mi-na *ehn ti-eh*-da *ku-in*-kuh   *Minä* en tiedä kuinka*
   kow-uhn *mi*-na *vii*-vün *taal*-la   *kauan minä* viivyn täällä.*

Is there a lift?
   on-ko *taal*-la *his*-si-a?   *Onko täällä hissiä?*
Where is the bathroom?
   mis-sa *on kül*-pü   *Missä on kylpyhuone*
   hu-o-neh (*vehs*-suh)?   *(vessa)?*
Is there hot water all day?
   on-ko *koo*-mah *veht*-ta   *Onko kuumaa vettä*
   ko-ko *pai*-van?   *koko päivän?*
Do you have a safe where
I can leave my valuables?
   on-ko *tayl*-la *sa*-ilü-tüs-*lo*-kehrr-   *Onko teillä säilytyslokeroa*
   oy-tuh *arr*-vo-*tuh*-vuhrr-uhl-le?   *arvotavaralle?*
Is there somewhere to wash clothes?
   voy-ko *taal*-la *yos*-sain   *Voiko täällä jossain*
   pehs-ta *vaht*-tay-tuh?   *pestä vaatteita?*
Can I use the kitchen?
   voyn-ko *ka-üt*-taa *kayt*-ti-er-ta?   *Voinko käyttää keittiötä?*
Can I use the telephone?
   voyn-ko *ka-üt*-taa *pu*-heh-lin-tuh?   *Voinko käyttää puhelinta?*
Is your sauna warm?
   on-ko *sow*-nuh *lam*-min?   *Onko sauna lämmin?*
Do you have a smoke sauna?
   on-ko *tayl*-la *suh*-vu-*sow*-nah?   *Onko teillä savusaunaa?*

SIGNS

HOTELLI	**HOTEL**
MATKUSTAJAKOTI	**GUESTHOUSE**
MOTELLI	**MOTEL**
RETKEILYMAJA	**YOUTH HOSTEL**

FINNISH

Requests & Complaints

Please wake me up at ...
voyt-teh-ko *heh*-rrat-taa   *Voitteko herättää*
mi-nut *kehl*-lo ...   *minut kello ...*

The room needs to be cleaned.
hu-o-neh *ta-ü*-tü-i-si *see*-vo-tuh   *Huone täytyisi siivota.*

Please change the sheets.
voyt-teh-ko *vaikh*-tah   *Voitteko vaihtaa*
luh-kuh-nuht   *lakanat.*

I can't open/turn on ...   *ehn* sah ... *ow*-ki   *En saa ... auki.*
I can't close/turn off ...   *ehn* saa ... *keen*-ni   *En saa ... kiinni.*
  the window   *ik*-ku-nah   *ikkunaa*
  the door   *o*-veh-uh   *ovea*
  the heating   *puht*-teh-rri-uh   *patteria*
  the TV   *tee*-veeh-ta   *TV:ta*

I left my key in the room.
uh-vai-meh-ni *ya-i*   *Avaimeni jäi*
hu-o-neeh-seehn   *huoneeseen.*

The toilet won't flush.
vehs-suh *ay* veh-da   *Vessa ei vedä.*

I don't like this room.
mi-na *ehn* oy-kayn *pi*-da   *Minä* en oikein*
tas-ta *hu-o*-neehs-tuh   *pidä tästä huoneesta.*

It's too small.   *se* on lee-uhn *pi-eh*-ni   *Se on liian pieni.*
It's noisy.   *si-ehl*-la on *meh*-lu-uh   *Siellä on melua.*
It's too dark.   *se* on lee-uhn *pi*-meh-a   *Se on liian pimeä.*
It's expensive.   *se* on *kuhl*-lis   *Se on kallis.*

Some Useful Words & Phrases

I'm/We're leaving now/tomorrow.

mi-na luh-dehn/meh   *Minä* lähden/Me*
lakh-deh-taan *nüt/hu-o*-mehn-nuh   *läh-detään nyt/huomenna.*

I'd like to pay the bill.

mi-na *muhk*-sai-sin *luhs*-kun   *Minä* maksaisin laskun.*

name	*ni*-mi	*nimi*
given names	*eh*-tu *ni*-meht	*etunimet*
surname	*su*-ku-*ni*-mi	*sukunimi*
address	*o*-soy-teh	*osoite*
room number	*hu-o*-neen	*huoneen*
	nu-meh-rro	*numero*
air-conditioned	*il*-muhs-toy-tu	*ilmastoitu*
balcony	*puhrr*-veh-keh	*parveke*
bathroom	*kül*-pü-*hu-o*-neh	*kylpyhuone*
bed	*san*-kü	*sänky*
bill	*luhs*-ku	*lasku*
blanket	*payt*-to	*peitto*
candle	*künt*-ti-la	*kynttilä*
chair	*tu-o*-li	*tuoli*
clean	*puh*-duhs	*puhdas*
cupboard	*kahp*-pi	*kaappi*
dirty	*li*-kai-nehn	*likainen*
double bed	*puh*-rri-*san*-kü	*parisänky*
electricity	*sakh*-ker	*sähkö*
excluded	ay *koo*-lu *hin*-tahn	*ei kuulu hintaan*
included	*koo*-loo *hin*-tahn	*kuuluu hintaan*
key	*uh*-vain	*avain*
lift (elevator)	*his*-si	*hissi*
light bulb	heh-ku-*luhmp*-pu/	*hehkulamppu/*
	luhmp-pu	*lamppu*
a lock	*luk*-ko	*lukko*
mattress	*puht*-yuh	*patja*
mirror	*pay*-li	*peili*
padlock	mu-nuh-*luk*-ko	*munalukko*

pillow	*tüü*-nü	tyyny
quiet	*hil*-jai-nehn	hiljainen
room (in hotel)	*hu-o*-neh / *ho*-tehl-li-*hu-o*-neh	huone/hotelli huone
sauna	*sow*-nuh	sauna
sheet	*luh*-kuh-nuh	lakana
shower	*su-ih*-ku	suihku
soap	*saip*-pu-uh	saippua
suitcase	*muht*-kuh-*lowk*-ku	matkalaukku
swimming pool	*u-i*-muh-*uhl*-luhs	uima-allas
table	*per-ü*-ta	pöytä
toilet	*veeh*-seeh / *vehs*-suh	WC/vessa
toilet paper	*vehs*-suh-*puh*-peh-rri	vessapaperi
towel	*püü*-heh	pyyhe
(some) water	*veht*-ta	vettä
cold water	*kül*-muh vesi	kylmä vesi
hot water	*koo*-mah vet-ta	kuumaa vettä
window	*ik*-ku-nuh	ikkuna

FINNISH

STRAIGHT TO THE POINT

When buying a pack of cigarettes or a beer, you just state the merchandise. Pitkä! means 'Could you give me a large glass of beer, please!'.

AROUND TOWN

Where is ...?	*mis-sa on ...?*	*Missä on ...?*
the art gallery	*tai-deh-guhl-leh-rri-ah/*	*taidegalleriaa/*
	tai-deh-guhl-leh-rri-uh	*taidegalleria*
a bank	*puhnk-ki-uh/ puhnk-ki*	*pankkia/pankki*
the church	*kirrk-ko-uh/ kirrk-ko*	*kirkkoa/kirkko*
the city centre	*kehs-kus-tah/*	*keskustaa/*
	kehs-kus-tuh	*keskusta*
the ...embassy	*...-n soorr*	*...-n suur*
	la-heh-tüs-ter-a/	*lähetystöä/*
	...-n soorr la-heh-tüs-ter	*suurlähetystö*
my hotel	*ho-tehl-li-ni*	*hotellini*
a mail box	*pos-ti-lah-tik-ko-uh/*	*postilaatikkoa/*
	pos-ti-lah-tik-ko	*postilaatikko*
the market	*to-rri-uh/ to-rri*	*oria/tori*
the museum	*mu-seh-o-tuh/ mu-seh-o*	*museota/museo*
the police	*po-lee-si-uh/ po-lee-si*	*poliisia/poliisi*
the post office	*pos-ti-uh/ pos-ti*	*postia/posti*
a public toilet	*ü-lays-ta vehs-sah/*	*yleistä vessaa/*
	ü-lay-nehn vehs-suh	*yleinen vessa*
a telephone	*pu-heh-lin-tuh/*	*puhelinta/*
	pu-heh-lin	*puhelin*
the tourist	*muht-kay-lu*	*matkailu*
information	*toy-mis-to-uh/*	*toimistoa/*
office	*toy-mis-to*	*toimisto*

What time does it open/close?
mil-loyn seh uh-vuh-tahn/	*Milloin se avataan/*
sul-jeh-tahn?	*suljetaan?*

What ... is this?	*mi-ka ... ta-ma on?*	*Mikä ... tämä on?*
street	*kuh-tu*	*katu*
suburb	*kow-pung-ngin-o-suh/*	*kaupunginosa/*
	eh-si-kow-pung-ki	*esikaupunki*

For directions, see the Getting Around section, page 144.

For directions, see the Getting Around section, page 144.

FINNISH

At the Post Office

I'd like to send ...	*huh*-lu-ai-sin	*Haluaisin*
	la-heht-taa ...	*lähettää ...*
a fax	*fuhk*-sin	*faksin*
a letter	*kirr*-yeehn	*kirjeen*
a postcard	*pos*-ti-*korr*-tin	*postikortin*
a parcel	*puh*-keh-tin	*paketin*
a telegram	*sakh*-keehn	*sähkeen*

I'd like some stamps.

    huh-lu-ai-sin   *Haluaisin*
    pos-ti-*mehrrk*-keh-ja   *postimerkkejä.*

How much does it cost
to send this to ...?

    puhl-yon-ko *muhk*-sah   *Paljonko maksaa*
    la-heht-taa ta-ma ...?   *lähettää tämä*
                                ...vowel + n?

an aerogram	*uh-eh*-rro-grruhm-mi	*aerogrammi*
air mail	*lehn*-to-*pos*-ti-nuh	*lentopostina*
envelope	*kirr*-jeh	*kirje*
registered mail	*kirr*-juht-tu *kirr*-jeh	*kirjattu kirje*
surface mail	*mah-pos*-ti-nuh	*maapostina*

FINNISH

Telephone & Internet

I want to ring ...
huh-lu-ai-sin *soyt*-tah ...   *Haluaisin soittaa ...*
The number is ...
pu-heh-lin-*nu*-meh-rro *on* ...   *Puhelinnumero on ...*

How much does a
three-minute call cost?
puhl-yon-ko *muhk*-sah   *Paljonko maksaa*
kol-mehn *mi*-noo-tin *pu*-heh-lu?   *kolmen minuutin puhelu?*
How much does each
extra minute cost?
puhl-yon-ko *muhk*-sah   *Paljonko maksaa*
jo-kai-nehn *li*-sa-*mi*-noot-ti?   *jokainen lisäminuutti?*

I'd like to speak to (Mr Nieminen).
huh-lu-ai-sin *pu*-hu-uh   *Haluaisin puhua*
(*hehrr*-rruh *ni*-eh-mi-sehn)   (*herra Niemisen*)
kuhns-suh   *kanssa.*
I want to make a
reverse-charges phone call.
huh-lu-uhn *soyt*-tah   *Haluan soittaa*
vuhs-tuh-*pu*-heh-lun   *vastapuhelun.*
It's engaged.
seh on vuh-rruht-tu   *Se on varattu.*
I've been cut off.
pu-heh-lu *kuht*-keh-si   *Puhelu katkesi.*

cellular phone
kan-nük-ka   *kännykkä*

Where can I access the Internet?
mis-sa *paa*-sehn   *Missä pääsen*
in-tehrr-neht-tiin?   *Internettiin?*
I'd like to send an e-mail.
huh-lu-ai-sin *la*-heht-taa   *Haluaisin lähettää*
suh-ker-*pos*-ti-uh   *sähköpostia.*

At the Bank

I want to change some money/
travellers cheques.

huh-lu-ai-sin *vaikh*-tah *rruh*-hah/　　*Haluaisin vaihtaa rahaa/*
muht-kuh *shehk*-keh-ja　　　　　　*matkashekkejä.*

What is the exchange rate?

mi-ka on *kurrs*-si?　　　　　　　*Mikä on kurssi?*

How many marks per dollar?

puhl-yon-ko *dol*-luh-rril-luh　　　　*Paljonko dollarilla*
sah muhrrk-ko-yuh?　　　　　　　*saa markkoja?*

Can I have money transferred
here from my bank?

voyn-ko *mi*-na *sah*-duh　　　　　*Voinko minä* saada*
rruh-hah *seö*-rreht-tü-a　　　　　*rahaa siirrettyä*
o-muhs-tuh *puhn*-kis-tuh-ni?　　　　*omasta pankistani?*

How long will it take to arrive?

kow-uhn-ko *sehn* tu-lo *kehs*-taa?　*Kauanko sen tulo kestää?*

Has my money arrived yet?

on-ko *mi*-nun *rruh*-huh-ni　　　　*Onko minun rahani*
sah-pu-nut *vi*-eh-la?　　　　　　*saapunut vielä?*

(some) banknotes	*seh*-teh-leh-i-ta	*seteleitä*
cashier	*kuhs*-suh	*kassa*
some coins	*ko*-li-koy-tuh	*kolikoita*
credit card	*lu*-ot-to-korrt-ti	*luottokortti*
exchange	*rruh*-huhn-*vaikh*-to	*rahanvaihto*
loose change	*pik*-ku-*rruh*-hah/	*pikkurahaa/*
	vaikh-to-*rruh*-hah	*vaihtorahaa*
money transfer	*ti*-li-*seer*-to	*tilisiirto*
signature	*uhl*-leh-*kirr*-yoy-tus	*allekirjoitus*

INTERESTS & ENTERTAINMENT
Sightseeing

Do you have a guidebook/
local map?
    on-ko *si*-nul-luh *muht*-kuh-*o*-
    puhs-tuh/ *kuhrrt*-tah?

*Onko sinulla matkao
pasta/karttaa?*

What are the main attractions?
    mit-ka *o*-vuht *tarr*-kaym-mat
    nakh-ta-vüü- deht?

*Mitkä ovat tärkeimmät
nähtävyydet?*

What is that?
    mi-ka *tu-o* on?

Mikä tuo on?

How old is it?
    ku-in-kuh *vuhn*-huh *seh* on?

Kuinka vanha se on?

Can I take photographs?
    voyn-ko *mi*-na *ot*-tah
    vuh-lo-*ku*-vi-uh?

Voinko minä ottaa
valokuvia?*

What time does it open/close?
    mil-loyn *seh* ow-keh-ah/
    sul-yeh-tahn?

*Milloin se aukeaa/
suljetaan?*

ancient	*vuhn*-huh	*vanha*
archaeological	*uhrr*-keh-o-lo-gi-nehn	*arkeologinen*
beach	*u-i*-muh *rruhn*-tuh	*uimaranta*
building	*rruh*-kehn-nus	*rakennus*
castle	*lin*-nuh	*linna*
cathedral	tu-o-mi-o-*kirrk*-ko/	*tuomiokirkko/*
	kuh-tehd-rrah-li	*katedraali*
church	*kirrk*-ko	*kirkko*
concert hall	kon-sehrrt-ti-*huhl*-li	*konserttihalli*
library	*kirr*-juhs-to	*kirjasto*
main square	*kehs*-kus to-rri	*keskustori*
market	to-rri/ kowp-puh-*to*-rri/	*tori/kauppatori/*
	muhrrk-ki-nuht	*markkinat*
monastery	*lu-os*-tuh-rri	*luostari*
monument	mu-*is*-to-mehrrk-ki/	*muistomerkki/*
	mo-nu-mehnt-ti	*monumentti*

mosque	*mos*-kay-yuh	*moskeija*
old city	*vuhm*-huh-*kow*-pun-ki	*vanhakaupunki*
palace	*puh*-luht-si	*palatsi*
opera house	*orrp*-peh-rruh-*tuh*-lo	*oopperatalo*
ruins	*rrow*-ni-ot	*rauniot*
stadium	*stuh*-di-on	*stadion*
some statues	*puht*-sai-tuh	*patsaita*
synagogue	*sü*-nuh-gorr-guh	*synagooga*
temple	*tehmp*-peh-li	*temppeli*
university	*ü-li-o*-pis-to/	*yliopisto/*
	korr-keh-uh *koh*-lu	*korkeakoulu*

Going Out

What's there to do in the evening?
| *mi*-ta *taal*-la *voy teh*-da *il*-tai-sin? | *Mitä täällä voi tehdä iltaisin?* |

Are there any discos?
| *on*-ko *taal*-la *üch*-taan *dis*-ko-uh? | *Onko täällä yhtään diskoa?* |

Are there places where you
can hear local folk music?
| *voy*-ko *taal*-la *mis*-saan *kool*-luh | *Voiko täällä missään kuulla* |
| *pai*-kal-lis-tuh *mu*-seek-ki-uh? | *paikallista musiikkia?* |

How much does it cost to get in?
| *puhl*-yon-ko *on paa*-sü *muhk*-su? | *Paljonko on pääsymaksu?* |

cinema	*eh*-lo-ku-vuh-	*elokuvateatteri*
	teh-uht-teh-rri	
concert	*kon*-sehrrt-ti	*konsertti*
discotheque	*dis*-ko	*disko*
theatre	*teh*-uht-teh-rri	*teatteri*

FRIENDS FOREVER

Traditionally Finns had to make a deal, sinunkaupat, to call each other sinä instead of Te. The deal involved an exchange of names and a formal handshake, after which you were friends forever.

FINNISH

Sports & Interests

What do you do in your spare time?

mi-ta *si*-na *teeht*	*mitä sinä teet*
va-pah-*ai*-kuh-nuh-si?	*vapaa-aikanasi?*

What sport do you play?

mi-ta *urr*-hay-lu-*luh*-yi-uh	*mitä urheilulajia*
huhrr-rruhs-tat?	*harrastat?*

art	*tai*-deh	*taide*
basketball	*ko*-rri-puhl-lo	*koripallo*
boxing	*nürrk*-kay-lü	*nyrkkeily*
cooking	*rru*-uuhn-*lait*-to	*ruuanlaitto*
fishing	*kuh*-luhs-tus	*kalastus*
football	*yuhl*-kuh-puhl-lo	*jalkapallo*
going out	*ul*-ko-nuh-*ka*-ün-ti	*ulkonakäynti*
going to	*eh*-lo-ku-vis-	*elokuvissakäynti*
the cinema	suh-*ka*-ün-ti	
music	*mu*-seek-ki	*musiikki*
photography	*vuh*-lo-kuv-ows	*valokuvaus*
reading	*luk*-ehm-in-ehn	*lukeminen*
shopping	*shop*-pai-luu	*shoppailu*
soccer	*yuhl*-kuh-puhl-lo	*jalkapallo*
sport	*orr*-hay-loo	*urheilu*
the theatre	*the*-uht-teh-rri	*teatteri*
travelling	*muht*-kust-uh-min-ehn	*matkustaminen*
writing	*kirr*-yoy-tuh-min-ehn	*kirjoittaminen*

FINNISH

Festivals

The best film festival is held in Sodankylä (above the Arctic Circle) in June. The longest-established summer events are both held in July: **Pori Jazz** and the huge festival of world and traditional music at Kaustinen in Ostrobothnia. The biggest rock festivals are held near Turku (Ruisrock, July) and Seinäjoki (Provinssirock, June). One of Europe's leading and most remarkable Chamber Music events is held in Kuhmo on the Eastern border (July). To hear some of the best choirs for which the Nordic countries are famous, go to the Choirs Festival in Vaasa in May.

IN THE COUNTRY
Weather

What's the weather like?	*mi*-ka *on saa ti*-luh?/ *mil*-lai-nehn *saa on*?	*Mikä on säätila?*/ *Millainen sää on*?
It's ... today.	*ta*-naan *on* ...	*Tänään on* ...
Will it be ... tomorrow?	*on*-ko *hu-o*-mehn-nuh?	*Onko huomenna*... ?
cloudy	*pil*-vis-ta	*pilvistä*
cold	*kül*-maa	*kylmää*
foggy	*su*-mu-is-tuh	*sumuista*
forest fire alert	*meht*-sa-*puh*-lo-*vuh*-rroy-tus	*metsäpalo varoitus*
frosty	*puhk*-kuhs-tuh	*pakkasta*
hot	*koo*-muh	*kuuma*
raining	*suh*-deht-tuh	*sadetta*
snowing	*lun*-tuh/ *lu*-mih-*suh*-deht-tuh	*lunta*/ *lumisadetta*
summer night frost	*huhl*-lah	*hallaa*
sunny	*ow*-rrin-koys-tuh	*aurinkoista*
thunderstorm	*uk*-kos-tuh	*ukkosta*
sleet	*rran*-taa	*räntää*
windy	*too*-lihs-tuh	*tuulista*

FINNISH

Camping

Am I allowed to camp here?
sah-ko *taal*-la *lay*-rri-ü-tü-a?   *Saako täällä leiriytyä?*
Is there a campsite nearby?
on-ko *taal*-la *yos*-sain *la*-hehl-la   *Onko täällä jossain lähellä*
lay-rrint-tuh-*uh*-luh-eh?   *leirintäaluetta?*

backpack	*rrehp*-pu	*reppu*
can opener	*purr*-kin-*uh*-vah-yuh	*purkinavaaja*
compass	*kom*-puhs-si	*kompassi*
some firewood	*polt*-to-*poo*-tuh	*polttopuuta*
foam mattress	*muh*-koo-*uh*-lou-tuh	*makuualusta*
gas cartridge	*kah*-su-*sa*-*i*-li-ö	*kaasusäiliö*
mattress	*puht*-yuh	*patja*
penknife	*link*-ku-*vayt*-si	*linkkuveitsi*
rope	*ker*-ü-si	*köysi*
tent	*tehlt*-tuh	*teltta*
torch (flashlight)	*tuhs*-ku-*luhmp*-pu	*taskulamppu*
sleeping bag	*muh*-koo-*pus*-si	*makuupussi*
stove	*rreht*-ki-*kay*-tin	*retkikeitin*
water bottle	*veh*-si-*pul*-lo	*vesipullo*

SIGNS

LEIRINTÄALUE	CAMPING GROUND

FINNISH

FOOD
Some Useful Words & Phrases

breakfast	*ah*-mi-ai-nehn	*aamiainen*
lunch	*loh*-nuhs	*lounas*
early/late dinner	*pa-i*-val-li-nehn/	*päivällinen/*
	il-luhl-li-nehn	*illallinen*

Table for ..., please.
　　sah-dahn-ko meh per-*ü*-ta ...?　　*Saadaanko me pöytä ... lle?*
Can I see the menu please?
　　voyn-ko *mi*-na　　　　　　　　*Voinko minä**
　　nakh-da meh-nun?　　　　　　　*nähdä menun?*
I'd like the set lunch, please.
　　sahn-ko *pa-i*-van *loh*-nahn　　*Saanko päivän lounaan.*
What does it include?
　　mi-ta *see*-hehn *koo*-loo?　　　*Mitä siihen kuuluu?*
Service is included in the bill.
　　tuhrr-yoy-lu *koo*-loo *hin*-tahn　*Tarjoilu kuuluu hintaan.*

ashtray	*tuh*-kuh-*kup*-pi	*tuhkakuppi*
the bill	*luhs*-ku	*lasku*
a cup	*kup*-pi	*kuppi*
dessert	*yal*-ki-*rru-o*-kuh	*jälkiruoka*
a drink	*yu-o*-muh	*juoma*
a fork	*hah*-rruk-kuh	*haarukka*
fresh	*tu-o*-rreh	*tuore*
a glass	*luh*-si	*lasi*
a knife	*vayt*-si	*veitsi*
a plate	*low*-tuh-nehn	*lautanen*
spicy	*tu*-li-nehn	*tulinen*
spoiled	*pi*-lahn-tu-nut	*pilaantunut*
a spoon	*lu*-sik-kuh	*lusikka*
sweet	*muh*-keh-uh	*makea*
teaspoon	*teeh*-lu-sik-kuh	*teelusikka*
toothpick	*huhm*-muhs-*tik*-ku	*hammastikku*

Vegetarian Meals

I'm a vegetarian.
    o-lehn *kuhs*-vis-*sü-er*-ya   *Olen kasvissyöjä.*
I don't eat meat.
    ehn sü-er *li*-hah   *En syö lihaa.*
I don't eat chicken, fish, or ham.
    ehn sü-er *kuh*-nah *kuh*-lah   *En syö kanaa, kalaa*
    ehn-ka *kink*-ku-uh   *enkä kinkkua.*

Staple Foods

bread	*lay*-paa	*leipää*
macaroni	*muh*-kuh-rro-ni	*makaroni*
oats	*kow*-rruh	*kaura*
rice	*rree*-si	*riisi*
rye	*rru*-is	*ruis*

Breakfast Menu

butter	*voi*	*voi*
boiled egg	*kay*-teht-tu *mu*-nuh	*keitet munah*
cereal	*hiu*-tuh-lay-ta	*hiualeitä*
cheese	*yuus*-to	*juusto*
coffee	*kuh*-vi	*kahvi*
fresh juice	*tuo*-rreh-*meh*-hu	*tuoremehu*
fried egg	*pais*-teht-tu *mun*-uh	*paisettu munah*
marmalade	*ap*-pehl-see-ni-*hil*-lo	*appelsiinihillo*
milk	*mai*-to	*maito*
oatmeal/porridge	*poo*-rro	*puuro*
orange juice	*ap*-pehl-see-ni-*meh*-hu	*appelsiinimehu*
sugar	*so*-kehrr-i	*sokeri*
tea	*teeh*	*tee*
toast	*pah*-to-*lay*-pa	*paahtoleipä*
yoghurt	*yog*-urrt-ti	*jogurtti*

FINNISH

Meat

beef	*now*-tuh/*harr*-ka	nauta/härkä
chicken	*kuh*-nuh/*brroy*-leh-rri	kana/broileri
ham	*kink*-ku	kinkku
liver	*muhk*-suh	maksa
minced meat	*yow*-heh-*li*-huh	jauheliha
pork	*porr*-sahs/*pos*-su	porsas/possu
reindeer	*po*-rron	poron
sausage	*muhk*-kuh-rruh	makkara
steak	*pih*-vi	pihvi

Seafood

Baltic herring	*si*-luhk-kuh	silakka
fish	*kuh*-lah	kala
herring	*sil*-li	silli
salmon	*loh*-hi	lohi
seafood (not fish)	*a*-ü-rri-ai-nehn	äyriäinen
shrimp	*kuht*-kuh-rruh-pu	katkarapu

Vegetables

cabbage	*kah*-li	kaali
carrot	*porrk*-kuh-nuh	porkkana
cucumber	*kurrk*-ku	kurkku
garlic	*val*-ko-*si*-pu-li	valkosipuli
mushroom	*si*-ehn-i	sieni
onion	*si*-pu-li	sipuli
pea	*hehrr*-ne	herne
potato	*peh*-rru-nuh	peruna
swede	*luhm*-tu	lanttu
tomato	*to*-maht-ti	tomaatti
vegetable	*vi*-huhn-nehs	vihannes

Fruit

apple	*om*-ehn-a	omena
banana	bah-*nah*-ni	banaani
blueberry	*mus*-tik-kuh	mustikka
grapes	*vee*-ni-*rü*-pa-leh	viinirypäle
lemon	*si*-troo-nah	sitruuna
lingonberry	*puo*-kuk-kuh	puolukka
orange	*ap*-pehl-see-ni	appelsiini
pear	*paa*-rü-na	päärynä
pineapple	*uhn*-uhn-uhs	ananas
strawberry	*muhn*-sik-kuh	mansikka

MENU DECODER

Prepared Food

kiisseli laatikko   *kees*-seh-li *lah*-tik-ko
  berry or fruit soup minced vegetables and/or meat,
  baked in an oven

rieska   *rrieh*-ska
  thin barley bread, like chappati

herkku	*hehrrk*-ku	tidbit
kastike	*kuhs*-ti-keh	sauce
keitto/soppa	*kayt*-toh/*sop*-puh	soup
munakas	*mu*-nuh-kuhs	omelette
paistos	*pais*-tos	scalloped food or pie
pannu	*puhn*-nu	pan-fried food
piiras	*pee*-rruhs	pie
salaatti	*suh*-laht-ti	salad
sämpylä	*sam*-pü-la	roll
voileipä	*voy*-*lay*-pa	open sandwich

'Grilli' Food

The grilli can also be called katukeittiö, snägäri or nakkikioski.
Enormously popular, they prepare fast food by order until the early
hours when everything else is closed. You can also find local spe-
cialities, such as mikkeliläinen in Mikkeli.

atomi   *uh*-to-mi
  meat pie with ham or fried egg

kebakko   *keh*-buhk-ko
  finger-shaped meat ball

lihapiirakka   *li*-huh-*pee*-rruhk-kuh
  pie with meat & rice filling

makkaraperunat   *muhk*-kuh-rruh-*peh*-rrun-uht
  sausage with French fries

munakukkaro   *mu*-nuh-*kuk*-kuh-rro
  hamburger with fried egg

nakkipiiras   *nuhk*-ki-*pee*-rruhs
  small sausage inside a pie

porilainen   *po*-rri-lai-nehn
  thick slice of sausage in a burger roll

FINNISH

reissumies   *rrays*-su-*miehs*
  two slices of rye bread with filling
vety   *veh*-tü
  meat pie with ham and eggs

camping	*kuhm*-ping	sausage
kalapuikot	*kuh*-luh-pu-i-kot	fish fingers
kuumakoira	*koo*-muh-*koi*-rruh	hot dog
nakki/nakit	*nuhk*-ki/*nuh*-kit	small sausage
publiski	*pub*-lis-ki	kind of hot dog
ranskalaiset	*rruhn*-skuh-lai-seht	French fries

Other Meals
janssonin kiusaus *yuhns*-son-in *kiu*-sows
  potato and herring prepared in oven
kaalikääryleet   *kah*-li-*kaa*-rrü-leeht
  minced meat covered with cabbage leaves
kesäkeitto   *ke*-sa-*kayt*-to
  vegetable soup (lit. 'summer soup')
lihamureke   *li*-huh-*mu*-rreh-keh
  seasoned minced meat prepared in the oven
metsästäjänpihvi   *mehts*-ast-ay-an-*pih*-vi
  minced meat with mushroom sauce (lit. 'Hunter's steak')
pyttipannu   *püt*-ti-*puhn*-nu
  ham and potatoes fried in butter

lihapullat	*li*-huh-*pul*-luht	meatballs
lipeäkala	*li*-peh-a-*kuh*-luh	lutefish

Local Specialities
karjalanpiirakka   *kuhrr*-yuh-luhn-*pee*-rruhk-kuh
  rye pie with rice, barley or potato filling (Eastern)
lanttusupikas   *luhnt*-tu-su-*pik*-uhs
  kind of rye pita bread with swede filling (Savo)
lörtsy   *lert*-sü
  flat doughnut with apple or meat filling (Eastern)
kukkonen   *kuk*-ko-nehn
  rice porridge on bread (Karelian)

leipäjuusto   *lay*-puh-*joo*-sto
  flat dessert cheese eaten with jam in the west and north of the country (Pohjanmaa & Kainuu)
loimulohi   *loi*-mu-lo-hi
  salmon prepared on open fire (Eastern)
mustamakkara   *mus*-tuh-*muhk*-kuh-rruh
  rice-filled black sausage (Tampere)
muurinpohjalettu   *muu*-rrin-*poh*-yuh-*leht*-tu
  thin large fried pancake (Eastern)
neulamuikut   *neh*-ul-uh-*mu*-ik-ut
  small whitefish (Karelian)
poronkäristys   *po*-rron-*ka*-rris-tüs
  reindeer casserole (Lapland)
rönttönen   *rrernt*-tern-ehn
  round pie with rye, potato and lingon filling (Kuhmo)
sultsina   *sult*-si-na
  kind of chappati bread stuffed with porridge (Karelian)
vatruska   *vuht*-rrus-kuh
  thick pancake made of mashed potato and wheat flour (Karelian)

kukko   *kuk*-ko
  large rye bread loaf with filling (Eastern)

ahvenkukko	*uh*-vehn-*kuk*-ko	pork and perch
kalakukko	*kuh*-luh-*kuk*-ko	pork and fish
lanttukukko	*luhnt*-tu-*kuk*-ko	pork and swede
muikkukukko	*muik*-ku-*kuk*-ko	pork and whitefish
perunakukko	*peh*-rru-nuh-*kuk*-ko	pork and potato

Alcoholic Drinks
kossu   *kos*-su
  another name for strong Koskenkorva spirit
kotikal ja   *ko*-ti-*kuhl*-yuh
  lit. 'home-brewed malt drink'
lonkero   *lon*-keh-rro
  another name for a long gin and lemon
pitkä   *pit*-ka
  large glass of strong beer (lit. 'long')
huurteinen   *huurr*-tay-nehn
  cold beer, (lit. 'frosty')

Non-Alcoholic Drinks

berry drink	*meh*-hu	mehu
coffee	*kuh*-vi	kahvi
(drinking) water	(*juo*-muh-)*veh*-si	(juoma)vesi
fresh juice	*tuo*-rreh-*meh*-hu	tuoremehu
hot chocolate	*kah*-kao	kaakao
iced water	*yaa*-veh-si	jäävesi
milk	*mai*-to	maito
soft drink	*lim*-on-uh-di/	limonadi/
	li-mu/*limp*-puh-rri/	limu/
	lim-suh	limppari/limsa
soured milk	*pee*-ma	piimä
tea	teeh	tee

Alcoholic Drinks

beer	*o*-lut/*kuhl*-yuh	olut/kalja
		(lit. 'malt drink')
cocktail	*drrink*-ki	drinkki
light beer	*ük*-kers *o*-lut	I-olut/ykkös olut
medium strong beer	*kehs*-ki-*kuhl*-ya/	keskikalja/
	kol-mon-ehn/	kolmonen/
	kol-mos *o*-lut	III-olut
red wine	pu-nuh-*vee*-ni	punaviini
strong alcohol, vodka	*vee*-nah	viina
strong beer	*neh*-los-*o*-lut	IV A-olut/
		nelosolut
white wine	*vuhl*-ko-*vee*-ni	valkoviini

TIME FOR A COFFEE BREAK

A kahvila is a normal cafe, whereas a kahvio serves coffee in, say, a petrol station or a supermarket, but basically these two are similar places, also called kuppila.

FINNISH

AT THE MARKET

Basics

bread	*lay-paa*	*leipää*
butter	*voi*	*voi*
cereal	*hiu-tuh-lay-ta*	*hiuvaleitä*
cheese	*yuus-to*	*juusto*
chocolate	*suk-lah*	*suklaa*
eggs	*kuh-nuh-mu-ni-uh*	*kanamunia*
flour	*yow-ho-uh*	*jauhoa*
margarine	*muhrr-guhrr-een-i-uh*	*margariinia*
marmalade	*ap-pehl-see-ni-*	*appelsiinihilloa*
milk	*mai-to*	*maito*
macaroni	*mah-kah-ro-ni*	*makaroni*
olive oil	*ol-ee-vi-erl-yü-uh*	*oliiviöljyä*
rice	*ree-si*	*riisi*
sugar	*so-kehrr-i*	*sokeri*
(drinking) water	*(juo-muh-)veh-si*	*(juoma)vesi*
yoghurt	*yog-urrt-ti*	*jogurtti*

Meat & Poultry

beef	*now-tuh/harr-ka*	*nauta/härkä*
chicken	*kuh-nuh/brroy-leh-rri*	*kana/broileri*
ham	*kink-ku*	*kinkku*
pork	*porr-sahs/pos-su*	*porsas/possu*
reindeer	*po-rron*	*poron*
sausage	*muhk-kuh-rruh*	*makkara*

AT THE MARKET

Vegetables

cabbage	*kah-li*	*kaali*
carrot	*porrk-kuh-nuh*	*porkkana*
cucumber	*kurrk-ku*	*kurkku*
garlic	*val-ko-si-pu-li*	*valkosipuli*
mushroom	*si-ehn-i*	*sieni*
onion	*si-pu-li*	*sipuli*
pea	*hehrr-ne*	*herne*
potato	*peh-rru-nuh*	*peruna*
swede	*luhnt-tu*	*lanttu*
tomato	*to-maht-ti*	*tomaatti*
vegetable	*vi-huhn-nehs*	*vihannes*

Seafood

Baltic herring	*si-luhk-kuh*	*silakka*
fish	*kuh-lah*	*kala*
herring	*sil-li*	*silli*
salmon	*loh-hi*	*lohi*
seafood (not fish)	*a-ü-rri-ai-nehn*	*äyriäinen*
shrimp	*kuht-kuh-rruh-pu*	*katkarapu*

Fruit

apple	*om-ehn-a*	*omena*
banana	*bah-nah-ni*	*banaani*
grapes	*vee-ni-rü-pa-leh*	*viinirypäle*
lemon	*si-troo-nah*	*sitruuna*
orange	*ap-pehl-see-ni*	*appelsiini*
pear	*paa-rü-na*	*päärynä*
strawberry	*muhn-sik-kuh*	*mansikka*

SHOPPING

bookshop	*kirr*-yuh *kowp*-puh	*kirjakauppa*
camera shop	*vuh*-lo-*ku*-vows-*lee*-keh	*valokuvausliike*
clothing store	*vah*-the-*kowp*-puh	*vaatekauppa*
delicatessen	*hehrrk*-ku-*kowp*-puh	*herkkukauppa*
general store, shop	*kowp*-puh	*kauppa*
laundry	*peh*-su-luh	*pesula*
market	*kowp*-puh *to*-rri/	*kauppatori*/
	muhrrk-ki-*nuht*/	*mark-kinat*/
	buh-sah-rri	*basaari*
newsagency/	*lekh*-ti *ki*-os-ki/	*lehtikioski*/
stationers	*puh*-peh-*rri*-*kowp*-puh	*paperikauppa*
pharmacy	*uhp*-teehk-ki	*apteekki*
shoe shop	*kehn*-ka-*kowp*-puh	*kenkäkauppa*
souvenir shop	*muht*-kuh *mu*-is-to	*matkamuisto-*
	müü-ma-la	*myymälä*
supermarket	*su*-pehrr *muhrr*-keht	*supermarket*
vegetable shop	*vi*-huhn-nehs-*kowp*-puh	*vihanneskauppa*

I'd like to buy ...
   huh-lu-ai-sin *os*-tah ...   *Haluaisin ostaa* ...
Do you have others?
   on-ko *tayl*-la *mu*-*i*-tuh?   *Onko teillä muita?*
I don't like it.
   ehn oy-kayn *pi*-da *see*-ta   *En oikein pidä siitä.*
Can I look at it?
   voyn-ko mi-na *kuht*-so-uh *si*-ta?   *Voinko minä* katsoa sitä?*

I'm just looking.
mi-na *vain kuht*-seh-lehn   Minä* vain katselen.
How much is it?
puhl-yon-ko *seh muhk*-sah?   Paljonko se maksaa?
Can you write down the price?
voyt-teh-ko *kirr*-yoyt-tah   Voitteko kirjoittaa
hin-nuhn?   hinnan?

Do you accept credit cards?
voy-ko *muhk*-sah   Voiko maksaa
lu-ot-to-*korrt*-til-luh?   luottokortilla?
Could you lower the price?
voyt-ko *luhs*-keh-uh *hin*-tah?   Voitko laskea hintaa?
I don't have much money.
mul-luh *ay* o-leh
puhl-yon *rruh*-hah   Mulla ei ole paljon rahaa.

Can I help you?
voyn-ko *owt*-tah?   Voinko auttaa?
Will that be all?
yuh tu-leeh-ko *moo*-tuh?   Ja tuleeko muuta?
Sorry, this is the only one.
ta-ma *on may*-dan *ai*-no-uh   Tämä on meidän ainoa.
How much/many do you want?
puhl-yon-ko *si*-na *huh*-lu-uht?/ Paljonko sinä* haluat?/
ku-in-kuh *mon*-tuh *pis*-teh-taan? Kuinka monta pistetään?

SAMI HANDICRAFTS

Sami handicrafts, made according to Sami tradi-
tions, make great souvenirs. They're made in the
traditional way, using traditional materials such
as bone, wood, metals and hides. Check for a
token with the word Duodji, as this indicates that
the item is genuine.

FINNISH

Essential Groceries

I'd like ...	*huh*-lu-ai-sin ...	*Haluaisin* ...
batteries	*puhrr*-is-to-ya	*paristoja*
bread	*lay*-paa	*leipää*
butter	*voi*-tuh	*voita*
cheese	*yuus*-to-uh	*juustoa*
chocolate	*suk*-lah	*suklaa*
eggs	*kuh*-nuh-*mu*-ni-uh	*kanamunia*
flour	*yow*-ho-uh	*jauhoa*
gas cylinder	*kah*-su-*sai*-li-er	*kaasusäiliö*
ham	*kink*-ku-uh	*kinkkua*
honey	*hun*-uh-yah	*hunajaa*
margarine	*muhrr*-guhrr-een-i-uh	*margariinia*
marmalade	*ap*-pehl-see-ni-*hil*-lo-uh	*appelsiinihilloa*
matches	*tu*-li-*tik*-ku-yuh	*tulitikkuja*
milk	*mai*-to-uh	*maitoa*
olive oil	*ol*-ee-vi-*erl*-yü-uh	*oliiviöljyä*
pepper	*pip*-pu-rri-uh	*pippuria*
salt	*su*-ol-ah	*suolaa*
shampoo	*sam*-porr-tuh	*shampoota*
soap	*saip*-pu-uh	*saippua*
sugar	*so*-kehrr-iuh	*sokeria*
toilet paper	*vehs*-suh-*puhp*-ehrr-iuh	*vessapaperia*
toothpaste	*huhm*-muhs-*tuh*-nah	*hammastahnaa*
washing powder	*peh*-su-*yow*-heht-tuh	*pesujauhetta*

Souvenirs

some earrings	*korr*-vuh-*ko*-rru-yuh	*korvakoruja*
some handicrafts	*ka*-si-*ter*-*i*-ta	*käsitöitä*
necklace	*kow*-luh-*ko*-rru	*kaulakoru*
pottery	*keh*-rruh-meek-*kuh*	*keramiikka*
ring	*sorr*-mus	*sormus*
rug	*muht*-to/*rrah*-nu	*matto/raanu*

Clothing

clothing	*vaht*-teeht	vaatteet
coat	*tuhk*-ki	takki
dress	*pu*-ku	puku
jacket	*tuhk*-ki	takki
jumper (sweater)	*pu*-seh-rro/	pusero/
	vil-luh-*pai*-tuh	villapaita
shirt	*pai*-tuh	paita
shoes	*kehng*-ngat	kengät
skirt	*huh*-meh	hame
trousers	*hoh*-sut	housut

It doesn't/They don't fit.

ta-ma/*na*-ma *ay muhkh*-du	Tämä/Nämä ei mahdu.

It's too ...	*seh* on *lee*-uhn ...	Se on liian ...
big/small	*i*-so/*pi-eh*-ni	iso/pieni
short/long	*lü*-hüt/*peet*-ka	lyhyt/pitkä
tight/loose	*ki*-rreh-a/*ler-ü*-sa	kireä/löysä

Materials

cotton	*poo*-vil-lah	puuvillaa
handmade	*ka*-sin-*teh*-tüh/	käsintehty/
	ka-si-*tü-er*-ta	käsityötä
leather	*nuhkh*-kah	nahkaa
brass	*mehs*-sin-ki-a	messinkiä
gold	*kul*-tah	kultaa
silver	*ho*-peh-ah	hopeaa
flax	*pehl*-luh-vah	pellavaa
pure alpaca	*uhl*-puhk-kah	alpakkaa
silk	*silk*-ki-a	silkkiä
wool	*vil*-lah	villaa

Colours

black	*mus*-tuh	*musta*
blue	*si*-ni-nehn	*sininen*
brown	*rrus*-keuh	*ruskea*
green	*vih*-rreh-a	*vihreä*
orange	*o*-rruhns-si	*oranssi*
pink	*vah*-leh-uhn-*pu*-nai-nehn (*pink*-ki)	*vaaleanpunainen (pinkki)*
purple	*vi*-o-leht-ti	*violetti*
red	*pu*-nai-nehn	*punainen*
white	*vuhl*-koy-nehn	*valkoinen*
yellow	*kel*-tai-nehn	*keltainen*

Toiletries

comb	*kuhm*-pa	*kampa*
some condoms	*kon*-do-meh-yuh	*kondomeja*
deodorant	*deh*-o-do-rruhnt-ti	*deodorantti*
hairbrush	*hi*-us-*huhrr*-yuh	*hiusharja*
moisturising cream	*kos*-te-us-*voy*-deh	*kosteusvoide*
razor	*puhrr*-tuh *teh*-rra	*partaterä*
sanitary napkins	*tehrr*-veh-üs-*si*-deh/ *pik*-ku-*hoh*-sun-su-o-yuh	*terveysside/ pikkuhousun-suoja*
shampoo	*suhmp*-porr	*shampoo*
shaving cream	*puhrr*-tuh-*vahh*-to	*partavaahto*
some tampons	*tuhm*-po-neh-yuh	*tamponeja*
tissues	*neh*-na-*lee*-nuh	*nenäliina*
toilet paper	*vehs*-suh-*puh*-peh-rri	*vessapaperi*
toothbrush	*huhm*-muhs-*huhrr*-yuh	*hammasharja*
toothpaste	*huhm*-muhs-*tuh*-nuh	*hammastahna*

Stationery & Publications

map	*kuhrrt-tuh*		*kartta*
newspaper	*(ehng-luhn-nin*		*(englannin*
(in English)	*ki-eh-li-nehn)*		*kielinen)*
	suh-no-muh-lekh-ti		*sanomalehti*
novels in English	*ehng-luhn-nin ki-eh-li-si-a*		*englannin kielisiä*
	rro-mah-neh-yuh		*romaaneja*
paper	*puh-peh-rri*		*paperi*
pen (ballpoint)	*kü-na*		*kynä*
	(koo-luh-karr-ki-kü-na)		*(kuulakärkikynä)*
scissors	*suhk-seht*		*sakset*

Photography

How much is it to process this film?

puhl-yon-ko muhk-sah   *Paljonko maksaa*
keh-hit-taa ta-ma fil-mi?   *kehittää tämä filmi?*

When will it be ready?

kos-kuh seh on vuhl-mis?   *Koska se on valmis?*

I'd like a film for this camera.

mi-na huh-lu-ai-sin fil-min   *Minä* haluaisin filmin*
ta-han kuh-meh-rrahn.   *tähän kameraan.*

B&W (film)	*mus-tuh-vuhl-koy-nehn*	*mustavalkoinen*
camera	*kuh-meh-rruh*	*kamera*
colour (film)	*va-rri-fil-mi*	*värifilmi*
film	*fil-mi*	*filmi*
flash	*suh-luh-muh*	*salama*
lens	*ob-yehk-tee-vi/lins-si*	*objektiivi/linssi*
light meter	*vuh-lo-tus-mit-tuh-rri*	*valotusmittari*

HOLY MOLEY!

Pyhä, 'holy', is used of Sundays, religious festivals and holidays like May Day and Midsummer when nearly everything is shut and special timetables apply. The day before these events, often used for heating up the sauna and celebrating, is aatto 'eve'.

FINNISH

Smoking

A packet of cigarettes, please.
sahn-ko *tu*-puhk-kuh	*Saanko tupakka*
uhs-kin *kee*-toss	*askin, kiitos.*

Are these cigarettes strong/mild?
o-vuht-ko *na*-ma *tu*-puh-kuht	*Ovatko nämä tupakat*
vakh-vo-yuh/*mi-eh*-to-yuh?	*vahvoja/mietoja?*

Do you have a light?
on-ko *sul*-luh *tul*-tuh?	*Onko sinulla tulta?*

cigarette papers	*suh*-vu-keh-*puh*-peh-rri-uh	*savuke paperia*
some cigarettes	*tu*-puhk-kah	*tupakkaa*
filtered	*filt*-teh-rri	*filtteri*
lighter	*sü*-tü-tin/*süt*-ka	*sytytin/sytkä* (inf)
matches	*tu*-li-*ti*-kut/*ti*-kut	*tulitikut/tikut* (inf)
menthol	*menth*-torr-li	*menthol*
pipe	*peep*-pu	*piippu*
tobacco	*tu*-puhk-kuh	*tupakka*

Sizes & Comparisons

small	*pi-eh*-ni	*pieni*
big	*soo*-rri/*i*-so	*suuri/iso*
heavy	*pai*-nuh-vuh	*painava*
light	*keh*-vüt	*kevyt*
more	*eh*-nehm-man	*enemmän*
less	*va*-hehm-man	*vähemmän*
too much/many	*lee*-kah/*lee*-uhn *mon*-tuh	*liikaa/liian monta*
many	*mon*-tuh	*monta*
enough	*tuhrr*-peehk-si	*tarpeeksi*
also	*mü*-ers	*myös*
a little bit	*va*-han	*vähän*

FINNISH

ALL DAY

Finns use Päivää! (lit. 'Day!') as a general greeting during most of the day.

HEALTH

Where is the ...?	*mis*-sa on ...?	*Missä on ...?*
doctor	*la*-a-ka-rri	*lääkäri*
hospital	*sai*-rrah-luh	*sairaala*
chemist	*uhp*-teehk-ki	*apteekki*
dentist	*huhm*-muhs-*laa*-ka-rri	*hammaslääkäri*

I'm/My friend is sick.
   o-lehn/*üs*-ta-va-ni on *sai*-rruhs   *Olen/Ystäväni on sairas.*
Could I see a female doctor?
   on-ko muhkh-dol-lis-tuh   *Onko mahdollista*
   saa-duh *nais laa*-ka-rri?   *saada naislääkäri?*

What's the matter?	*mi*-ka on ha-*ta*-na?	*Mikä on hätänä?*
Where does it hurt?	*mis*-ta *suht*-too?	*Mistä sattuu?*
My ... hurts.	*mi*-nun ...	*Minun ...*
	on *ki*-peh-a	*on kipeä.*

Parts of the Body

ankle	*nilk*-kuh	*nilkka*
arm	*ka*-si	*käsi*
back	*sehl*-ka	*selkä*
chest	*rrin*-tuh/*rrin*-tuh-*keh*-ha	*rinta/rintakehä*
ear	*korr*-vuh	*korva*
eye	*sil*-ma	*silmä*
finger	*sorr*-mi	*sormi*
foot	*yuhl*-kuh	*jalka*
hand	*ka*-si	*käsi*
head	*paa*	*pää*
heart	*sü*-dan	*sydän*
leg	*saa*-rri	*sääri*
mouth	*soo*	*suu*
nose	*neh*-na	*nenä*
ribs	*kül*-ki-*loot*	*kylkiluut*
skin	*i*-ho	*iho*
stomach	*muh*-huh/*vuht*-suh	*maha/vatsa*
teeth	*huhm*-paht	*hampaat*
throat	*kurrk*-ku	*kurkku*

Ailments

I have (a/an) ...	*mul*-luh on ...	*Minulla on ...*
allergy	*uhl*-lehrr-gi-uh	*allergia*
anaemia	*uh*-neh-mi-uh	*anemia*
blister	*rruhk*-ko	*rakko*
burn	*puh*-lo-*vuhm*-muh	*palovamma*
cold	*fluns*-suh	*flunssa*
constipation	*um*-meh-tus-tuh	*ummetusta*
cough	*üs*-ka	*yskä*
diarrhoea	*rri*-pu-li	*ripuli*
fever	*koo*-meht-tuh	*kuumetta*
headache	*paan sarr*-kü	*päänsärky*
hepatitis	*muhk*-suh-*tu*-leh-dus/	*maksatulehdus/*
	heh-puh-teet-ti	*hepatiitti*
indigestion	*rroo*-uhn-*su*-luh-tos	*ruuansulatus-*
	ha-i-rri-er	*häiriö*
infection	*tu*-leh-dus	*tulehdus*
influenza	*in*-flu-ehns-suh	*influenssa*
lice	*ta*-i-ta	*täitä*
low/high	*muh*-tuh-luh/	*matala/*
blood pressure	*korr*-keh-uh	*korkea*
	veh-rrehn-*pai*-neh	*verenpaine*
sore throat	*kurrk*-ku *ki*-peh-a	*kurkku kipeä*
sprain	*nilk*-kuh	*nilkka*
	nürr-yakh-ta-nüt	*nyrjähtänyt*
stomachache	*muh*-huh *ki*-pu	*mahakipu*
sunburn	*i*-ho *puh*-luh-nut	*iho palanut*
venereal disease	*su*-ku *pu*-o-li-*tow*-ti	*sukupuolitauti*

Some Useful Words & Phrases

I'm pregnant.
o-lehn *rruhs*-kah-nuh   *Olen raskaana.*

I'm on the pill.
sü-ern *eh*-pil-lehrr-ayt-a   *Syön e-pillereitä*

I haven't had my period for ... months.
mul-luh *ay* o-leh *ol*-lut   *Minulla ei ole ollut*
koo-kow-ti-si-uh ...   *kuukautisia ...vowel + n*
koo-kow-teehn   *kuukauteen.*

I have been vaccinated.
min-ut *on* rro-ko-teht-tu   *Minut on rokotettu.*

I have my own syringe.
mul-luh *on* o-muh   *Minulla on oma*
rru-is-ku/*neh-u*-luh   *ruisku/neula.*

I feel better/worse.
voyn-ti-ni *on* puh-rrehm-pi/   *Vointini on parempi/*
hu-o-nom-pi   *huonompi.*

I'm ...	*o*-lehn ...	*Olen ...*
asthmatic	*uhst*-mah-tik-ko	*astmaatikko*
diabetic	*di-uh*-beeh-tik-ko	*diabeetikko*
epileptic	*eh*-pi-lehp-tik-ko	*epileptikko*

I'm allergic to ...   *mi*-na *o*-lehn   *Minä* olen*
uhl-lehrr-gi-nehn ...   *allerginen ...*
   antibiotics   *uhn*-ti-bi-orr-tayl-leh   *antibiooteille*
   penicillin   *peh*-ni-sil-lee-nil-leh   *penisilliinille*

accident	*on*-neht-to-moos	*onnettomuus*
addiction	*rreep*-pu-voos	*riippuvuus*
antiseptic	*uhn*-ti-sehp-ti-nehn	*antiseptinen*
aspirin	*uhs*-pi-rree-ni	*aspiriini*
bandage	*si*-deh	*side*
blood test	*veh*-rri-*ko*-eh	*verikoe*
contraceptive	*ehk*-ka-i-sü-*va*-li-neh	*ehkäisyväline*
injection	*rru-is*-keh	*ruiske*
injury	*vuhm*-muh	*vamma*
medicine	*laa*-keh	*lääke*
nausea	*puh*-hoyn-*voyn*-ti	*pahoinvointi*
oxygen	*huhp*-pi	*happi*
some vitamins	*vi*-tuh-mee-neh-yuh	*vitamiineja*

FINNISH

At the Chemist

I need medication for ...
tuhrr-vit-sen *laa*-ki-tüs-ta ...-uh/
a *vuhrr*-tehn

*Tarvitsen lääkitystä ...-a/
ä varten.*

I have a prescription.
mi-nul-luh *on* rreh-sehp-ti

Minulla on resepti.

At the Dentist

I have a toothache.
mi-nun *huhm*-muhs-tuh-ni
sarr-keeh

*Minun hammastani
särkee.*

I've lost a filling.
mi-nul-tuh *on*
irr-rron-nut *paik*-kuh

*Minulta on irronnut
paikka.*

I've broken a tooth.
mi-nul-tuh *on*
loh-yehn-nut *huhm*-muhs

*Minulta on
lohjennut hammas.*

My gums hurt.
i-keh-neh-ni *o*-vuht *ki*-peh-uht

Ikeneni ovat kipeät.

I don't want it extracted.
ehn huh-lu-uh *eht*-ta
huhm-muhs *poys*-teh-tahn

*En halua, että
hammas poistetaan.*

Please give me an anaesthetic.
voyt-teh-ko *poo*-dut-tah

Voitteko puuduttaa.

SOCK IT TO ME COLD & STEAMY

In the traditional Finnish smoke sauna, savusauna,
water is thrown over the log-heated stove to produce
steam. You may see people lightly hit themselves with
small, leafy birch branches, to improve circulation.
Then, it's outside to jump into a lake or the sea, even
in winter, when they may first cut a hole in the ice.

TIME & DATES

What date is it today?
   mi-ka *pa-i*-va *ta*-naan *on*?   *Mikä päivä tänään on?*
What time is it?
   puhl-yon-ko *kehl*-lo on?   *Paljonko kello on?*

It's in the ...	*kehl*-lo on ...	*Kello on ...*
morning	*ah*-mul-luh	*aamulla*
afternoon	*il*-tuh-*pa-i*-val-la	*iltapäivällä*
evening	*il*-luhl-luh	*illalla*

Days of the Week

Monday	*mah*-nuhn-tai	*maanantai*
Tuesday	*tees*-tai	*tiistai*
Wednesday	*kehs*-ki-*veek*-ko	*keskiviikko*
Thursday	*torrs*-tai	*torstai*
Friday	*pehrr*-yuhn-tai	*perjantai*
Saturday	*low*-uhn-tai	*lauantai*
Sunday	*sun*-nun-tai	*sunnuntai*

Months

January	*tuhm*-mi-koo	*tammikuu*
February	*hehl*-mi-koo	*helmikuu*
March	*mah*-lis-koo	*maaliskuu*
April	*huh*-ti-koo	*huhtikuu*
May	*toh*-ko-koo	*toukokuu*
June	*keh*-sa-koo	*kesäkuu*
July	*hay*-na-koo	*heinäkuu*
August	*eh*-lo-koo	*elokuu*
September	*süüs*-koo	*syyskuu*
October	*lo*-kuh-koo	*lokakuu*
November	*muhrr*-rruhs-koo	*marraskuu*
December	*yoh*-lu-koo	*joulukuu*

FINNISH

Seasons

summer	*keh*-sa	*kesä*
autumn	*sük*-sü	*syksy*
winter	*tuhl*-vi	*talvi*
spring	*keh*-vat	*kevät*

Present

today	*ta*-naan	*tänään*
this morning	*ta*-na *ah*-mu-nuh	*tänä aamuna*
tonight	*ta*-na *il*-tuh-nuh	*tänä iltana*
this week	*tal*-la *vee*-kol-luh	*tällä viikolla*
this year	*ta*-na *vu-on*-nuh	*tänä vuonna*
now	*nüt*	*nyt*

Past

yesterday	*ay*-lehn	*eilen*
day before yesterday	*toys*-suh-*pa-i*-va-na	*toissapäivänä*
yesterday morning	*ay*-lehn *ah*-mul-luh	*eilen aamulla*
last night	*vee*-meh *ü-er*-na	*viime yönä*
last week	*vee*-meh *vee*-kol-luh	*viime viikolla*
last year	*vee*-meh *vu-on*-nuh	*viime vuonna*

Future

tomorrow	*hu-o*-mehn-nuh	*huomenna*
day after tomorrow	*ü*-li *hu-o*-mehn-nuh	*ylihuomenna*
tomorrow morning	*hu-o*-mehn *ah*-mu-nuh	*huomen aamuna*
tomorrow afternoon	*hu-o*-mehn-nuh *il*-tuh-*pa-i*-val-la	*huomenna iltapäivällä*
tomorrow evening	*hu-o*-mehn *il*-tuh-nuh	*huomeniltana*
next week	*ehn*-si *vee*-kol-luh	*ensi viikolla*
next year	*ehn*-si *vu-on*-nuh	*ensi vuonna*

During the Day

afternoon	*il-tuh-pa-i-val-la*	*iltapäivällä*
dawn	*ah-mun koyt-to*	*aamunkoitto*
very early morning	*ah-mul-luh ai-kai-sin*	*aamulla aikaisin*
day	*pa-i-va*	*päivä*
early	*ai-kai-sin*	*aikaisin*
midnight	*kehs-ki-ü-er*	*keskiyö*
morning	*ah-mu*	*aamu*
night	*ü-er*	*yö*
noon	*kehs-ki-pa-i-va*	*keskipäivä*
sunset	*ow-rring-ngon-luhs-ku*	*auringonlasku*
sunrise	*ow-rring-ngon-noh-su*	*auringonnousu*

NUMBERS & AMOUNTS

0	*nol-luh*	*nolla*
1	*ük-si*	*yksi/yks* (inf)
2	*kuhk-si*	*kaksi/kaks* (inf)
3	*kol-meh*	*kolme*
4	*nehl-ya*	*neljä*
5	*vee-si*	*viisi/viis* (inf)
6	*koo-si*	*kuusi/kuus* (inf)
7	*sayt-seh-man*	*seitsemän/seittemän* (inf)
8	*kuhkh-dehk-suhn*	*kahdeksan/kasi/kaheksan* (inf)
9	*ükh-dehk-san*	*yhdeksän/ysi/yheksän* (inf)
10	*küm-meh-nehn*	*kymmenen*
11	*ük-si-toys-tuh*	*yksitoista*
12	*kuhk-si-toys-tuh*	*kaksitoista*
13	*kol-meh-toys-tuh*	*kolmetoista*
14	*nehl-ya-toys-tuh*	*neljätoista*
15	*vee-si-toys-tuh*	*viisitoista*
20	*kuhk-si-küm-mehn-ta*	*kaksikymmentä*
30	*kol-meh-küm-mehn-ta*	*kolmekymmentä*
40	*nehl-ya-küm-mehn-ta*	*neljäkymmentä*
50	*vee-si-küm-mehn-ta*	*viisikymmentä*
60	*koo-si-küm-mehn-ta*	*kuusikymmentä*
70	*sayt-seh-man-küm-mehn-ta*	*seitsemänkymmentä*

80	*kuhkh*-dehk-suhn-*küm*-mehn-ta	kahdeksankymmentä
90	*ükh*-dehk-san-*küm*-mehn-ta	yhdeksänkymmentä
100	*suh*-tuh	sata
1000	*tu*-huht	tuhat
one million	*mihl*-yorr-nuh	miljoona
1st	*ehn*-sin-ma-i-nehn/*eh*-kuh	ensimmäinen/eka (inf)
2nd	*toy*-nehn/*to*-kuh	toinen/toka (inf)
3rd	*kol*-muhs	kolmas
1/4	*nehl*-yas *o*-suh/*nehl*-yan-nehs	neljäsosa/neljännes
1/3	*kol*-muhs *o*-suh/*kol*-muhn-nehs	kolmasosa/kolmannes
1/2	*pu*-*o*-leht	puolet
3/4	*kol*-meh *nehl*-yas *o*-sah	kolme neljäsosaa

Some Useful Words

Enough!	*rreet*-taa!	Riittää!
a little	*va*-han	vähän
double	*tup*-luht	tuplat
a dozen	*tu*-si-nuh	tusina
few	*huhrr*-vuh	harva
less	*va*-hehm-man	vähemmän
many	*mon*-tuh/*mo*-ni-uh	monta/monia
more	*eh*-nehm-man	enemmän
once	*kehrr*-rruhn	kerran
a pair	*puh*-rri	pari
percent	*prro*-sehnt-ti	prosentti
some	*yo*-tuh-kin/*va*-han/*yon*-kin *vehrr*-rruhn	jotakin/vähän/jonkin verran
too much	*lee*-kah/*lee*-uhn *puhl*-yon	liikaa/liian paljon
twice	*kuhkh*-dehs-ti/*kuhk*-si *kehrr*-tah	kahdesti/kaksi kertaa

FINNISH

ABBREVIATIONS

ALE – alennusmyynti	sale
ark – arkisin	on weekdays (Monday to Saturday)
as. – asema	station
eiL – ei lauantaisin	not on Saturdays
EP – erikoispikajuna	special express train
EU – Euroopan Unioni	European Union
FIN/fi.	Official abbreviations of Finland
Hki	Helsinki
IC	Intercity
k. – katu	Street
ke – keskiviikko	Wednesday
-kj. – -kuja	Alley
kpl – kappaletta	amount of something, or pieces
la – lauantai	Saturday
ma – maanantai	Monday
mk – markka	Finnish marks (currency)
n:o/nro – numero	number
pe – perjantai	Friday
PL – Postilokero	PO Box
puh./p. – puhelinnumero	telephone number
-t. – -tie	Road
SRM – Suomen Retkeilymajajärjestö	Finnish YHA
SS	(in timetables only) when there are two consecutive holidays, buses run on the second holiday only
su – sunnuntai	Sunday
ti – tiistai	Tuesday
Tku	Turku
to – torstai	Thursday
Tre	Tampere
v. – vuonna	year
VR – Valtion Rautatiet	National Railways

FINNISH

EMERGENCIES

Help!
   uh-pu-uh!
   Apua!

It's an emergency!
   ta-ma on *ha*-ta-tuh-pows!
   Tämä on hätätapaus!

SIGNS
POLIISI **POLICE**
POLIISIASEMA **POLICE STATION**

There's been an accident!
   nüt on *tuh*-puh-tu-nut
   on-neht-to-moos!
   Nyt on tapahtunut onnettomuus!

Call a doctor!
   kut-su-kah *laa*-ka-rri!
   Kutsukaa lääkäri!

Call an ambulance!
   soyt-tuh-kah *uhm*-bu-luhns-si!
   Soittakaa ambulanssi!

I've been raped.
   mi-nut on *rrais*-kuht-tu
   Minut on raiskattu.

I've been robbed.
   mi-nut on *rrü-ers*-teht-tü
   Minut on ryöstetty.

Call the police!
   soyt-tuh-kah po-lee-si!
   Soittakaa poliisi!

Where is the police station?
   mis-sa on po-*lee*-si *uh*-seh-muh?
   Missä on poliisiasema?

Go away!
   meh-neh *poys!*/*ha-i*-vü!
   Mene pois!/*Häivy!* (inf)

I'll call the police!
   mi-na *kut*-sun po-*lee*-sin!
   Minä kutsun poliisin!*

Thief!
   vuh-rruhs!
   Varas!

I'm/My friend is ill.
   mi-na o-lehn/
   mun *üs*-ta-va on *sai*-rruhs
   Minä olen/*
   Minun ystäväni on sairas.

I'm lost.
   mi-na o-lehn *ehk*-sü-nüt
   Minä olen eksynyt.*

Where are the toilets?
    mis-sa *on vehs*-suh?   *Missä on vessa?*

Could you help me please?
    voyt-teh-ko (*voyt*-ko) *owt*-tah   *Voitteko (voitko) auttaa.*

Could I please use the telephone?
    sahn-ko *ka-üt*-taa   *Saanko käyttää*
    pu-heh-lin-tuh?   *puhelinta?*

I'm sorry. I apologise.
    oh-lehn *puh*-hoyl-luh-ni.   *Olen pahoillani.*
    püü-dan *uhn*-teehk-si   *Pyydän anteeksi.*

I didn't realise I was doing
anything wrong.
    ehn tuh-yun-nut *teh*-keh-va-ni   *En tajunnut tekeväni*
    mi-taan *vaa*-rrin   *mitään väärin.*

I didn't do it.
    ehn teh-nüt *si*-ta   *En tehnyt sitä.*

I wish to contact my
embassy/consulate.
    huh-lu-uhn *ot*-tah *ükh*-teh-üt-ta   *Haluan ottaa yhteyttä*
    soorr-*la*-heh-tüs-ter-ni/   *suurlä-hetystööni/*
    kon-su-laht-teen   *konsulaattiin.*

I speak English.
    pu-hun *ehng*-luhn-ti-uh   *Puhun englantia.*

I have medical insurance.
    mi-nul-luh *on vuh*-koo-tus   *Minulla on vakuutus.*

FINNISH

My possessions are insured.
tuh-vuh-rruh-ni *on*   *Tavarani on*
vuh-koo-teht-tu   *vakuutettu.*

My ... was stolen.
mi-nul-tuh *on*   *Minulta on*
vuh-rruhs-teht-tu   *varastettu ...*

I've lost my...   *mi*-na *o*-lehn   *Minä* olen*
                         hu-kuhn-nut ...   *hukannut ...*
bag   *lowk*-ku-ni   *laukkuni*
handbag   *ka*-si *-owk*-ku-ni   *käsilaukkuni*
money   *rruh*-huh-ni   *rahani*
travellers   *muht*-kuh-*shehk*-ki-ni   *matkashekkini*
  cheques
passport   *puhs*-si-ni   *passini*

FINNISH

ICELANDIC

ICELANDIC

QUICK REFERENCE

Hello.	hahl-loh	Halló.
Goodbye.	blehs	Bless.
Yes./No.	yow/nay	Já./Nei.
Excuse me. (forgive me)	ahf-sahk-ith	Afsakið.
Sorry.	myehrr thi-kirr thahth layth	Mér þykir það leitt.
Please.	gyer-thö svo vehl	Gjörðu svo vel.
Thank you.	tahk firr-irr	Takk fyrir.
You're welcome.	ehk-ehrrt ahth thahk-ah	Ekkert að þakka.
I'd like ...	gyai-ti yehkh fayn-khith ...	Gæti ég fengið ...
a one-way ticket	mith-ah/ahth-rrah layth-in-ah	miða/aðra leiðina
a return ticket	mith-ah/bowth-ahrr layth-irr	miða/báðar leiðir

I (don't) understand.
yehkh skil (ehk-i) — *Ég skil (ekki).*

Do you speak English?
tah-lahrr thoo ehn-skö? — *Talar þú ensku?*

Where is ...?
kvahrr ehrr ...? — *Hvar er ...?*

Go straight ahead.
fahrr-thö baynt owfrram — *Farðu beint áfram.*

Turn left/right.
baykh-thö til vinst-rri/haikh-rri. — *Beygðu til vinstri/hægri.*

Do you have any rooms available?
ehrr-ö hehrr-behrr-khi leörs? — *Eru herbergi laus?*

I'm looking for a public toilet.
yehkh ehrr ahth lay-tah ahth ahl-mehn-inkhs-sahl-ehrr-dni — *Ég er að leita að almenningssalerni.*

1	aydn	einn	6	sehks	sex
2	tvayrr	tveir	7	syer	sjö
3	thrreer	þrír	8	owt-dah	átta
4	fyoh-rrirr	fjórir	9	nee-ö	níu
5	fimm	fimm	10	tee-ö	tíu

ICELANDIC

Icelandic is a North Germanic language. Iceland was settled primarily by Norwegians in the 9th and 10th centuries. By the 14th century Icelandic (Old Norse) and Norwegian had grown apart considerably. This was due to changes in Norwegian, while Icelandic changed remarkably little through the centuries. In fact, it has an unbroken literary tradition, dating from about 1100. The treasures of the Sagas and the poetic Edda, written about 700 years ago, can be enjoyed by a modern-day speaker of Icelandic.

Icelanders are proud of their literary heritage. They are particularly conservative when it comes to the written word. Borrowed vocabulary is ill tolerated and the policy of keeping the language pure is very strong. After all, Icelandic is spoken by a mere 280,000 people, and outside pressures on the language, in these times of easy travel and worldwide communications, are enormous.

The practice of creating neologisms (new words) instead of adopting foreign words is well established in Iceland. Neologisms, such as útvarp, 'radio', sjónvarp, 'television', tölva, 'computer', and þota, 'jet', are just a few that have become part of the Icelandic vocabulary in the last 50 years.

Icelanders are a rather informal people. A person is very rarely addressed by title and/or surname. Icelanders use the ancient patronymic system, where son, 'son' or dóttir, 'daughter' is attached to the genitive form of the father's or, less commonly, the mother's, first name. The telephone book entries are listed according to first names.

As one might expect, most Icelanders speak English, and often as many as three or four other languages, although among themselves they only converse in Icelandic. Your efforts to speak Icelandic will most certainly be met with great enthusiasm.

STRESS

Stress is generally on the first syllable.

ICELANDIC

PRONUNCIATION

Double consonants are pronounced as such. The Icelandic alphabet consists of 33 letters: a, á, b, d, ð, e, é, f, g, h, i, í, j, k, l, m, n, o, ó, p, r, s, t, u, ú, v, x, y, ý, z, þ, æ, ö.

Pronunciation is given in the general pronunciation guide at the front of this book, with the following exceptions:

Diphthongs

ICELANDIC	GUIDE	SOUNDS
au ö̈	eör	there is no equivalent sound in English

Semiconsonants

é	yeh	as in the 'ye' in 'yes'

Consonants

f	f	as in English. When between vowels or at the end of a word it's pronounced as 'v'. When followed by *l* or *n* it's pronounced as 'b'.
g	g	as the 'g' in 'get'
	kh	between vowels or before *r* or *ð*, *g* has a guttural sound, as the 'ch' in Scottish 'loch'
h	h	as in English, except when followed by *v*, when it's pronounced as 'k'
þ	th	as the 'th' in 'thin'
ð	th	as the 'th' in 'lather'

PRONOUNS		
SG		
I	yehkh	ég
you	thoo	þú
she/he/it	hoon/hahn/thahth	hún/hann/það
PL		
we	vith	við
you (pol)	thoo	þú
you (pl)	thith	þið
they	thayrr/thairr/theör	þeir/þær/þau

MIND YOUR þ's & ð's

Remember, the Icelandic letter þ, represented as <u>th</u> in the pronunciation guide, is pronounced as the 'th' in 'thin', while ð, represented as th, is pronounced as the 'th' in 'lather'.

ICELANDIC

GREETINGS & CIVILITIES
Top Useful Phrases

Hello.	hahl-loh	*Halló.*
Goodbye.	blehs	*Bless.*
Yes./No.	yow/nay	*Já./Nei.*
Excuse me. (forgive me)	ahf-sahk-ith	*Afsakið.*
Sorry.	myehrr <u>th</u>i-kirr <u>th</u>ahth layht	*Mér þykir það leitt.*
Please.	gyer-thö svo vehl	*Gjörðu svo vel.*
Thank you.	tahk firr-irr	*Takk fyrir.*
That's fine.	ahlt ee lai-i	*Allt í lagi.*
You're welcome.	ehk-ehrrt ahth <u>th</u>ahk-ah	*Ekkert að þakka.*

Forms of Address

Madam/Mrs	frroo	*frú*
Sir/Mr	hehrr-rrah	*herra*
Miss	frrer-kehn	*fröken*
companion/friend	vin-ko-nah/vin-örr	*vinkona/vinur* (f/m)

Greetings

Good morning.	gohth-ahn dai-in	*Góðan daginn.*
Good afternoon.	gohth-ahn dai-in	*Góðan daginn.*

Good evening/night.
| khot kverld/khoh-<u>th</u>-ah noht | *Gott kvöld./Góða nótt.* |

| How are you? | kvehrr-dnikh heh-vörr <u>th</u>oo <u>th</u>ahth? | *Hvernig hefur þú það?* |
| Well, thanks. | khot tahk | *Gott, takk.* |

ICELANDIC

SMALL TALK
Meeting People

What's your name?	kvahth hay-tirr-<u>thoo</u>?	*Hvað heitir þú?*
My name is ...	yehkh hay-ti ...	*Ég heiti ...*
I'm pleased to meet you.	kon-dö sail/saidl	*Komdu sæl/sæll.* (f/m)

> **DID YOU KNOW ...** Family names are illegal in Iceland, unless they were adopted before the Personal Names Act which was passed by Iceland's parliament, Alþing, in 1925.

Nationalities

Where are you from?   kvahth-ahn ehrrt <u>thoo</u>   *Hvaðan ert þú?*

I'm from ...	yehkh ehrr frrow ...	*Ég er frá ...*
Australia	owst-rrah-lee-ö	*Ástralíu*
Canada	kaha-nah-dah	*Kanada*
England	aynkh-lahn-di	*Englandi*
Ireland	eer-lahn-di	*Írlandi*
New Zealand	nee-ah syow-lahn-di	*Nýa Sjálandi*
Scotland	skot-lahn-di	*Skotlandi*
the USA	bahnd-ah-rree-kyö-nöm	*Bandaríkjunum*

Age

How old are you?
    kvahth ehrr-dö ger-möl/   *Hvað ertu gömul/*
    gahm-ahdl?   *gamall?* (f/m)
I'm ... years old.
    yehkh ehrr ... ow-rrah   *Ég er ... ára.*

ICELANDIC

Occupations

What do you do?	kvahth gehrr-irr <u>th</u>oo?	*Hvað gerir þú?*

I'm (a/an) ...	yehkh ehrr ...	*Ég er ...*
in business	ee vith-skift-öm	*í viðskiptum*
journalist	frryeht-ah-mahth-örr	*fréttamaður*
manual worker	vehrrk-ah-mahth-örr	*verkamaður*
nurse	hyook-rrön-ahrr-frraith-ing-örr	*hjúkrunarfræðingur*
office worker	skrrif-stof-ö-mahth-örr	*skrifstofumaður*
scientist	vee-sin-dah-mahth-örr	*vísindamaður*
student	nowms-mahth-örr	*námsmaður*
teacher	kehn-ah-rri	*kennari*
waiter	<u>th</u>yohdn/ <u>th</u>yohn-ös-dö-stool-kah	*þjónn/ þjónustustúlka*
writer	rrit-hehrf-önd-örr	*rithöfundur*

Religion

What is your religion?		
	kvehrr-ahrr trroo-ahrr ehrrt <u>th</u>oo?	*Hverrar trúar ert þú?*
I'm not religious.		
	yehkh ehrr ehk-i trroo-öth/ trroo-ahth-örr	*Ég er ekki trúuð/ trúaður.* (f/m)

I'm ...	yehkh ehrr ...	*Ég er ...*
Buddhist	boo-dah-trroo-ahrr	*búddatrúar*
Catholic	kah-<u>th</u>olsk/ kah-<u>th</u>ol-skörr	*kaþólsk/ kaþólskur* (f/m)
Christian	krrist-in-ahrr trroo-ahrr	*kristinnar trúar*
Hindu	hin-doo trroo-ahrr	*hindú trúar*
Jewish	gith-ing-örr	*gyðingur*
Muslim	moo-hah-mehths-trroo-ahrr	*múhameðstrúar*

ICELANDIC

Family

Are you married?
ehrrt-ö gift/gift-örr?
Ert þú gift/giftur? (f/m)

I'm single.
yehkh ehrr ayn-hlayp/
ayn-hlayp-örr
*Ég er einhleyp/
einhleypur.* (f/m)

I'm married.
yehkh ehrr gift/gift-örr
Ég er gift/giftur. (f/m)

How many children do you have?
kvahth owt thoo merg berdn?
Hvað átt þú mörg börn?

I don't have any children.
yehkh ow ayn-gin berdn
Ég á engin börn.

Do you have a boyfriend/girlfriend?
owt thoo kairr-ahs-dah/
kairr-ös-dö?
*Átt þú kærasta/
kærustu?*

brother	brroh-thirr	*bróðir*
children	berdn	*börn*
daughter	doht-irr	*dóttir*
family	fyerl-skil-dah	*fjölskylda*
father	fahth-irr	*faðir*
grandfather	ah-vi	*afi*
grandmother	ahm-mah	*amma*
husband	ay-in-mahth-örr	*eiginmaður*
mother	mohth-irr	*móðir*
sister	sist-irr	*systir*
son	son-örr	*sonur*
wife	ay-in-ko-nah	*eiginkona*

Kids' Talk

How old are you?
kvahth ehrr-tö ger-möl/
gahm-ahdl?
*Hvað ertu gömul/
gamall?* (f/m)

When's your birthday?
kveh-nayrr owh-tö ahm-mai-li?
Hvenær áttu afmæli?

What do you do after school?
kvath geh-rrirr-thoo ehf-tirr skoh-la?
Hvað gerirðu eftir skóla?

Do you have a pet at home?
    owt-tö gyai-lö-deer hehi-ma?   *Áttu gæludýr heima?*

I have a ...	yehkh ow ...	*Ég á ...*
bird	fögl	*fugl*
budgerigar	pow-va-geörk	*páfagauk*
canary	kah-nah-rree-fögl	*kanarífugl*
cat	kerht	*kött*
dog	hönd	*hund*
frog	frrosk	*frosk*

ICELANDIC

Feelings

I (don't) like ...
    yehkh ehrr (ehk-i) hrri-vin ahv ...   *Ég er (ekki) hrifinn af ...*
I'm cold/hot.
    myehrr ehrr kahlt/hayt   *Mér er kalt/heitt.*

I'm ...	yehkh ehrr ...	*Ég er ...*
angry	rrayth/rrayth-örr	*reið/reiður* (f/m)
grateful	thahk-lowt/	*þakklát/*
	thahk-law-törr	*þakklátur* (f/m)
happy	ow-naikhth/	*ánægð/*
	aw-naikhth-örr	*ánægður* (f/m)
hungry	sveörnkh/svown-görr	*vöng/svangur* (f/m)
sad	hrrig/hrrig-görr	*hrygg/hryggur* (f/m)
tired	thrrayt/thrrayt-örr	*þreytt/þreyttur* (f/m)
well	frreesk/frrees-görr	*frísk/frískur* (f/m)

I'm worried.
    yehkh hehf ow-hig-yörr   *Ég hef áhyggjur.*
I'm sorry. (condolence)
    myehrr thik-irr thahth layht   *Mér þykir það leitt.*

Some Useful Phrases

Sure.	viss-ö-lehkh-ah	*Vissulega.*
Just a minute.	bee-dö ahth-ayns	*Bíddu aðeins.*
Good luck!	gown-gi thyehrr vehl!	*Gangi þér vel!*

ICELANDIC

BREAKING THE LANGUAGE BARRIER

Do you speak English?
    tah-lahrr <u>th</u>oo ehn-skö?   *Talar þú ensku?*
Does anyone speak English?
    tah-lahrr ayn-kvehrr ehn-skö?   *Talar einhver ensku?*
I speak a little Icelandic.
    yehkh tah-lah svoh lit-lah   *Ég tala svolitla*
    ees-lehn-skö   *íslensku.*
I don't speak ...
    yehkh tah-lah ehki ...   *Ég tala ekki ...*
I (don't) understand.
    yehkh skil (ehk-i)   *Ég skil (ekki).*
Could you speak more slowly please?
    gyai-tirr <u>th</u>oo tah-lah<u>th</u>   *Gætir þú talað*
    svo-lee-ti<u>th</u> haikh-ahrr?   *svolítið hægar?*

Could you repeat that?
    gyai-tirr <u>th</u>oo   *Gætir þú*
    ehn-dörr-tehk-ith <u>th</u>eht-ah?   *endurtekið þetta?*
How do you say ...?
    kvehrr-dnikh say-irr   *Hvernig segir*
    mahth-örr ...?   *maður ...?*
What does ... mean?
    kvahth <u>th</u>eeth-irr?   *Hvað þýðir ...?*

I speak ...   yehkh tah-lah ...   *Ég tala ...*
    English   ehn-skö   *ensku*
    French   frrern-skö   *frönsku*
    German   <u>th</u>ees-kö   *þýsku*
    Italian   ee-terl-skö   *ítölsku*
    Spanish   spern-skö   *spönsku*

ICELANDIC

BODY LANGUAGE

Icelandic society is small and it's possible to recognise Icelanders abroad because of the way they watch people directly, even in a big city, as if they expect to meet someone they know. Icelanders also tend – or at least used to, they're becoming more sophisticated now – to stare at foreigners.

Possibly the reason Icelanders crowd each other is that they have a different sense of bodily space from other westerners. An interesting idea, which may also account for the large number of automobile collisions, is that they have a different sense of 'car space' – a sense that there is much more space around themselves and their cars than in fact there is.

In the old Icelandic rural culture, people used to kiss a lot when they met. Nowadays most people only shake hands or put a little kiss on one cheek only. Icelanders are rather reserved and it takes time to get to know them, but they're known for their hospitality and they're used to fixing things (for themselves or anyone who needs it), so even if they don't seem very friendly you may experience their helpfulness all the same.

SIGNS	
AÐGANGUR BANNAÐUR	NO ENTRY
BANNAÐ	PROHIBITED
FARANGUR	BAGGAGE COUNTER
FRÁTEKIÐ	RESERVED
INNGANGUR/INN	ENTRANCE
INNRITUN	CHECK-IN COUNTER
KONUR/KARLAR	LADIES/GENTLEMEN
NEYÐARÚTGANGUR	EMERGENCY EXIT
OPIÐ/LOKAÐ	OPEN/CLOSED
ÓKEYPIS	FREE ADMISSION
REYKINGAR BANNAÐAR	NO SMOKING
SÍMI	TELEPHONE
SNYRTING	TOILETS
TOLLUR	CUSTOMS
UPPLÝSINGAR	INFORMATION
ÚTGANGUR/ÚT	EXIT

ICELANDIC

PAPERWORK

address	hay-mil-is-fowng	heimilisfang
age	ahld-örr	aldur
birth certificate	faith-ing-ahrr-vot-orrth	fæðingarvottorð
car owner's title	ayg-nahrr-voth-orrth	eignarvottorð
car registration	biv-rrayth-ah-skoth-ön	bifreiðaskoðun
customs	todl-skoth-ö	tollskoðun
date of birth	faith-ing-ahrr-dahkh-örr	fæðingardagur
driver's licence	er-kö-skeer-tay-ni	ökuskírteini
identification	skil-rree-ki	skilríki
immigration	vehkh-ah-brryehvs-skoth-ön	vegabréfsskoðun
name	nahbn	nafn
nationality	<u>th</u>yohth-ehrr-dni	þjóðerni
passport	vehkh-ah-brryehv	vegabréf
(number)	(s-noo-ehrr)	(snúmer)
place of birth	faith-ing-ahrr-stahth-örr	fæðingarstaður
profession	aht-vin-ah	atvinna
reason for travel	ow-staith-ah fehrrth-ah-lahkhs-ins	ástæða ferðalagsins
religion	trroo	trú
sex	kin	kyn
tourist card	fehrrth-ah-mahn-ah-spyahld	ferðamannaspjald
visa	vehkh-ah-brryehvs-ow-rrit-ön	vegabréfsáritun

GETTING AROUND

What time does the ... leave/arrive?	kveh-nayrr fehrr/ keh-mörr ...?	Hvenær fer/ kemur ...?
aeroplane	flökh-vyehl-in	flugvélin
boat	bow-törr-in	báturinn
(city)bus	vahgn-in	vagninn
tram	sporr-vahgn-in	sporvagninn

ICELANDIC

Directions

Where is ...?
    kvahrr ehrr ...?   *Hvar er ...?*

How do I get to ...?
    kvehrr-dnikh kyehmst   *Hvernig kemst*
    yehkh til ...?   *ég til ...?*

Is it far from here?
    ehrr <u>thath</u> lowngt hyehth-ahn?   *Er það langt héðan?*

Can I walk there?
    ehrr <u>thath</u> ee gern-gö fai-rri?   *Er það í göngufæri?*

Can you show me (on the map)?
    geh-törr <u>thoo</u> seent myehrr   *Getur þú sýnt mér*
    (ow korrt-in-ö)?   *(á kortinu)?*

I want to go to ...
    migh lown-gahrr ahth   *Mig langar að*
    fah-rrah til ...   *fara til ...*

Go straight ahead.
    fahrr-thö baynt owfrram   *Farðu beint áfram.*

It's two blocks down.
    <u>thath</u> ehrr tvaym-örr   *það er tveimur*
    gert-öm nehth-ahrr   *götum neðar.*

Turn left/right	baykh-thö til	*Beygðu til*
at the ...	vinst-rri/haikh-rri vith ...	*vinstri/hægri við ...*
next corner	nais-dah horrdn	*næsta horn*
traffic lights	öm-fehrrth-ahrr-ljohs-in	*umferðarljósin*
behind	firr-irr ahft-ahn	*fyrir aftan*
in front of	firr-irr frrahm-ahn	*fyrir framan*
far	lownkht ee börr-dö	*langt í burtu*
near	now-laikht	*nálægt*
opposite	ow moh-ti	*á móti*

ICELANDIC

Booking Tickets

Where can I buy a ticket?
kvahrr geht yehkh kayft mith-ah?   *Hvar get ég keypt miða?*

I want to go to ...
yehkh vil fah-rrah til ...   *Ég vil fara til ...*

Do I need to book?
<u>th</u>ahrrf yehkh ahth pahn-tah?   *Þarf ég að panta?*

I'd like to book a seat to ...
gyai-ti yehkh pahn-tahth fahrr til ...   *Gæti ég pantað far til ...*

I'd like ...	gyai-ti yehkh fayn-khith ...	*Gæti ég fengið ...*
a one-way ticket	mith-ah/	*miða/*
	ahth-rrah layth-in-ah	*aðra leiðina*
a return ticket	mith-ah/	*miða/*
	bowth-ahrr layth-irr	*báðar leiðir*
two tickets	tvo mith-ah	*tvo miða*
a student's fare	nowms-mahn-	*námsmanna-*
	ah-mith-ah	*miða*
1st class	firrst-ah fahrr-rreem-i	*fyrsta farrými*
2nd class	ahn-ahth fahrr-rreem-i	*annað farrými*

Is it completely full?
ehrr ahl-vehkh fölt?   *Er alveg fullt?*

Can I get a stand-by ticket?
gyeht yehkh fayn-gith
forr-fahd-lah-mith-ah?   *Get ég fengið
forfallamiða?*

Can I have a refund?
gyeht yehkh fayn-gith
ehnd-örr-grrayths-lö?   *Get ég fengið
endurgreiðslu?*

DID YOU KNOW ...   There are no trains in Iceland,
but there are plenty of buses!

ICELANDIC

SIGNS

BROTTFÖR	DEPARTURES
KOMA	ARRIVALS
MIÐASALA	TICKET OFFICE
STRÆTISVAGNABIÐSTÖÐ	BUS STOP
STÖÐ	STATION
TÍMAÁÆTLUN	TIMETABLE

Air

Is there a flight to ...?
   ehrr flo-yith til ...?   *Er flogið til ...?*
How long does the flight take?
   kvahth ehrr <u>the</u>h-tah lowngt flüg? *Hvað er þetta langt flug?*

airport tax	flü-vadla-skah-türr	*fluhvallaskattur*
boarding pass	brroht-fah-rrahrr-spyald	*brottfaraspjald*

Bus

Where is the bus stop?
   kvahrr ehrr bith-sterth-in? *Hvar er biðstöðin?*
Which bus goes to ...?
   kvahth-ah vahkhn fehrr til ...? *Hvaða vagn fer til ...?*
Could you let me know
when we get to ...?
   gyai-tirr <u>thoo</u> low-tith mikh *Gætir þú látið mig*
   vi-tah <u>the</u>hkh-ahrr *vita þegar*
   vith kom-öm til ...? *við komum til ...?*
I want to get off!
   yehkh vil fah-rrah oot! *Ég vil fara út!*

What time is	kveh-nairr	*Hvenær*
the ... bus?	kehm-örr ... vahgn-in?	*kemur ... vagninn?*
first	firrst	*fyrst*
next	naist	*næst*
last	seeth-ahst	*síðast*

ICELANDIC

Taxi

Please take me to ...
gyai-tir thoo ehkith myehrr til ...?
Gætir þú ekið mér til ...?

How much does it cost to go to ...?
kvahth kost-ahrr aht
fah-rrah til ...?
*Hvað kostar að
fara til ...?*

Here is fine, thank you.
hyehrr-dnah ehrr ow-gyait tahk
Hérna er ágætt, takk.

The next street to the left/right.
nais-tah gah-tah til
vinst-rri/haikh-rri
*Næsta gata til
vinstri/hægri.*

Continue.   hahl-dö ow-frrahm   *Haltu áfram.*
Stop here!   stahn-sah hyehrr-dnah!   *Stansa hérna!*

Car

Where's the next petrol station?
kvahrr ehrr nais-dah
behn-seen-sterth?
*Hvar er næsta
bensínstöð?*

The battery is flat.
gaym-irr-in ehrr
rahv-mahgns-leös
*Geymirinn er
rafmagnslaus.*

The radiator is leaking.
vahs-kahs-in leh-körr
Vatnskassinn lekur.

I have a flat tyre.
thahth ehrr
sprroon-ghith hyow myer
*Það er
sprungið hjá mér.*

It's overheating.
hahn heh-vör of-hit-nath
Hann hefur ofhitnað.

It's not working.
hahn virrk-ahrr ehk-i
Hann virkar ekki.

ICELANDIC

air (for tyres)	loft (ee dehk)	*loft (í dekk)*
battery	rrahf-gay-mirr	*rafgeymir*
brakes	brrehm-sörr	*bremsur*
clutch	koop-leeng	*kúpling*
driver's licence	ehr-kö-skeer-tay-ni	*ökuskírteini*
engine	vyehl	*vél*
lights	lyohs	*ljós*
radiator	vahss-kahss-i	*vatnskassi*
road map	vehkh-ah-korrt	*vegakort*
tyres	dehk	*dekk*
windscreen	frrahm-rrooth-ah	*framrúða*

SIGNS

ALLUR AKSTUR BANNAÐUR	NO ENTRY
BIÐSKYLDA	GIVE WAY
BLÝLAUST	UNLEADED
EÐLILEGT	NORMAL
EINSTEFNA	ONE WAY
ENGIN BÍLASTÆÐI	NO PARKING
SJÁLFSAFGREIÐSLA	SELF SERVICE
STANS	STOP
SUPER	SUPER
VERKSTÆÐI	GARAGE
VÉLVIRKI	MECHANIC
VIÐGERÐIR	REPAIRS

ACCOMMODATION

Where is a ...	kvahrr ehrr ...	*Hvar er ...*
hotel?	ho-tehl?	*hótel?*
cheap	oh-deert	*ódýrt*
nearby	now-laikht	*nálægt*
clean	hrraynt	*hreint*

What is the address?
kvahth ehr hay-mil-is-fówn-gith? *Hvað er heimilisfangið?*

Could you write the address, please?
gyai-tirr <u>thoo</u> skrrif-ahth *Gætir þú skrifað*
nith-örr hay-mil-is fówn-gith? *niður heimilisfangið?*

ICELANDIC

At the Hotel

Do you have any rooms available?
ehrr-ö hehrr-behrr-khi leörs? *Eru herbergi laus?*

I'd like ...	gyai-ti yehkh fayn-khith ...	*Gæti ég fengið ...*
a single room	ayn-stahk-lings-hehrr-behrr-khi	*einstaklingsherbergi*
a double room	tvehg-yah-mahn-ah-hehrr-behrr-gi	*tveggjamannaherbergi*
a room with a bathroom	hehrr-behrr-khi mehth bahth-i	*herbergi með baði*
to share	ahth day-lah	*að deila*
a dorm	hehrr-behrr-khi mehth erth-rröm	*herbergi með öðrum*
a bed	rroom	*rúm*

I'm going to stay for ...	yehkh vehrrth ee ...	*Ég verð í ...*
one day	aydn dahkh	*einn dag*
two days	tvo dahkh-ah	*tvo daga*
one week	ay-nah vi-kö	*eina viku*

Sorry, we're full.
myehrr thi-kirr thahth layt thahth ehrr födl boh-kahth *Mér þykir það leitt, það er fullbókað.*

How long will you be staying?
kvahth ait-lahrr thoo ahth veh-rra layn-gi? *Hvað ætlar þú að vera lengi?*

How many nights?
kvahth mahrr-gahrr nai-törr? *Hvað margar nætur?*

How much is it per night/ per person?
kvahth kost-ahrr noht-in firr-irr mahn-in? *Hvað kostar nóttin fyrir manninn?*

Requests & Complaints

Can I see it?
mow yehkh syow thahth? — *Má ég sjá það?*

Are there any other/cheaper rooms?
eh-rrö nok-örr ern-örr/
oh-deer-ah-rri hehrr-behrr-gi? — *Eru nokkur önnur/
ódýrari herbergi?*

Is there a reduction for
students/children?
ehrr ahf-slowt-örr firr-irr
nowms-mehn/berdn? — *Er afsláttur fyrir
námsmenn/börn?*

Does it include breakfast?
ehrr morrkh-ön-maht-örr
in-i-fahl-in? — *Er morgunmatur
innifalinn?*

It's fine, I'll take it.
thahth ehrr ow-gyait
yehkh fai thahth — *Það er ágætt,
ég fæ það.*

I'm not sure how long I'm staying.
yehkh ehrr ehk-i viss öm
kvahth yehkh vehrrth layn-gi — *Ég er ekki viss um
hvað ég verð lengi.*

Where is the bathroom?
kvahrr ehrr
bahth-hehrr-behrr-gith? — *Hvar er
baðherbergið?*

May I leave these in your safe?
mow yehkh gay-mah theh-dah
ee er-ikh-is-hohl-vi? — *Má ég geyma þetta
í öryggishólfi?*

Is there somewhere to wash clothes?
ehrr ayn-kvehrrs-stahth-ahrr
haikht ahth thvo thvoht? — *Er einhversstaðar
hægt að þvo þvott?*

Can I use the kitchen?
mow yehkh no-tah
ehld-hoo-sith? — *Má ég nota
eldhúsið?*

Can I use the telephone?
mow yehkh no-tah
see-mahn? — *Má ég nota
símann?*

ICELANDIC

Some Useful Words & Phrases

We're leaving now/tomorrow.
> vith ehrr-öm ahth fah-rrah   *Við erum að fara*
> noo-nah/ow morr-goon   *núna/á morgun.*

I'd like to pay the bill.
> yehkh vil borr-khah   *Ég vil borga*
> rraykn-inkh-in   *reikninginn.*

bathroom	bahth-hehrr-behrr-gi	*baðherbergi*
bed	rroom	*rúm*
blanket	teh-bi	*teppi*
clean	hrraydn	*hreinn*
dirty	ow-hrraydn	*óhreinn*
double bed	tvee-brrayt rroom	*tvíbreitt rúm*
electricity	rrahv-mahgn	*rafmagn*
excluded	firr-irr öt-ahn	*fyrir utan*
fan	vif-dah	*vifta*
included	in-i-fahl-ith	*innifalið*
key	li-kidl	*lykill*
lift (elevator)	lif-dah	*lyfta*
light bulb	lyow-sah-peh-rrah	*ljósapera*
a lock	lows	*lás*
mirror	spay-idl	*spegill*
pillow	kod-di	*koddi*
quiet	hlyoht	*hljótt*
sheet	lahk	*lak*
shower	störr-dah	*sturta*
soap	sow-pah	*sápa*
toilet	kloh-seht/sahl-ehrr-dni	*klósett/salerni*
toilet paper	klow-seht-pah-peer	*klósettpappír*
towel	hahnd-klai-thi	*handklæði*
(cold/hot) water	(kahlt/hayt) vahtn	*(kalt/heitt) vatn*
window	khlö-khi	*gluggi*

AROUND TOWN

I'm looking for a/the ...	yehkh ehrr ahth lay-tah ahth ...	*Ég er að leita að ...*
bank	bown-kah	*banka*
city centre	mith-bai-nöm	*miðbænum*
... embassy	... sehn-di-rrow-thi-nö	*... sendiráðinu*
hotel	hoh-tehl-i-nö mee-nö	*hótelinu mínu*
market	mahrrk-ahth-nöm	*markaðnum*
police	lerkh-rrehgl-ö-ni	*lögreglunni*
post office	pohst-hoos-i-nö	*pósthúsinu*
public toilet	ahl-mehn-inkhs-sahl-ehrr-dni	*almennings-salerni*
telephone centre	seem-sterthin-i	*símstöðinni*
tourist information office	öp-lees-een-gah-thjohn-öst-ö firr-irr fehrrth-ah-fohlk	*upplýsinga-þjónustu fyrir ferðafólk*

ICELANDIC

What time does it open/close?
   kveh-nairr ehrr op-nahth/ lo-kahth?   *Hvenær er opnað/ lokað?*

What street/suburb is this?
   kvahth-ah gah-tah/ kvehrr-vi ehrr theh-dah?   *Hvaða gata/ hverfi er þetta?*

For directions, see the Getting Around section, page 207.

SIGNS	
FARFUGLAHEIMILI	YOUTH HOSTEL
GISTIHEIMILI	GUESTHOUSE
GISTIHÚS	MOTEL
HÓTEL	HOTEL

ICELANDIC

At the Post Office

I'd like	yehkh ait-lah	*Ég ætla*
to send a ...	ahth sehn-dah ...	*að senda ...*
letter	brreef	*bréf*
postcard	korrt	*kort*
parcel	pahk-ah	*pakka*
telegram	skay-ti	*skeyti*

I'd like some stamps.
    yehkh aid-lah ahth fow   *Ég ætla að fá*
    nok örr frree-mehrr-gi   *nokkur frímerki.*

How much does it cost
to send this to ...?
    kvahth kos-dahrr ahth   *Hvað kostar að*
    sehn-dah <u>theh</u>-dah til ...?   *senda þetta til ...?*

an aerogram	flökh-brreef	*flugbréf*
airmail	flookh-pohst-örr	*flugpóstur*
envelope	öm-slahkh	*umslag*
mailbox	pohst-kahss-i	*póstkassi*
registered mail	ow-birrth-ahrr-pohst-örr	*ábyrgðarpóstur*
surface mail/sea mail	syoh-pohst-örr	*sjópóstur*

Telephone & Internet

I want to ring ...
    yehkh <u>thahrrv</u> ahth hrreen-gya ...   *Ég þarf að hringja ...*
The number is ...
    noo-mehrr-ith ehrr ...   *Númerið er ...*
How much does a three-minute
call cost?
    kvahth kos-dahrr   *Hvað kostar*
    <u>thrr</u>i-khjah-meen-oot-nah   *þriggja mínútna*
    sahm-tahl?   *samtal?*
How much does each extra minute cost?
    kvahth kos-dahrr   *Hvað kostar*
    kvehrr meen-oo-tah?   *hver mínúta?*

ICELANDIC

I'd like to speak to (Jón Pálsson).
> gyai-ti yehkh fayn-gith ahth
> tahlah vith (yohn powls-sohn)?

*Gæti ég fengið að
tala við (Jón Pálsson)?*

I want to make a reverse-charges
phone call.
> yehkh ait-lah ahth hrreen-khyah
> okh vith-tahk-ahn-di borr-gahrr

*Ég ætla að hringja
og viðtakandi borgar.*

It's engaged. <u>thahth</u> ehrr ow tah-li *Það er á tali.*
I've been cut off. <u>thahth</u> slit-nahth-i *Það slitnaði.*

Where can I get Internet access?
> kvahr gyeht yehkh fayn-gyith
> ahth noh-tah in-tehrr-neh-tith?

*Hvar get ég fengið
að nota internetið?*

I'd like to send an email.
> Mig lown-guhrr til ahth
> sen-duh terl-vü-pohst

*Mig langar til að
senda tölvupóst.*

At the Bank

I want to exchange some money/
travellers cheques.
> yehkh <u>thahrrf</u> ahth skif-dah
> pehn-inkh-öm/fehrrth-ah-tyehköm

*Ég þarf að skipta
peningum/ferðatékkum.*

What is the exchange rate?
> kvehrrt ehrr gehngith?

Hvert er gengið?

How many kronas per dollar?
> kvahth ehrr-ö mahrr-gahrr
> krrohn-örr ee dol-ah-rrah-nöm?

*Hvað eru margar
krónur í dollaranum?*

bank notes	sehth-lahrr	*seðlar*
cashier	gyahld-kehrr-i	*gjaldkeri*
coins	smow-mint	*smámynt*
credit card	grrayth-slö-korrt	*greiðslukort*
exchange	skif-dah	*skipta*
loose change	rrayth-ö-fyeh	*reiðufé*
signature	ön-dirr-skrrift	*undirskrift*

ICELANDIC

INTERESTS & ENTERTAINMENT
Sightseeing

Do you have a guidebook/local map?
owt-ö fehrrth-ah-hahnd-bohk/
korrt ahv stahth-nöm?
Áttu ferðahandbók/
kort af staðnum?

What are the main attractions?
kvahth ehrr mahrrk-vehrrt
ahth syow?
Hvað er markvert
að sjá?

What is that?
kvahth ehrr <u>th</u>eh-dah?
Hvað er þetta?

How old is it?
kvahth ehrr <u>th</u>ahth gahm-ahlt?
Hvað er það gamalt?

Can I take photographs?
mow yehkh tah-kah mind-irr?
Má ég taka myndir?

What time does it open/close?
klök-ahn kvahth op-nahrr/
lok-ahrr?
Klukkan hvað opnar/
lokar?

Going Out

What's there to do in the evenings?
kvahth ehrr haikht ahth
gyeh-rra ow kverl-din?
Hvað er hægt að
gera á kvöldin?

Is there a local entertainment guide?
ehrr til baik-leen-görr öm
skiehm-tah-nirr hyehrr
ow stahth-nöm?
Er til bæklingur um
skemmtanir hér
á staðnum?

I feel like	mig lowngarr	*Mig langar*
going to a/the ...	til ahth fahrrah ...	*til að fara ...*
cinema	ee bee-oh	*í bíó*
opera	ee oh-peh-rrö-nah	*í óperuna*
theatre	ee layk-hoo-sith	*í leikhúsið*
bar	ow bahrr	*á bar*
cafe	ow kahffi-hoos	*á kaffihús*
concert/gig	ow tohn-lay-kah	*á tónleika*
disco	ow diskoh-tehk	*á diskótek*
nightclub	ow nai-törr-kloobb	*á næturklúbb*
restaurant	ow vay-teen-gah-hoos	*á veitingahús*

Sports & Interests

What sports do you play?
kvah-thah ee-<u>th</u>roh-tirr
stön-dahrr <u>th</u>oo?

*Hvaða íþróttir
stundar þú?*

What are your interests?
kvehrr eh-rrö <u>th</u>een
ow-högah-mowl?

*Hver eru þín
áhugamál?*

ICELANDIC

art	lis-tirr	*listir*
basketball	ker-fö-bol-ti	*körfubolti*
chess	skowk	*skák*
collecting things	ahth sab-nah hlö-töm	*að safna hlutum*
dancing	ahth dahnsah	*að dansa*
food	mah-törr	*matur*
football	fohd-bol-ti	*fótbolti*
hiking	geörn-gö-fehrr-thirr	*gönguferðir*
martial arts	bahrr-dahgah-ee-<u>th</u>roh-tirr	*bardagaíþróttir*
meeting friends	ahth hih-tah vi-ni	*að hitta vini*
movies	kvik-min-dirr	*kvikmyndir*
music	tohn-list	*tónlist*
nightclubs	nai-törr-kloob-bahrr	*næturklúbbar*
photography	lyohs-min-dön	*ljósmyndun*
reading	lehs-törr	*lestur*
shopping	ahth fah-rrah ee boo-thirr	*að fara í búðir*
skiing	ahth fah-rrah ow skee-thi	*að fara á skíði*
swimming	sönd	*sund*
tennis	tehn-nis	*tennis*
travelling	ahth fehrr-thahst	*að ferðast*
TV/videos	syohn-vahrrp/ mind-bernd	*sjónvarp/ myndbönd*
visiting friends	ahth haym-sai-kyah vi-ni	*að heimsækja vini*

ICELANDIC

Festivals

During Þorri, the fourth month of winter (from mid-January to mid-February), it's common to hold a party called þorrablót, where people gather to sing and eat traditional Icelandic food.

Seven weeks before Easter is bolludagur 'bun-day', so-called because people are supposed to have all kinds of buns on this day. Children wake their parents in the morning with bolluvöndur, a decorated birch-rod. The last day before the beginning of the traditional Lenten fast (Shrove Tuesday) is sprengidagur. The name refers to sprenging (explosion) because people are supposed to eat as much saltkjöt og baunir (salted lamb/mutton, served with split pea soup) as they can, even so much that they may 'explode'.

A very old tradition in Iceland is celebrating the first day of summer, sumardagurinn fyrsti. It's an old custom to give sumargjöf (a summer gift) to close relatives.

Sautjándi júní, 17 June, is Iceland's National Independence Day. It's celebrated in front of the Parliament where the fjallkona, a female symbol of Iceland (usually a young actress in national costume), recites a poem.

The most important day of preparation for Jólin (Christmas), is 23 December, called Þorláksmessa after the only officially canonised Icelandic saint. The main Christmas celebration starts with a Christmas church service on Christmas Eve, aðfangadagskvöld, followed by a family dinner. To wish someone a merry Christmas you say gleðileg jól.

IN THE COUNTRY
Weather
What's the weather like?
  kvehrr-dnikh ehrr vehth-rrith?
  Hvernig er veðrið?

SIGNS	
TJALDSTÆÐI	CAMPING GROUND

It's ... today.	vehth-rrith ehrr ... ee dahkh	*Veðrið er ... í dag.*
Will it be ...	vehrrth-örr ...	*Verður ...*
tomorrow?	ow morr-khön?	*á morgun?*
cloudy	skee-yahth	*skýjað*
cold	kahlt	*kalt*
hot	hayt	*heitt*
raining	rrikh-neenkh	*rigning*
snowing	snyohrr	*snjór*
sunny	sohl-skin	*sólskin*
windy	kvahst	*hvasst*

Camping
Am I allowed to camp here?
  mow yehkh tyahl-dah hyehrr?   *Má ég tjalda hér?*
Is there a campsite nearby?
  ehrr tyahld-staith-i hyehrr now-laikht?   *Er tjaldstæði hér nálægt?*

backpack	bahk-po-ki	*bakpoki*
can opener	doh-sah-op-nah-rri	*dósaopnari*
firewood	ehld-i-vith-örr	*eldiviður*
gas cartridge	gahs-koo-törr	*gaskútur*
mattress	dee-nah	*dýna*
penknife	vah-sah-hneev-örr	*vasahnífur*
rope	snai-rri	*snæri*
tent (pegs)	tyahld(-hai-lahrr)	*tjald(hælar)*
torch/flashlight	vah-sah-lyohs	*vasaljós*
sleeping bag	svehbn-po-ki	*svefnpoki*
stove	ehld-ah-veel	*eldavél*
water bottle	vahs-flahs-ga	*vatnsflaska*

ICELANDIC

FOOD

breakfast	morr-gön-mah-törr	*morgunmatur*
lunch	how-day-is-maht-örr	*hádegismatur*
dinner	kverld-maht-örr	*kvöldmatur*

Table for ..., please.
gyeht yehkh fayn-gith ...   *Get ég fengið ...*
mah-nah borrth?   *manna borð?*

Can I see the menu please?
gyeht-yehkh fayn-gith ahth   *Get ég fengið að*
syow maht-sehth-il-in?   *sjá matseðilinn?*

What does it include?
kvahth ehrr in-i-fahl-ith?   *Hvað er innifalið?*

Is service included in the bill?
ehrr <u>thyoh</u>-nös-dah in-i-fahl-in?   *Er þjónusta innifalin?*

ashtray	ers-kö-bah-khi	*öskubakki*
the bill	rrayk-ninkh-örr-in	*reikningurinn*
a cup	bod-li	*bolli*
a drink	drrik-örr	*drykkur*
a fork	khahf-adl	*gaffall*
a glass	khlahs	*glas*
a knife	hnee-vörr	*hnífur*
a plate	disk-örr	*diskur*
a spoon	skayth	*skeið*
teaspoon	teh-skayth	*teskeið*

Vegetarian Meals

I'm a vegetarian.
yehkh ehrr grrain-meht-is-ai-tah   *Ég er grænmetisæta.*

I don't eat meat.
yehkh borr-thah ehk-i kyert   *Ég borða ekki kjöt.*

Staple Foods & Condiments

bread	brreörth	*brauð*
cream	rryoh-mi	*rjómi*
eggs	ehg	*egg*

ICELANDIC

fish	fis-körr	*fiskur*
fruit	ow-vehg-stirr	*ávextir*
ketchup	toh-mahts-soh-sah	*tómatsósa*
meat	kyert	*kjöt*
mustard	sin-nehp	*sinnep*
pepper	pi-pahrr	*pipar*
potatoes	kahrr-ter-blörr	*kartöflur*
rice	hrrees-grryohn	*hrísgrjón*
salt	sahlt	*salt*
sauce	soh-sah	*sósa*
seasoning	krridd	*krydd*
sugar	si-görr	*sykur*
vegetables	grrain-meh-ti	*grænmeti*

Breakfast Menu

boiled egg	so-thith ehg	*soðið egg*
bread	brreörth	*brauð*
bread roll	rroon-stih-kyi	*rúnstykki*
butter	smyeörrr	*smjör*
cereal	morr-gün-korrdn	*morgunkorn*
cheese	ostörr	*ostur*
coffee	kahf-fi	*kaffi*
fruit juice	ow-vahgs-tah-sah-vi	*ávaxtasafi*
honey	hö-nowng	*hunang*
jam	söl-tah	*sulta*
marmalade	mahrr-meh-lah-thi	*marmelaði*
milk	myohlk	*mjólk*
muesli	müsl	*müsl*
oatmeal	hahv-rrah-grrehü-türr	*hafragrautur*
orange juice	ah-pehl-see-n-sah-vi	*appelsínsafi*
sour milk	soorr-myohlk	*súrmjólk*
(type of yoghurt)		
sugar	si-görr	*sykur*
tea	teh	*te*
toast	rris-tahth brrehüth	*ristað brauð*
yoghurt	yoh-goorrt	*jógúrt*

ICELANDIC

Meat & Poultry

beef	neör-tah-kyert	*nautakjöt*
chicken	kyooh-kleen-görr	*kjúklingur*
ham	skin-kah	*skinka*
lamb	lahm-bah-kyert	*lambakjöt*
pork	svee-nah-kyert	*svínakjöt*
reindeer	hrrayn-dee-rrah-kyert	*hreindýrakjöt*
sausage	pil-sah	*pylsa*
turkey	kahl-koodn	*kalkúnn*

Fish

cod	<u>th</u>orr-skörr	*þorskur*
haddock	ee-sah	*ýsa*
halibut	loo-thah	*lúða*
herring	seeld	*síld*
lobster	hö-mahrr	*humar*
(smoked) salmon	(rraykh-dörr) lahks	*(reyktur) lax*
scallop	her-rr-pö-dis-körr	*hörpudiskur*
shrimp	rrai-kyah	*rækja*

Fruit

apples	ehb-li	*epli*
apricots	ah-prree-koh-sörr	*apríkósur*
bananas	bah-nah-nahrr	*bananar*
blueberries	blow-behrr	*bláber*
crowberries	krrai-kyi-behrr	*krækiber*
grapes	veen-behrr	*vínber*
lemon	see-trroh-nah	*sítróna*
oranges	ah-pehl-see-nörr	*appelsínur*
peaches	fehrrs-kyörr	*ferskjur*
pears	peh-rrörr	*perur*
pineapple	ah-nah-nahs	*ananas*
strawberries	yahrr-thahrr-behrr	*jarðarber*

ICELANDIC

Vegetables

cabbage	kveet-kowl	*hvítkál*
carrots	göl-rrai-törr	*gulrætur*
cauliflower	blohm-kowl	*blómkál*
cucumber	goorr-kah	*gúrka*
garlic	kveet-leör-körr	*hvítlaukur*
green peas	grrai-nahrr beör-nirr	*grænar baunir*
green pepper	grrain pah-prri-kah	*græn paprika*
lettuce	sah-lahd	*salat*
mushrooms	sveh-pirr	*sveppir*
onion	leör-körr	*laukur*
potatoes	kahrr-ter-blörr	*kartöflur*

Desserts

biscuits	smow-ker-körr/kehgs	*smákökur/kex*
cake	kahkah	*kaka*
fruit	ow-vehgs-tirr	*ávextir*
ice cream	ees/rryoh-mah-ees	*ís/rjómaís*
pancakes	per-nö-ker-körr	*pönnukökur*
pudding	boo-theen-görr	*búðingur*
chocolate	sooh-kö-lah-thi	*súkkulaði*
stewed fruit	ow-vahg-stah-grreör-törr	*ávaxtagrautur*

Drinks

coffee	kahf-fi	*kaffi*
(white/black)	(mehth myolk/svahrrt)	*(með mjólk/svart)*
fruit juice	ow-vahgs-tah-sah-vi	*ávaxtasafi*
ice	klah-kyi	*klaki*
soft drinks	gos-drrih-kyirr	*gosdrykkir*
tea	teh	*te*
water	vahdn	*vatn*

DID YOU KNOW ... Alcohol was prohibited in Iceland in 1912. Beer wasn't legalised again until 1 March 1989, now known as Bjórdagurinn, 'beer day'.

ICELANDIC

MENU DECODER

Starters

flatkökur	flahd-ker-körr	thin unsweet bread
og hangikjöt	og hown-gyi-kyert	made of rye flour, eaten with butter and slices of smoked lamb
grafinn lax	grrahv-inn lahks	grav lax
harðfiskur	harrth-fis-görr	dried fish, stockfish

Main Meals

bjúgu   byoo-ö
  smoked minced meat sausage. Served hot or cold with potatoes in white sauce.

flatkökur   flaht-ker-körr
  rye pancakes, also popular with *hangikjöt*

hangikjöt   hown-gyi-kyert
  smoked lamb, leg or shoulder. Served hot or cold, with potatoes in bechamel sauce and green peas. Also popular as a luncheon meat.

harðfiskur   hahrrth-fis-körr
  dried fish; haddock, cod or catfish. It does not require cooking but is enjoyed as snack food, often spread with a little butter.

kjötsúpa   kyert-soo-pah
  soup, made of a small quantity of vegetables and a large quantity of lamb meat and rice. Always served hot.

ICELANDIC

saltkjöt   sahlt-kyert
   salted lamb/mutton, served with potatoes or swede turnips
   and often accompanied by split pea soup

slátur   slow-törr
   blood and liver puddings. Prepared in the months of Sep-
   tember and October, when slaughtering is at its peak. Blood
   pudding, blóðmör (blohth-mehrr), and liver pudding,
   lifrarpylsa (liv-rrahrr-pil-sah), are eaten sliced hot or cold.
   Traditionally, the slátur that could not be eaten fresh was
   pickled in whey and enjoyed throughout the winter months.

svið   svith
   singed sheep heads. Eaten hot or cold, with either plain
   boiled potatoes, mashed potatoes or swede turnips. The
   pressed and gelled variety is popular for packed lunches.
   seytt rúgbrauð saiht rroo-brreörth cooked rye bread,
   moist and chewy. Popular with hangikjöt.

Desserts

pönnukökur með   pern-nö-ker-körr mehth
sykri eða   si-grri ehth
með sultu og rjóma   mehth söl-tö og rryo-mah
   pancakes with sugar or with jam and cream

skyr   skyirr
   dairy product similar to yoghurt, it's very low in fat. Eaten
   as dessert with sugar and milk and with fresh berries,
   when in season.

Alcoholic Drinks

aqua vitae (brandy)	brreh-ni-veen	*brennivín*
beer	byohrr	*bjór*
cognac	ko-nee-ahk	*koníak*
liqueur	lee-kyer	*líkjör*
whisky	vis-kee	*whisky*
red/ white wine	rreörth-veen/ kveet-veen	*rauðvín/* *hvítvín*

ICELANDIC

SHOPPING

general store, shop	booth	*búð*
laundry	thvo-hdah-hoos	*þvottahús*
market	mahrr-kahth-örr	*markaður*
newsagency/	blah-thah-sah-lah/	*blaðasala/*
stationers	boh-kah-booth	*bókabúð*
pharmacy	ahp-oh-tehk	*apótek*
shoe shop	skoh-booth	*skóbúð*
supermarket	stohrr-mahrr-kahth-örr	*stórmarkaður*
vegetable shop	grrain-meht-is-booth	*grænmetisbúð*

I'd like to buy ...
mikh lown-khahrr *Mig langar*
ahth keör-pah ... *að kaupa ...*
Can you write down the price?
gyeht-örr-ö skrri-vahth *Gætir þú skrifað*
nith-örr vehrrthith? *niður verðið?*

Essential Groceries

batteries	rrahv-hler-thör	*rafhlöður*
bread	brreörth	*brauð*
butter	smyer-rr	*smjör*
cheese	os-törr	*ostur*
chocolate	sooh-kö-lah-thi	*súkkulaði*
eggs	ehg	*egg*
flour	kvay-ti	*hveiti*
gas cylinder	gahs-hihl-kyi	*gashylki*
honey	hö-nowng	*hunang*
marmalade	mahrr-meh-lah-thi	*marmelaði*
matches	ehld-spee-törr	*eldspýtur*
milk	myohlk	*mjólk*
olive oil	oh-lee-vö-o-lee-ö	*ólífuolíu*
pepper	pi-pahrr	*pipar*
salt	sahlt	*salt*
shampoo	syahm-poh	*sjampó*

soap	sow-pö	*sápu*
sugar	si-körr	*sykur*
toilet paper	kloh-seht-pah-pirr	*klósettpappír*
toothbrush	tahn-bös-di	*tannbursti*
washing powder	tvoh-tah-dooft	*þottaduft*

Souvenirs

Typically Icelandic souvenirs include lopapeysur (lo-pah-pay-sör), woollen sweaters and all kinds of woollen articles; pieces of jewellery made of icelandic resources, such as chains with a lava cube covered with gold; body lotion and other cosmetics made of the clay from the Blue Lagoon; Icelandic brennivín (brrehn-ni-veen), schnapps, not least hvannarótar-brennivín (kvahn-nah-rroh-tahrr-brrehn-ni-veen), schnapps flavoured with angelica.

Clothing

clothing	fert	*föt*
coat	kow-pah	*kápa*
dress	kyohdl	*kjóll*
jacket	yah-kyi	*jakki*
jumper/sweater	pay-sah	*peysa*
shirt	skyirr-tah	*skyrta*
shoes	skohrr	*skór*
skirt	pils	*pils*
trousers	bög-sörr	*buxur*

Materials

cotton	boh-mödl	*bómull*
handmade	hahnd-gyehrrt	*handgert*
leather	leh-thörr	*leður*
brass	oorr mehs-eeng	*messing*
gold	oorr göd-li	*gulli*
silver	oorr sil-vrri	*silfri*
flax	herrr	*hör*
silk	sil-kyi	*silki*
wool	ödl	*ull*

ICELANDIC

Colours

black	svahrrt	*svart*
blue	blowt	*blátt*
brown	brroont	*brúnt*
green	grraint	*grænt*
red	rreört	*rautt*
white	kveet	*hvítt*
yellow	gölt	*gult*

Toiletries

comb	grray-thah	*greiða*
condoms	smok-ahrr	*smokkar*
deodorant	svi-tah-likt-ahrr-ay-thirr	*svitalyktareyðir*
razor	rrahk-vyehl	*rakvél*
sanitary napkins	der-mö-bin-di	*dömubindi*
shampoo	syahm-poh	*sjampó*
shaving cream	rrahk-krrehm	*rakkrem*
soap	sow-pah	*sápa*
tampons	vaht-tahp-ahrr/	*vatttappar/*
	tahm-poh-nahrr	*tampónar*
tissues	brryehv-<u>th</u>örr-körr	*bréfþurkur*
toilet paper	kloh-seht-pah-peer	*klósettpappír*
toothpaste	tahn-krrehm	*tannkrem*

Stationery & Publications

map	korrt	*kort*
newspaper	dakh-blahth	*dagblað*
(in English)	(ow ehn-skö)	*(á ensku)*
paper	pah-peer	*pappír*
pen (ballpoint)	pehn-ni/koo-lö-pehn-ni	*penni/kúlupenni*

Photography

How much is it to process this film?

kvahth kos-tahrr ath
frrahm-kahdlah thehs-sah fil-mö?

*Hvað kostar að
framkalla þessa filmu?*

When will it be ready?

kveh-nairr vehrr- thörr
hoon til-boo-in?

*Hvenær verður
hún tilbúin?*

I'd like a film for this camera.

mikh vahn-tahrr fil-mö ee
thehs-sah min-dah-vyehl

*Mig vantar filmu í
þessa myndavél.*

camera	min-dah-vyehl	*myndavél*
develop	frrahm-kad-lah	*framkalla*
film	fil-mah	*filma*
ready	til-boo-ith	*tilbúið*

Smoking

A packet of cigarettes, please.

aydn see-gahrr-eh-dö-pahk-ah
tahk

*Einn sígarettupakka,
takk.*

Do you have a light?

ow-dö ehld?

Áttu eld?

cigarette papers	see-gahrr-eh-dö-brryehv	*sígarettubréf*
cigarettes	see-gahrr-eh-dörr	*sígarettur*
filtered	mehth see-ö/fil-tehrr	*með síufilter*
lighter	kvay-kyah-rri	*kveikjari*
matches	ehld-speet-örr	*eldspýtur*
menthol	mehnt-ohl	*mentól*
tobacco	toh-bahk	*tóbak*

Sizes & Comparisons

big	stohrrt	*stórt*
small	lee-tith	*lítið*
heavy	thoont	*þungt*
light	lyeht	*létt*
less	mi-nah	*minna*
more	may-rrah	*meira*

ICELANDIC

HEALTH

Where is a ...?	kvahrr ehrr ...?	*Hvar er ...?*
doctor	laik-nirr	*læknir*
hospital	syook-rrah-hoos	*sjúkrahús*
chemist	ah-poh-tehk	*apótek*
dentist	tahn-laik-nirr	*tannlæknir*

Could I see a female doctor?
gyai-ti yehkh fayn-gith ahth	*Gæti ég fengið að*
tah-lah vith kvehn layk-ni?	*tala við kvenlækni?*

What's the matter?
| kvahth ehrr ahth? | *Hvað er að?* |

Where does it hurt?
| kvahrr fin-örr <u>thoo</u> til? | *Hvar finnur þú til?* |

It hurts here.
| mikh vehrrk-yahrr hyehrr | *Mig verkjar hér.* |

Parts of the Body

ankle	erh-kli	*ökkli*
arm	hahnd-lehg-görr	*handleggur*
back	bahk	*bak*
chest	brreeng-gah	*bringa*
ear	ay-rrah	*eyra*
eye	eör-gah	*auga*
finger	feen-görr	*fingur*
feet/legs	fai-törr	*fætur*
hands	hehn-dörr	*hendur*
head	her-vöth	*höfuð*
heart	hyarr-tah	*hjarta*
hips	myath-mirr	*mjaðmir*
mouth	mön-nörr	*munnur*
neck	howls	*háls*
ribs	rriv-bayn	*rifbein*
skin	hooth	*húð*
stomach	mai-i	*magi*
teeth	tehn-nörr	*tennur*
thighs	lai-rri	*læri*

ICELANDIC

Ailments

I have (a)...	yehkh ehrr mehth ...	Ég er með ...
cold	kvehf	kvef
constipation	hahrrth-lee-vi	harðlífi
diarrhoea	nith-örr-gowng	niðurgang
fever	hi-tah	hita
headache	her-vöth-vehrrk	höfuðverk
indigestion	mehlt-eeng-ahrr-trröb-lön	meltingartruflun
influenza	flehn-sö	flensu
low/high	low-ahn/how-ahn	lágan/háan
blood pressure	blohth-<u>th</u>rreest-eeng	blóðþrýsting
sore throat	howls-bohl-gö	hálsbólgu
sprain	tokh-nön	tognun
stomachache	mahkh-ah-vehrrk	magaverk
sunburn	sohl-brrö-ni	sólbruni

I'm sunburnt.	yehk hehrr sohl-brrön-in	Ég er sólbrunninn.

Some Useful Words & Phrases

I'm ...	yehkh ehrr ...	Ég er ...
asthmatic	mehth ahs-mah	með asma
diabetic	sik-örr-syoo-körr	sykursjúkur
epileptic	flokh-ah-vay-körr	flogaveikur

I'm allergic to antiobiotics/penicillin.
yehkh ehrr mehth ov-nai-mi firr-irr foo-kah-liv-yöm/ pehn-si-lee-ni	Ég er með ofnæmi fyrir fúkalyfjum/ pensilíni.

I'm pregnant.
yehkh ehrr oh-frreesk	Ég er ófrísk.

ICELANDIC

I've been vaccinated.
yehkh fyehk oh-nai-mis-sprreör-tö   *Ég fékk ónæmissprautu.*
I feel better/worse.
myehrr leeth-örr beh-törr/vehrr   *Mér líður betur/verr.*

antibiotics	foo-kah-lif	*fúkalyf*
antiseptic	soht-hrrayns-ahndi	*sótthreinsandi*
blood pressure	blohth-<u>th</u>rreest-ing-örr	*blóðþrýstingur*
blood test	blohth-prrövah	*blóðprufa*
contraceptive	gyeht-nahth-ahrr-verdn	*getnaðarvörn*
injection	sprreör-tah	*sprauta*
medicine	lif	*lyf*
menstruation	blaith-eeng-ahrr	*blæðingar*
nausea	oh-khleh-thi	*ógleði*
toothache	tahn-pee-nah	*tannpína*

At the Chemist

I need medication for ...
yehkh <u>th</u>ahrrf lif vith ...   *Ég þarf lyf við ...*
I have a prescription.
yehkh ehrr mehth lif-sehth-il   *Ég er með lyfseðil.*

At the Dentist

I have a toothache.
yehkh ehrr mehth tahn-pee-nö   *Ég er með tannpínu.*
I've lost a filling.
yehkh hehv misst fid-leen-gö   *Ég hef misst fyllingu.*
I've broken a tooth.
yehkh hehv brro-tith tern   *Ég hef brotið tönn.*
My gums hurt.
mikh vehrr-kyarr ee   *Mig verkjar í*
tahn-hol-dith   *tannholdið.*
Please give me an anaesthetic.
gyehrr-thö svo vehl   *Gerðu svo vel*
ath day-vah mikh   *að deyfa mig.*

ICELANDIC

TIME & DATES

What date is it today?
kvahth-ah dahkh-örr   *Hvaða dagur*
ehrr ee dahkh?   *er í dag?*

What time is it?
kvahth ehrr klök-ahn?   *Hvað er klukkan?*

It's ... am/pm.
hoon ehrr ... firr-irr how-day-i/   *Hún er ... fyrir hádegi/*
ehf-dirr how-day-i   *eftir hádegi.*

in the morning   ahth mo-dni   *að morgni*
in the evening   ahth kverl-di   *að kvöldi*

Days of the Week

Monday	mow-nö-dahkh-örr	*mánudagur*
Tuesday	thrrith-yö-dahkh-örr	*þriðjudagur*
Wednesday	mith-vik-ö-dahkh-örr	*miðvikudagur*
Thursday	fim-tö-dahkh-örr	*fimmtudagur*
Friday	fers-dö-dahkh-örr	*föstudagur*
Saturday	leörkh-ah-dahkh-örr	*laugardagur*
Sunday	sön-ö-dahkh-örr	*sunnudagur*

Months

January	yah-noo-ahrr	*janúar*
February	fehb-rroo-ahrr	*febrúar*
March	mahrrs	*mars*
April	ah-prreel	*apríl*
May	mai	*maí*
June	yoo-nee	*júní*
July	yoo-lee	*júlí*
August	ow-goost	*ágúst*
September	sehft-ehm-behrr	*september*
October	okt-oh-behrr	*október*
November	noh-vehm-behrr	*nóvember*
December	dehs-ehm-behrr	*desember*

ICELANDIC

Seasons

summer	sö-mahrr	*sumar*
autumn	heörst	*haust*
winter	veh-törr	*vetur*
spring	vorr	*vor*

Present

today	ee dahkh	*í dag*
this morning	ee morr-gön	*í morgun*
tonight	ee kverld	*í kvöld*
this week	<u>the</u>hs-ah vi-kö	*þessa viku*
this year	<u>the</u>ht-ah owrr	*þetta ár*
now	noo-nah	*núna*

Past

yesterday	ee gyairr	*í gær*
two days ago	firr-irr tvay-mörr derkh-öm	*fyrir tveimur dögum*
last night	seeth-öst-ö noht	*síðustu nótt*
last week	(ee) seeth-öst-ö vi-kö	*(í) síðustu viku*
last year	seeth-ast-lith-ith owrr	*síðastliðið ár*

Future

tomorrow	ow morr-gön	*á morgun*
in two days	ehf-dirr tvo dahg-ah	*eftir tvo daga*
next week	(ee) nais-tö vi-kö	*(í) næstu viku*
next month	(ee) nais-tah mown-öthi	*(í) næsta mánuði*
next year	(ow) nais-tah ow-rri	*(á) næsta ár*

During the Day

afternoon	ehf-dirr how-day-i	*eftir hádegi*
day	dahkh-örr	*dagur*
midnight	mithnait-i	*miðnætti*
morning	morr-gön	*morgunn*
night	noht	*nótt*
noon	how-day-i	*hádegi*

NUMBERS & AMOUNTS

0	nool	*núll*
1	aydn	*einn*
2	tvayrr	*tveir*
3	<u>th</u>rreer	*þrír*
4	fyoh-rrirr	*fjórir*
5	fimm	*fimm*
6	sehks	*sex*
7	syer	*sjö*
8	owt-dah	*átta*
9	nee-ö	*níu*
10	tee-ö	*tíu*
20	tö-tökh-ö	*tuttugu*
21	tö-tö-gö og aydn	*tuttugu og einn*
30	<u>th</u>rryow-tee-ö	*þrjátíu*
40	fyer-tee-ö	*fjörutíu*
50	fim-tee-ö	*fimmtíu*
60	sehks-tee-ö	*sextíu*
70	syer-tee-ö	*sjötíu*
80	ow-tah-tee-ö	*áttatíu*
90	nee-tee-ö	*níutíu*
100	ayt hön-drrahth	*eitt hundrað*
1000	ayt <u>th</u>oos-önd	*eitt þúsund*
one million	ayn mil-yohn	*ein milljón*

ICELANDIC

Some Useful Words

a little (amount)	lee-tith	*lítið*
few	fow-irr	*fáir*
more	may-rrah	*meira*
some	nok-rrirr	*nokkrir*
too much/many	ov mi-kith/mahrr-girr	*of mikið/margir*

ICELANDIC

ABBREVIATIONS

f.h./e.h. – fyrir hádegi/eftir hádegi	am/pm
h.f. – hlutafélag	Ltd./Inc.
S.V.R. – Strætisvagnar Reykjavíkur	Reykjavík Municipal Bus Company
f.kr./e.kr.	BC/AD
frk. – fröken	Miss
frú	Mrs
hr. – herra	Mr/Sir
Rvk. – Reykjavík	Reykjavík
FÍB – Félag íslenskra bifreiðaeigenda	The Icelandic Automobile Association
kl. – klukkan	o'clock
km/klst. – kílómetrar á klukkustund	kilometres per hour
kr. – króna	crown (Icelandic monetary unit)
v. – við	at
vsk. – virðisaukaskattur	tax (included in the price on all goods and services)
t.h. – til hægri	to the right (used in addresses)
hs. – heimasími	telephone at home
vs. – vinnusími	telephone at work
t.v. – til vinstri	to the left (used in addresses)
(1.) h. – hæð	(1st) floor

EMERGENCIES

Help!	hyowlp!	*Hjálp!*
Go away!	fahrr-thö!	*Farðu!*
Thief!	<u>th</u>yoh-vörr!	*þjófur!*

SIGNS

LÖGREGLA
POLICE

LÖGREGLUSTÖÐ
POLICE STATION

There's been an accident!
    <u>th</u>ahth hehf-örr orrth-ith slis! — *Það hefur orðið slys!*

Call a doctor/an ambulance!
    now-ith ee laik-ni/ — *Náið í lækni/*
    syook-rrah beel! — *sjúkrabíl!*

I've been raped.
    myehrr vahrr neörth-gahth — *Mér var nauðgað.*

I've been robbed!
    yehkh vahrr rraind/rrain-dörr! — *Ég var rænd/-ur!* (f/m)

Call the police!
    nowith ee lerg-rrehgl-ön-ah! — *Náið í lögregluna!*

Where is the police station?
    kvahrr ehrr — *Hvar er*
    lerkh-rrehkh-lö-sterth-in? — *lögreglustöðin?*

I'm/My friend is ill.
    yehkh ehrr/vin-örr min — *Ég er/vinur minn*
    ehrr vay-körr — *er veikur.*

I'm lost.
    yehkh ehrr vilt/vilt-örr — *Ég er villt/-ur.* (f/m)

Where are the toilets?
    kvahrr ehrr snirrt-inkh-in?/ — *Hvar er snyrtingin?/*
    kvahrr ehrr kloh-seht-ith? — *Hvar er klósettið?*

Could you help me please?
    gyai-tirr <u>th</u>oo hyowlp-ahth myehrr? — *Gætir þú hjálpað mér?*

Could I please use the telephone?
    gyai-ti yehkh fayn-khith — *Gæti ég fengið*
    ahth hrrin-gyah? — *að hringja?*

I'm sorry.
    myehrr <u>th</u>ik-irr <u>th</u>ahth layht — *Mér þykir það leitt.*

ICELANDIC

I didn't realise I was doing
anything wrong.

yehkh vi-si ehk-i ahth yehkh	*Ég vissi ekki að ég*
vai-rri ahth gyeh-rrah rrow-nt	*væri að gera rangt.*

I didn't do it.

yehkh gyehrr-thi <u>th</u>ahth ehk-i	*Ég gerði það ekki.*

I wish to contact my embassy/consulate.

yehkh vil hah-vah sahm-bahnd	*Ég vil hafa samband*
vith sehndi-rrowth mit/	*við sendiráð mitt/*
rraith-is -mahn min	*ræðismann minn.*

I speak English.

yehkh tah-lah ehn-skö	*Ég tala ensku.*

I have medical insurance.

yehkh hehf	*Ég hef*
syook-rrah-trrikh-een-gö	*sjúkratryggingu.*

My possessions are insured.

aykh-örr meen-ahrr	*Eigur mínar*
ehrr-ö trrikhth-arr	*eru tryggðar.*

My... was stolen.	... vahrr sto-lith	*... var stolið.*
I've lost my ...	yehkh teen-di ...	*Ég týndi ...*
bags	ter-skö-nöm mee-nöm	*töskunum mínum*
handbag	hahnd-tersk-ön-i mi-ni	*handtöskunni minni*
money	pehn-eeng-ön-öm mee-nöm	*peningunum mínum*
travellers cheques	fehrrth-ah-tyeh-kö-nöm mee-nöm	*ferðatékkunum mínum*
passport	vehg-ah-brryeh-vi-nö mee-nö	*vegabréfinu mínu*

NORWEGIAN

QUICK REFERENCE

NORWEGIAN

Hello.	gud-*dahg*	Goddag.
Goodbye.	*huh*-deh	Ha det.
Yes./No.	yah/nay	Ja./Nei.
Excuse me.	*un*-shül	Unnskyld.
Sorry.	*beh-klah*-gehrr	Beklager,
	til-yi mai	tilgi meg.
Please.	va sho *snil*	Vær så snill.
Thank you.	tuhk	Takk.
You're welcome.	*ing*-ön *or*-shahk	Ingen årsak.

I'd like a ...	yay vil *ya*-rrnö hah ...	Jeg vil gjerne ha ...
one-way ticket	*ehn*-kehlt-bi-*leht*	enkelt billett
return ticket	*too*-rrö-*toorr*	tur-retur

I (don't) understand.
    yay fosh-*tor-rr* (ik-kö)   Jeg forstår (ikke).
Do you speak English?
    snuh-kö du *ehng*-ölsk?   Snakker du engelsk?
Where is ...?
    voor arr ...?   Hvor er ...?
Go straight ahead.
    deh arr *rreht* frruhm   Det er rett fram.
Turn left/right.
    tah til *vehns*-trrö/*höy*-rrö. Ta til venstre/høyre.
Do you have any rooms available?
    hah du *lay*-di-ö *rrum*?   Har du ledige rom?
I'm looking for a public toilet.
    yay *leh*-törr eht-törr eht   Jeg leter etter et
    of-föntli too-a-*leht*   offentlig toalett.

1	ehn	en	6	sehks	seks
2	too	to	7	shu/süv	sju/syv
3	trreh	tre	8	ot-tö	åtte
4	*fee*-rrö	fire	9	nee	ni
5	fehm	fem	10	tee	ti

NORWEGIAN

Norway has two official written language forms. They are very similar, and every Norwegian learns both at school. Bokmål (BM), literally 'book-language', is the urban-Norwegian variety of Danish, the language of the former rulers of Norway. It's the written language of 80 percent of the population. Although many Norwegians speak a local dialect in the private sphere, most of them speak BM in the public sphere. BM is therefore very appropriate for the traveller who wants to communicate with Norwegians all over the country.

The other written language is Nynorsk (NN), or 'New Norwegian' – as opposed to Old Norwegian, the language in Norway before 1500 AD, that is, before Danish rule. It's an important part of Norwegian cultural heritage as it's the truly 'Norwegian' language, as opposed to the Danish-based BM. In order to preserve the language, Norway has a NN theatre in Oslo – Det Norske Teater. Traditionally, many NN writers also produce their works to be performed in the NN tongue; the language lends itself to theatre and song as it can be very lyrical. By law the national TV and radio channels also broadcast a certain percentage of their text in NN.

In speech the distinction between BM and NN is no problem since Norwegians understand either. Although both are used in the media, BM is predominant in the daily papers, television and radio. Many people are put off trying to speak Norwegian because of the two languages, but in reality, BM is the ruling language. This book uses BM only.

A striking feature of both written languages is that many words have two or more officially authorised forms of spelling in either language. One can choose according to one's speech or social aspirations. In many cases it's possible to choose spellings which are common to either language.

In the rural areas you may come across people who hardly speak a word of English, and if you show an effort to speak Norwegian, it will help a great deal to establish contact. Many Norwegians will answer you in English, as they are only too eager to show off their knowledge. Their use of English is usually very good.

PRONUNCIATION

Vowels

Length, as a distinctive feature of vowels, is very important in the pronunciation of Norwegian. Almost every vowel has a (very) long and a (very) short counterpart, when appearing in a stressed syllable. Generally, it's long when followed by one consonant, and short when followed by two or more consonants.

A few words, mainly function words like pronouns and auxilliaries, are 'mispronounced': the vowel is short in spite of the fact that it's followed by only one consonant.

Pronunciation is given in the pronunciation guide in the front of the book.

PRONOUNS		
SG		
I	yay	jeg
you	du	du
he/she/it		
PL	hun/hahn/deh	hun/han/det
we	vi	vi
you (pol)	*deh*-rreh	Dere
you (pl)	*deh*-rreh	dere
they	dem	dem

GREETINGS & CIVILITIES
Top Useful Phrases

Hello.	gud-*dahg*	*Goddag.*
Goodbye.	*hah*-deh	*Ha det.*
Yes.	yah	*Ja.*
No.	nay	*Nei.*
Excuse me.	*un*-shül	*Unnskyld.meg.*
Please.	va sho *snil*	*Vær så snill.*
Thank you.	tuhk	*Takk.*
Many thanks.	*tusn* tuhk	*Tusen takk.*
That's fine.	*ing*-ön or-shahk	*Ingen årsak.*
You're welcome.		

May I? Do you mind?
for-rr yay *lorv*? hah du
noo-ö i-*moot* deh?

*Får jeg lov? Har du
noe imot det?*

Sorry. (excuse me, forgive me)
behk-lah-gehrr til-yi mai

Beklager, tilgi meg.

Good morning.	gu *morr*-gon	*God morgen.*
Good afternoon.	gud-*dahg*	*Goddag.*
Good evening/night.	gu *kvehl*/*nuht*	*God kveld/natt.*
How are you?	voorr-duhn *hah* du deh?	*Hvordan har du det?*
Well, thanks.	brrah tuhk	*Bra, takk.*

Forms of Address

Madam/Mrs	frru	*fru*
Sir/Mr	harr	*herr*
Miss	*frrayrr*-kön	*frøken*
companion	kuh-muh-*rraht*	*kamerat*
friend	vehn-*nin*-nö/vehn	*venninne/venn* (f/m)

NORWEGIAN

SMALL TALK
Meeting People

What is your name?	vah *hay*-tö du?	*Hva heter du?*
My name is ...	yay *hay*-törr ...	*Jeg heter ...*

I'd like to introduce you to ...
    deh-tö arr ...   *Dette er ...*
I'm pleased to meet you.
    hü-gö-li o *trreh*-fö day   *Hyggelig å treffe deg.*

NORWEGIAN

Nationalities

Where are you from?   voorr *arr* du frrah?   *Hvor er du fra?*

I'm from ...	yay *arr* frruh ...	*Jeg er fra ...*
Australia	ow-*strrah*-li-uh	*Australia*
Canada	*kuh*-nuh-duh	*Kanada*
England	*ehng*-luhn	*England*
Ireland	*ee*-rrluhn	*Irland*
New Zealand	nü *say*-luhn	*Ny Zealand*
Norway	*norr*-gö	*Norge*
Scotland	*skot*-luhn	*Skottland*
the USA	a-mehrr-rrik-uha/ ü-wehs-*sah*	*Amerika/ USA*
Wales	vehls	*Wales*

Age

How old are you?
    voor *guhm*-muhl arr du?   *Hvor gammel er du?*
I'm ... years old.
    yay arr ...   *Jeg er ...*

Occupations

What do you do?
vah *drree-vö* du may?   *Hva driver du med?*

I'm a/an ...	yay arr ...	*Jeg er ...*
artist	*kunst*-nörr	*kunstner*
businesswoman/	fo-*rreht*-nings-	*foretnings*
man	kvin-nö/	*kvinne*/
	fo-*rreht*-nings-	*forretnings*
	muhn	*mann*
doctor	*lay*-gö	*lege*
engineer	in-shön-*yayrr*-rr	*ingeniør*
farmer	*gahrr*-brru-körr	*gardbruker*
journalist	shoo-rrnuh-*list*	*journalist*
lawyer	uhd-vo-*kuht*	*advokat*
manual worker	uhrr-*bay*-dörr	*arbeider*
mechanic	meh-*kah*-ni-körr	*mekaniker*
nurse	*sy*-kö-play-örr	*sykepleier*
office worker	koon-*toorr*-	*kontor*-
	uhrr-bay-dörr	*arbeider*
scientist	*vee*-tön-skahps-muhn	*vitenskapsmann*
student	stu-*deh*-nt	*student*
teacher	*la*-rrörr	*lærer*
waiter	*kehl*-nörr/sehrr-	*kelner*/
	vay-rrings-dah-mö	*serveringsdame*
writer	fo-rr-*fuht*-törr	*forfatter*

NORWEGIAN

THE LONG AND THE SHORT OF IT

Nearly all vowels in Norwegian have short and long versions. This can affect the meaning, so look at the word carefully.

NORWEGIAN

Religion

What is your religion?
    vah arr din rreh-li-*gyoon*?   *Hva er din religion?*
I'm not religious.
    yay arr *ik*-kö rreh-li-*yers*   *Jeg er ikke religiøs.*

I'm ...	yay arr ...	*Jeg er ...*
Buddhist	bud-*dist*	*buddhist*
Catholic	kuh-*tolsk*	*katolsk*
Hindu	*hin*-du	*hindu*
Jewish	*yayrr*-dö	*jøde*
Muslim	*mus*-lim	*muslim*
Protestant	prro-teh-*stuhnt*	*protestant*

Family

Are you married?   arr du *yift*?   *Er du gift?*

I'm...	yay arr ...	*Jeg er ...*
single	ehns-li	*enslig*
married	*yift*	*gift*

How many children do you have?
    voor muhng-ö *bah-rrn* hah du?   *Hvor mange barn har du?*
I don't have any children.
    yay huh *ik*-kö noon bah-rrn   *Jeg har ikke noen barn.*
I have a daughter/a son.
    yay hahrr ehn *duht-törr/sern*   *Jeg har en datter/sønn.*
How many brothers/sisters
do you have?
    voor muhng-ö *sers*-kön hah du?   *Hvor mange søsken har du?*
Is your husband/wife here?
    arr *muhn-n* din harr/   *Er mannen din her?/*
    arr koo-nuh di harr?   *Er kona di her?*
Do you have a boyfriend/girlfriend?
    hah du *fuhst* ferl-lö?   *Har du fast følge?*

brother	brroorr	*bror*
children	bah-rrn	*barn*
daughter	*duht*-törr	*datter*
family	fuh-*mee*-li-ö	*familie*
father	fahrr	*far*
grandfather	*behs*-tö-fahrr	*bestefar*
grandmother	*behs*-tö-moorr	*bestemor*
husband	muhn	*mann*
mother	moorr	*mor*
sister	sers-törr	*søster*
son	sern	*sønn*
wife	*koo*-nö	*kone*

Kids' Talk

How old are you?
voorr guh-mehl arr du?   *Hvor gammel er du?*
When's your birthday?
norr hahrr du *bush*-dahg?   *Når har du bursdag?*
What do you do after school?
vah *yer* du eh-tehrr skoo-leh-tid?   *Hva gjør du etter skoletid?*
Do you have a pet at home?
hahrr du eht *cha*-leh-dürr   *Har du et kjæledyr*
yeh-meh?   *hjemme?*

I have a ...	yay hahrr ehn ...	*Jeg har en ...*
bird	fool	*fugl*
budgerigar	un-du-*luht*	*undulat*
canary	kuh-*nuh*-rri-fool	*kanarifugl*
cat	kuht	*katt*
dog	hun	*hund*
frog	frrorsk	*frosk*

NORWEGIAN

Feelings

I (don't) like ...
yay *lee*-körr (*ik*-kö) ...   *Jeg liker (ikke) ...*
I feel cold/hot.
yay *frrüs*-ört/yay arr *vuh*-rrm   *Jeg fryser/Jeg er varm.*
I'm in a hurry.
yay hahrr *huhst*-varrk   *Jeg har hastverk.*
You're right.
du hah *rreht*   *Du har rett.*

I'm ...	*yay arr ...*	*Jeg er ...*
angry	*sin*-nuh	*sinna*
happy	*lük*-kö-li	*lykkelig*
hungry/thirsty	*shul*-tön/ter-sht	*sulten/tørst*
tired	trrer-t	*trøtt*
sad	oo-*lük*-kö-li/*nay*-forr	*ulykkelig/nedfor*
sleepy	*sherv*-ni	*søvnig*
well	brrah	*bra*
worried	oo-*rroo*-li	*urolig*

I'm sorry. (condolence)
kon-doo-*lay*-rrörr   *Kondolerer.*
I'm grateful.
yay arr *tuhk*-nehm-li   *Jeg er takknemlig.*

BREAKING THE LANGUAGE BARRIER

Do you speak English?
snuh-kö du *ehng*-ölsk?   *Snakker du engelsk?*
Does anyone speak English?
arr deh noon som snuh-körr   *Er det noen som snakker*
ehng-ölsk harr?   *engelsk her?*
I speak a little ...
yay snuh-kö lit ...   *Jeg snakker litt ...*
I don't speak ...
yay snuh-körr *ik*-kö ...   *Jeg snakker ikke ...*

I (don't) understand.
    yay fosh-*tor-rr* (*ik*-kö)   *Jeg forstår (ikke).*
Could you speak more slowly please?
    kuhn du snuh-kö luhng-   *Kan du snakke langsommere?*
    som-mö-rrö?
Could you repeat that?
    kuhn du *yehn*-tuh day?   *Kan du gjenta det?*
How do you say ...?
    vah hay-*törr* ... por noshk?   *Hva heter ... på norsk?*
What does ... mean?
    vah bö-*türr* ...?   *Hva betyr ...?*

I speak ...	yay snuh-kuhrr ...	*Jeg snakker ...*
English	*ehng*-ehlsk	*engelsk*
French	frruhnsk	*fransk*
German	tüsk	*tysk*
Norwegian	noshk	*norsk*
Spanish	spuhnsk	*spansk*

NORWEGIAN

Some Useful Phrases

Of course./Sure.	*sehl-ferrl-geh-li*/vist	*Selvfølgelig./Visst.*
Just a minute.	vehnt lit;	*Vent litt;*
	eht öy-eh-blik	*Et øyeblikk.*
It's (not) important.	deh arr (*ik*-kö)	*Det er (ikke)*
	vik-ti	*viktig.*
It's (not) possible.	deh arr (*ik*-kö)	*Det er (ikke)*
	moo-li	*mulig.*
Wait!	vehnt!	*Vent!*
Good luck!	*lük*-kö *til*!	*Lykke til!*

BODY LANGUAGE

It's considered good manners to shake hands with Norwegians when you meet. Remember, this includes both men and women; many Norwegian women feel ignored in English-speaking nations where usually only the men shake hands.

After having met a few times, a friendly hug or a peck on the cheek is common – this includes both women and men.

PAPERWORK

address	uh-*drreh*-sö	*adresse*
age	*uhl*-dörr	*alder*
birth certificate	*ferts*-ls-uht-tehst	*fødselsattest*
border	*grrehn*-sö	*grense*
car owner's title	*vongn*-ko-rt	*vognkort*
car registration	*chehn*-nö-tayn	*kjennetegn*
customs	*tol*	*toll*
date of birth	*fert*-söls-dah-tu	*fødselsdato*
driver's licence	*fayrr*-rrörr-kort	*førerkort*
identification	lay-gay-ti-*muh*-shon	*legitimasjon*
immigration	*in*-vuhn-drring	*innvandring*
marital status	si-*veel*-stuhn	*sivilstand*
name	nuhvn	*navn*
nationality	nuh-shu-nuh-li-*tayt*	*nasjonalitet*
passport (number)	*puhs*(-num-mörr)	*pass(nummer)*
place of birth	*fayrr*-dö-stay	*fødested*
profession	*ürr*-kö	*yrke*
reason for travel	*hehn*-sikt meh *rray*-sn	*hensikt med reisen*
religion	rreh-li-*gyoon*	*religion*
sex	chern	*kjønn*
tourist card	tu-*rrist*-kort	*turistkort*
visa	*vee*-sum	*visum*

GETTING AROUND

What time does ... leave/arrive?	norr gor-rr/ kom-mörr ...?	Når går/ kommer ...?
the (aero)plane	flü-yö	flyet
the boat	bor-tn	båten
the (city) bus	(bü-)busn	(by)bussen
the (intercity) bus	(lin-yö-)busn	(linje-)bussen
the train	tor-gö	toget
the tram	trrik-kön	trikken

Directions

Where is ...?
voor arr ...?   *Hvor er ...?*
How do I get to ...?
voor-duhn kom-mörr yay til ...?   *Hvordan kommer jeg til ...?*
Is it far from/near here?
arr deh *luhngt harr*-frruh?   *Er det langt herfra?*

NORWEGIAN

SIGNS

BAGASJEINNLEVERING	CHECK-IN COUNTER
DAMER/HERRER	LADIES/GENTLEMEN
FORBUDT	PROHIBITED
GRATIS ADGANG	FREE ADMISSION
INFORMASJON/ OPPLYSNINGER	INFORMATION
INGEN ADGANG	NO ENTRY
INNGANG	ENTRANCE
NØDUTGANG	EMERGENCY EXIT
REISEGODS	BAGGAGE COUNTER
RESERVERT	RESERVED
RØYKING FORBUDT	NO SMOKING
TELEFON	TELEPHONE
TOLL	CUSTOMS
UTGANG	EXIT
WC/TOALETTER	TOILETS
ÅPEN/STENGT	OPEN/CLOSED

NORWEGIAN

Can I walk there?
kuhn yay *gor* deet? — *Kan jeg gå dit?*

Can you show me (on the map)?
kuhn du *vee*-sö ma (po *kuh*-rtö)? — *Kan du vise meg (på kartet)?*

Are there other means of getting there?
arr deh ehn *ahn*-ön mor-tö or kom-mö *deet* po? — *Er det en annen måte å komme dit på?*

I want to go to ...
yay skuhl til ... — *Jeg skal til ...*

Go straight ahead.
deh arr *rreht* frruhm — *Det er rett fram.*

It's two blocks down.
deh arr *too* kvuh-rtahl *vee*-dö-rrö — *Det er to kvartal videre.*

Turn left/right at the ...	*tah* til *vehns*-trrö/ *höy*-rrö veh ...	*Ta til venstre/ høyre ved ...*
next corner	*nehs*-tö *yayrr*-nö	*neste hjørne*
traffic lights	*lüs*-krrüs-sö	*lyskrysset*

behind	bak	*bak*
in front of	fo-rruhn	*foran*
far	luhngt	*langt*
near	narr	*nær*
opposite	*or*-vörr-*forr*	*overfor*
next to	*veh*-si-dehn-*uhv*	*ved siden av*

SIGNS

ANKOMST	**ARRIVALS**
AVGANG	**DEPARTURES**
BILLETTKONTOR	**TICKET OFFICE**
JERNBANESTASJON	**TRAIN STATION**
RUTEPLAN	**TIMETABLE**
STASJON	**STATION**
T-BANE	**SUBWAY**

Booking Tickets

Excuse me, where is the
ticket office?

    un-shül voor *arr*
    bi-*leht*-lu-kuh?

Unnskyld, hvor er
billettluka?

Where can I buy a ticket?

    voor kuhn yay
    sher-peh bi-*leht?*

Hvor kan jeg
kjøpe billett?

I want to go to ...

    yay skuhl til ...

Jeg skal til ...

Do I need to book?

    arr deh nerd-*vehn*-di o
    bö-*stil*-lö pluhs?

Er det nødvendig å
bestille plass?

I'd like to book a seat to ...

    yay vil *ya*-rrnö bö-*stil*-lö
    si-*tö*-pluhs til ...

Jeg vil gjerne bestille
sitte-plass til ...

NORWEGIAN

I'd like ...	yay vil *ya*-rrnö hah ...	*Jeg vil gjerne ha ...*
a one-way ticket	*ehn*-kehlt-bi-*leht*	*enkelt billett*
a return ticket	*too*-rrö-*toorr*	*tur-retur*
two tickets	*too* bi-*leht*-tehrr	*to billetter*
tickets for all of us	bi-*leh*-tehrr til os	*billetter til oss*
	uhl-lö *suh*-mehn	*alle sammen*
a student's fare	stu-*dehnt*-rruh-buht	*studentrabatt*
a child's fare	*bah*-rrnö-bi-*leht*	*barnebillett*
a pensioner's fare	ho-*nayrr*-bi-*leht*	*honnør-billett*
1st class	*fersh*-tö kluhs-sö	*første klasse*
2nd class	*ahn*-ön kluhs-sö	*annen klasse*

Is it completely full?

    arr deh *halt* fult?

Er det helt fullt?

Can I get a stand-by ticket?

    kuhn yay for ehn
    shuhn-sö-bi-*leht?*

Kan jeg få en
sjansebillett?

NORWEGIAN

Air

Is there a flight to ...?
arr deh eht flü til ...?
Er det et fly til ...?

When is the next flight to ...?
norr gor *nehs*-tö flü-yö til ...?
Når går neste flyet til ...?

SIGNS	
BAGASJE	LUGGAGE PICKUP
INNSJEKKING	CHECK-IN

How long does the flight take?
voor *luhng*-ö tid tahrr
flüv-ning-ehn?

Hvor lang tid tar flyvningen?

What is the flight number?
vah arr *flait*-nu-mö-rrö?

Hva er flightnummeret?

You must check in at ...
du mor shehk-kö *in* veh ...

Du må sjekke inn ved ...

check-in desk	*in*-shehk-*in*-skrruhn-keh	*innsjekking skranke*
airport tax	*luft*-huhvn-*ahv*-yift	*lufthavnavgift*
boarding pass	um-*boorr*-steeg-(n)ing-sko-rt	*ombord-stig(n)ings-kort*
customs	tol	*toll*

Bus

Where is the bus/tram stop?
voor arr *bus*-hol-lö-pluhsn/
trrik-hol-lö-pluhsn?
Hvor er bussholdeplassen/ trikkholdeplassen?

SIGNS	
BUSSHOLDEPLASS	BUS STOP
TRIKKHOLDEPLASS	TRAM STOP

Which bus goes to ...?
vil-kön bus gor rtil ...?
Hvilken buss går til ...?

Does this bus go to ...?
gor *rdehn*-nö busn til ...?
Går denne bussen til ...?

How often do buses pass by?
voor muhng-ö *bus*-sörr gor-rdeh?
Hvor mange busser går det?

What time is the	no-rr kom-mör	Når kommer
... bus?	... busn?	... bussen?
next	*nehs-tö*	neste
first	*fer-shtö*	første
last	*sis-tö*	siste

NORWEGIAN

Train

Is this the right platform for ...?
arr *deht*-tö *rreht*-tö
pluht-forr-muh forr
tor-gö til ...?
*Er dette rette plattforma
for toget til ...?*

The train leaves from platform ...
tor-gö gor-rr frra spoorr ...   *Toget går fra spor ...*

Passengers must ...	*rray*-sön-dö mor ...	Reisende må ...
change trains	*büt*-tö torg	bytte tog
change platforms	*gor* til spoorr ...	gå til spor ...

dining car	*spee*-sö-vongn	spisevogn
express	ehks-*prrehs*-torg	ekspresstog
local	lu-*kahl*-torg	lokaltog
sleeping/	*sor*-vö-vongn/	sovevogn/
couchette car	*lig*-gö-vongn	ligge-vogn

Metro

Which line takes me to ...?
vil-kön *lin*-yö/*bah*-nö
mor yay tah til ...?

*Hvilken linje/bane
må jeg ta til ...?*

What is the next station?
vah arr *nehs*-tö stuh-*shoon?*

Hva er neste stasjon?

SIGNS	
T-BANE	METRO/UNDERGROUND
UTGANG	WAY OUT
VEKSLING	CHANGE (for coins)

NORWEGIAN

Taxi

Where can I get hold of a taxi?
vorr kuhn yay for
tahk i ehn drro-shö?

*Hvor kan jeg få
tak i en drosje?*

Please take me to ...
vil du *chayrr*-rrö ma teel ...?

Vil du kjøre meg til ...?

How much does it cost to go to ...?
vorr *mü*-yö *kos*-törr deh
o *chayrr*-rrö til ...?

*Hvor mye koster det
å kjøre til ...?*

Here is fine, thank you.
du kuhn *stop*-pö harr tuhk

Du kan stoppe her, takk.

Continue!
buh-rrö *furrt*-sheht!

Bare fortsett!

The next street to the left/right.
nehs-tö gah-teh til
vehn-strrö/*höy*-rrö

*Neste gate til
venstre/høyre.*

Stop here!
stop harr!

Stopp her!

Please slow down.
va sho snil o *cher*-rr
lit *suhk*-teh-rreh

*Vær så snill og kjør
litt saktere.*

Please wait here.
varr sor snil o *vehn*-tö harr

Vær så snill å vente her.

Car

Where can I rent a car?
voor kuhn yay lay-ö ehn *beel*?   *Hvor kan jeg leie en bil?*

How much is it daily/weekly?
vorr mü-yö *kos*-törr deh   *Hvor mye koster det*
parr *dahg/u*-kö?   *pr. dag/uke?*

Does that include insurance/mileage?
arr deh *in*-kloo-*dehrrt*   *Er det inkludert*
fo-*shik*-rring/frree   *forsikring/fri*
chayrr-rrö-ah-stuhn?   *kjøreavstand?*

Where's the next petrol station?
voor *arr* narr-mös-tö   *Hvor er nærmeste*
behn-seen-stuh-*shoon*?   *bensinstasjon?*

How long can I park here?
voor *lehng*-ö kan   *Hvor lenge kan*
beel-n min *stor* harr?   *bilen min stå her?*

Does this road lead to ...?
arr deh-tö *vay*-yön til ...?   *Er dette veien til ...?*

air (for tyres)	luft	*luft*
battery	buht-tö-*rree*	*batteri*
brakes	*brrehm*-sörr	*bremser*
clutch	klerch	*kløtsj*
driver's licence	*fayrr*-rrörr-kort	*førerkort*
engine	moo-turr	*motor*
lights	*lük*-törr	*lykter*
oil	ul-yö	*olje*
puncture	pung-*tay*-rring	*punktering*
radiator	rruh-di-*yah*-turr	*radiator*
road map	kuhrt	*kart*
tyres	dehk	*dekk*
windscreen	*frront*-rru-tö	*frontrute*

NORWEGIAN

SIGNS

BILVERKSTED	REPAIRS
BLYFRI	UNLEADED
ENVEISKJØRNING	ONE WAY
GARASJE	GARAGE
INNKJØRNING FORBUDT	NO ENTRY
MEKANIKER	MECHANIC
MOTORVEI	FREEWAY
NORMAL	NORMAL
OMKJØRNING	DETOUR
PARKERING FORBUDT	NO PARKING
SELVBETJENING	SELF SERVICE
STOPP	STOP
SUPER	SUPER
VIKEPLIKT	GIVE WAY

I need a mechanic.
   yay *trrehng*-ehrr ehn *Jeg trenger en*
   bil-meh-*kah*-ni-körr   *bilmekaniker.*
The battery is flat.
   buht-tö-*rree*-ö arr *fluht*   *Batteriet er flatt.*
The radiator is leaking.
   rruh-di-*ah*-toorrn arr *lehk*   *Radiatoren er lekk.*
I have a flat tyre.
   yu-lö arr pung-*tayrt*   *Hjulet er punktert.*
It's overheating.
   moo-toorrn *koo*-körr   *Motoren koker.*
It's not working.
   deh fung-*gay*-rrörr ik-kö   *Det fungerer ikke.*

Some Useful Phrases

The train is delayed/cancelled.
tor-gö arr fo-*shing*-keht/*in*-stilt   *Toget er forsinket/innstilt.*

How long will it be delayed?
voor *mü*-yö arr deh fo-*shing*-keht?   *Hvor mye er det forsinket?*

There is a delay of ... hours.
tor-gö arr ... *tee*-mörr   *Toget er ... timer*
eht-törr *rru*-tö   *etter rute.*

How long does the trip take?
voor *lehng*-ö tahrr *rray*-suh?   *Hvor lenge tar reisa?*

Is it a direct route?
arr deh eht di-*rrehk*-tö torg?   *Er det et direkte tog?*

Is that seat taken?
arr *dehm*-nö *stoo*-ln *up*-tuht?   *Er denne stolen opptatt?*

I want to get off at ...
yay vil gor *ahv* i ...   *Jeg vil gå av i ...*

Where can I hire a bicycle?
voor kuhn yay *lay*-ö   *Hvor kan jeg leie*
ehn *sük*-köl?   *en sykkel?*

ACCOMMODATION

Where is a ...?	voor arr eht ...?	Hvor er et ...?
cheap hotel	*bil*-li hu-*tehl*	*billig hotell*
good hotel	got hu-*tehl*	*godt hotell*
nearby hotel	hu-*tehl* i *narr*-haytn	*hotell i nærheten*
nice/quaint hotel	*koo*-shli/*guhm*-muhl-duhks hu-*tehl*	*koselig/gammel-dags hotell*

What is the address?
vah arr uh-*drrehs*-ehn?   *Hva er adressen?*

Could you write the address, please?
kuhn du *va*-rrö so snil   *Kan du være så snill*
o *skrree*-vö up uh-*drrehs*-ehn?   *å skrive opp adressen?*

NORWEGIAN

At the Hotel

Do you have any rooms available?
    hah du *lay*-di-ö *rrum*?   *Har du ledige rom?*

I'd like ...   yay vil *ya*-rrnö ...   *Jeg vil gjerne ...*
  a single room   hah eht *ehng*-költ-rrum   *ha et enkeltrom*
  a double room   hah eht *dob*-ölt-rrum   *ha et dobbeltrom*
  to share a dorm   *lig*-gö por *sor*-vö-sah-lön   *ligge på sovesalen*

NORWEGIAN

SIGNS	
GJESTGIVERI/PENSJONAT	GUESTHOUSE
HOTELL	HOTEL
VANDRERHJEM	YOUTH HOSTEL

Do you have identification?
    hah du lay-gi-ti-muh-*shoon*?   *Har du legitimasjon?*
Your membership card, please.
    may-lehms-ko-rtö dit *tuhk*   *Medlemskortet ditt, takk.*
Sorry, we're full.
    beh-*klah*-görr deh arr *fült*   *Beklager, det er fullt.*
How long will you be staying?
    voor *lehng*-ö *blee-rr* du harr?   *Hvor lenge blir du her?*
How many nights?
    voor muhng-ö *neht*-törr?   *Hvor mange netter?*
It's ... per day/per person.
    deh arr ... pa *rdahg*/parr pa-*shoon*   *Det er ... pr. dag/pr. person.*
There are (four) of us.
    vi arr (*fee*-rrö) *stük*-körr   *Vi er (fire) stykker.*

I want a room   yay vil *ya*-rrnö hah   *Jeg vil gjerne ha*
with a ...   eht *rrum* meh ...   *et rom med ...*
  bathroom   bahd   *bad*
  shower   dush   *dusj*
  television   *teh-veh*   *tv*
  window   *vin*-du   *vindu*

I'm going to stay for ...

yay hah *tehnkt* o blee harr i ...

Jeg har tenkt å bli her i ...

one day	*ehn dahg*	*en dag*
two days	*too dah*-gehrr	*to dager*
one week	*an u-kö*	*en uke*

How much is it per night/per person?
voor *mü*-yö arr deh parr dahg/
parr pa-*shoon*?

Hvor mye er det pr. dag/ pr. person?

Can I see it?
kuhn yay for *se* deh?

Kan jeg få se det?

Are there any others?
hah du *uhn*-drrö?

Har du andre?

Are there any cheaper rooms?
hah du *bil*-li-ö-rrö *rrum?*

Har du billigere rom?

Can I see the bathroom?
kuhn yay fo *se* bah-dö?

Kan jeg få se badet?

Is there a reduction for students/children?
yee du stu-*dehnt*-rruh-*buht*/
bah-rrnö-rruh-*buht*?

Gir du studentrabatt/ barnerabatt?

Does it include breakfast?
in-kloo-*deh*-rrehrr deh
frroo-kostn?

Inkluderer det frokosten?

It's fine, I'll take it.
brrah yay *tah* rdeh

Bra, jeg tar det.

I'm not sure how long I'm staying.
yay *veht* ik-kö voor
leh-ngö yay skuh blee harr

Jeg vet ikke hvor lenge jeg skal bli her.

Is there a lift?
fins deh ehn *hays* harr?

Finnes det en heis her?

Where is the bathroom?
voor arr *bah*-dö?

Hvor er badet?

Is there hot water all day?
arr deh *vuh*-rrnt
vuhn *döy*-nö rrunt?

Er det varmt vann døgnet rundt?

NORWEGIAN

Do you have a safe where
I can leave my valuables?
    hah du ehn sayf darr yay
    kan *lehg*-gö va-*rdee*-sah-kö-nö
    mee-nö?

Har du en safe der jeg
kan legge verdisakene
mine?

Is there somewhere to wash clothes?
    kuhn yay vuhs-kö *kla*-rrnö
    mee-nö noo-eh *steh*?

Kan jeg vaske klærne
mine noe sted?

Can I use the kitchen?
    arr deh *lorv* o *brru*-kö
    cherk-kö-nö?

Er det lov å bruke
kjøkkenet?

Can I use the telephone?
    kuhn yay for *lor*-nö
    tay-lay-*foon*-n?

Kan jeg få låne
telefonen?

Requests & Complaints

Please wake me up at ...
    va sho *snil* o *vehk*-kö ma ...

Vær så snill å vekke meg ...

The room needs to be cleaned.
    deht-tö *rrum*-mö bayrr
    yayrr-rrös *rraynt*

Dette rommet bør
gjøres reint.

Please change the sheets.
    va sho snil o *shift*-ö
    sehng-ö-töy

Vær så snill å skifte
sengetøy.

I can't open/close the window.
    yay *grray*-örr ik-kö *orp*-nö/
    luk-kö *vin*-du-ö

Jeg greier ikke åpne/
lukke vinduet.

I've locked myself out of my room.
    yay hah *lor-st* ma *oo*-tö
    ah *rrum*-mö mit

Jeg har låst meg ute
av rommet mitt.

The toilet won't flush.
    yay for-rr *ik*-kö spült
    nay po too-a-*leht*-tö

Jeg får ikke spylt
ned på toalettet.

I don't like this room.
    yay *lee*-körr ik-kö
    deht-tö *rrum*-ö

Jeg liker ikke
dette rommet.

It's ...	deh arr ...	Det er ...
expensive	*dürt*	*dyrt*
noisy	fo mü-yö *brrork*	*for mye bråk*
too dark	forr *mer-rrt*	*for mørkt*
too small	fo *lee*-tö	*for lite*

Some Useful Words & Phrases

I'm leaving now/tomorrow.
yay *rray*-sörr nor/i-*mo*-rn   *Jeg reiser nå/i morgen.*

I'd like to pay the bill.
kuhn yay for *rrehng*-ning-ehn   *Kan jeg få regningen,*
tuhk?   *takk?*

name	nuhvn	navn
surname	*eht*-tö-nuhvn	etternavn
address	uh-*drrehs*-sö	adresse
room number	*rrum*-num-mörr	romnummer
air-conditioning	*klee*-muh-uhn-lehg	klimaanlegg
balcony	buhl-*kong*	balkong
bathroom	bahd	bad
bed	sehng	seng
bill	*rray*-ning	regning
blanket	*tehp*-pö	teppe
chair	stool	stol
clean	rrayn	rein
cupboard	skahp	skap
dirty	*shit*-n	skitten
double bed	*dob*-bölt-sehng	dobbeltseng
electricity	strrerm	strøm
fan	*vif*-tö	vifte
key	*nerk*-köl	nøkkel
lift (elevator)	hays	heis
light bulb	*lüs*-pa-rrö	lyspære
a lock	lors	lås
mattress	muh-*drruhs*	madrass
mirror	spayl	speil
padlock	*hehng*-ö-lors	hengelås
pillow	*pu*-tö	pute

quiet	*stil*-lö	*stille*
room (in hotel)	rrum/*va*-rröl-sö	*rom/værelse*
sheet	*lah*-kön	*laken*
shower	dush	*dusj*
soap	*sor*-pö	*såpe*
suitcase	*kuf*-fört	*koffert*
swimming pool (indoor)	*sverm*-mö-huhl	*svømmehall*
table	boo-rr	*bord*
toilet	doo	*do*
toilet paper	*doo*-puh-*peerr*	*dopapir*
towel	*hong*-klö	*håndkle*
water	vuhn	*vann*
hot/cold water	*vuh*-rrnt/*kuhlt* vuhn	*varmt/kaldt vann*
window	*vin*-du	*vindu*

AROUND TOWN

I'm looking for ...	yay *leh*-törr eht-törr ...	*Jeg leter etter ...*
the art gallery	*kunst*-guhl-lö-*rree*-ö	*kunstgalleriet*
a bank	*buhng*-kön	*banken*
the church	*chirr*-kehn	*kirken*
the city centre	*sehn*-trrum	*sentrum*
the ... embassy	den ... uhm-buhs-*sah*-dö	*den ... ambassade*
my hotel	hu-*tehl*-lö mit	*hotellet mitt*
the market	*to*-rr-gö	*torget*
the museum	mu-*say*-ö	*museet*
the police	pu-li-*ti*-ö	*politiet*
the post office	*post*-kun-*too*-rrö	*postkontoret*
the chemist	*uh*-po-*tehk*	*apotek*
a public toilet	eht *of*-fönt-li too-a-*leht*	*et offentlig toalett*
the telephone centre	*tay*-lö-*varr*-kö	*televerket*
the tourist information office	tu-*rrist*-in-fo-rr-muh-*shoon*	*turistinformasjon*

What time does it open/close?
    norr orp-nö/*stehng*-ö rdehn?   *Når åpner/stenger den?*
What street/suburb is this?
    vilk-ön *gah*-tö/*forr*-stahd arr deh? *Hvilken gate/forstad er det?*

For directions, see the Getting Around section, page 253.

NORWEGIAN

At the Post Office

I'd like to send a ...	yay skuh *sehn*-nö ...	*Jeg skal sende ...*
letter	eht *brrayv*	*et brev*
postcard	eht *post*-kort	*et postkort*
parcel	ehn *puhk*-kö	*en pakke*
telegram	eht tay-lö-*grruhm*	*et telegram*

I'd like some stamps.
    yay vil *ya*-rrnö *hah* noon   *Jeg vil gjerne ha noen*
    frree-marr-kö   *frimerker.*
How much does it cost
to send this to ...?
    voor *mü*-yö kos-törr deh   *Hvor mye koster det*
    o *sehn*-nö deh-tö til ...?   *å sende dette til ...?*

air mail	*luft*-post	*luftpost*
envelope	kon-vu-*lut*	*konvolutt*
mail box	*post*-kuhs-sö	*postkasse*
registered mail	rreh-kom-muhn-*dayrt* post	*rekommandert post*
surface mail	or-*vörr*-flah-tö-*post*	*overflatepost*

NORWEGIAN

Telephone & Internet

I want to ring ...
 yay vil *rring*-ö til ...   *Jeg vil ringe til ...*
The number is ...
 num-mö-rrö arr ...   *Nummeret er ...*
How much does a
three-minute call cost?
 voor *mü*-yö *kos*-törr ehn *Hvor mye koster en*
 trray mi-*nut*-tehsh *suhm*-tah-lö? *tre minutters samtale?*
How much does each
extra minute cost?
 voor *mü*-yö *kos*-törr *vart* *Hvor mye koster hvert*
 ehks-trruh mi-*nut*?   *ekstra minutt?*
I'd like to speak to (Mr Olsen).
 yay skul-lö *ya*-rrnö for *Jeg skulle gjerne få*
 snuhk-kö may (harr *ol*-sehn) *snakke med (herr Olsen).*
I want to make a reverse-charges
phone call.
 yay vil bö-*stil*-lö ehn *Jeg vil bestille en*
 suhm-tah-lö meh   *samtale med*
 noo-*tay*-rrings-*or*-vörr-*fay*-rring *noteringsoverføring.*
It's engaged.
 deh arr *upp*-tuht   *Det er opptatt.*
I've been cut off.
 suhm-tah-lön blay *brrut* *Samtalen ble brutt.*

Where can I get Internet access?
 voor kuhn yay for *ahd*-gang til *Hvor kan jeg få adgang til*
 in-tehrr-neht?   *Internet?*
I'd like to send an email.
 yay vil *ya*-rrnö sehn-deh *Jeg vil gjerne sende*
 ehn *ee*-mayl   *en email.*

At the Bank

I want to exchange some money/
travellers cheques.

    yay vil *ya*-rrnö *vehks*-lö
    pehng-örr/*heh-vö* noon
    rray-sö-shehk-körr

*Jeg vil gjerne veksle
penger/heve noen
reisesjekker.*

What is the exchange rate?

    vah arr vuh-*loo*-tuh-ku-shön?

Hva er valutakursen?

How many Norwegian
kroner per dollar?

    voor *muhng*-ö *krroo*-nörr
    forr *ehn dol*-luhrr?

*Hvor mange kroner
for en dollar?*

Can I have money transferred
here from my bank?

    kuhn yay for or-vörr-fayrr-rt
    pehng-örr *heet* frrah
    buhng-kön min?

*Kan jeg få overført
penger hit fra
banken min?*

How long will it take to arrive?

    voor *lehng*-ö vil deh *tah*?

Hvor lenge vil det ta?

Has my money arrived yet?

    hahrr *pehng*-ö-nö mee-nö
    kom-möt nor?

*Har pengene mine
kommet nå?*

NORWEGIAN

autobank	*mi*-ni-buhnk	*minibank*
bank draft	vehk-sl/rreh-*mis*-sö	*veksel/remisse*
bank notes	*pehng*-ö-sehd-lörr	*pengesedler*
cashier	kuh-*say*-rrörr	*kasserer*
coins	*mün*-törr	*mynter*
credit card	krreh-*dit*-kort	*kredittkort*
exchange	*vehk*-sling	*veksling*
loose change	*vehk*-slö-pehng-örr	*vekslepenger*
signature	*un*-nörr-skrrift	*underskrift*

INTERESTS & ENTERTAINMENT
Sightseeing

Do you have a guidebook/local map?
| hah du ehn *gaid*/eht | *Har du en guide/et* |
| *lo-kuhl*-kuhrt? | *lokalkart?* |

What are the main attractions?
| *vah* arr di *vik*-ti-stö | *Hva er de viktigste* |
| say-*varr*-di-hay-törr? | *severdigheter?* |

What is that?
| vah arr *deh*? | *Hva er det?* |

How old is it?
| voor *guhm*-mölt arr deh? | *Hvor gammelt er det?* |

Can I take photographs?
| *kuhn* yay tah *bil*-dörr? | *Kan jeg ta bilder?* |

What time does it open/close?
| norr orp-nö/*stehng*-ö dehn? | *Når åpner/stenger den?* |

ancient	*guhm*-mehl	*gammel*
beach	strruhn	*strand*
castle	slot	*slott*
cathedral	kuh-teh-*drrahl*	*katedral*
church	*chirr*-kö	*kirke*
concert hall	kon-*sart*-hus	*konserthus*
library	bi-bli-yu-*tayk*	*bibliotek*
main square	(*stoo-rr*)-to-rrgö	*(stor)torget*
market	*to-rr*gö	*torget*
town hall	*rrord*-hus	*rådhus*
monastery	*klos*-törr	*kloster*
monument	his-*too*-rrisk *büg*-ning	*historisk bygning*
mosque	mos-*kay*	*moské*
old town	guhm-möl *bü*	*gammel by*
the old city	*guhm*-lö-bü-yön	*gamlebyen*
opera house	*oo*-pö-rruh-hus	*operahus*
palace	slot	*slott*
ruins	rroo-*ee*-nörr	*ruiner*

NORWEGIAN

stadium	*stah*-di-on	*stadion*
statues	*bil*-löd-ster-törr	*billedstøtter*
synagogue	sü-nuh-*goo*-gö	*synagoge*
temple	*hor-v/tehm*-pöl	*hov/tempel*
university	u-ni-va-shi-*tayt*	*universitet*

NORWEGIAN

Going Out

What's there to do in the evenings?
    vah kuhn muhn *yer*-rrö
    om *kvehl*-n?

Hva kan man gjøre
om kvelden?

Are there any discos?
    arr deh noon dis-ku-*tayk*?

Er det noen diskotek?

Are there places where you
can hear local folk music?
    arr deh noo-ön stay-dörr darr
    ehn kuhn *her*-rrö po noshk
    fol-kö-mu-*sik*?

Er det noen steder der
en kan høre på norsk
folkemusikk?

How much does it cost to get in?
    voor *mü*-yö kost-örr deh
    forr o ko-mö *in*?

Hvor mye koster det
for å komme inn?

cinema	*chee*-nu	*kino*
concert	kon-*sart*	*konsert*
discotheque	dis-ku-*tayk*	*diskotek*
theatre	tay-*ah*-törr	*teater*

Sports & Interests

What do you do in your spare time?
vah yer rdu i frree-ti-dehn? *Hva gjør du i fritiden?*

What sport do you play?
vah shluhgs id-rreht *Hva slags idrett*
drri-vehrr du? *driver du?*

art	kunst	*kunst*
basketball	*buh*-skeht-*buhl*	*basketball*
boxing	*buk*-sing	*boksing*
cooking	*muht-luhg*-ing	*matlaging*
fishing	*fee*-sking	*fisking*
football/soccer	*fut*-buhl	*fotball*
going out	gor *ut*	*gå ut*
going to the cinema	gor por *chee*-nu	*gå på kino*
music	mu-*sik*	*musikk*
photography	foo-too-grruh-*fee*-rring	*fotografering*
reading	*lehs*-ning	*lesning*
shopping	*huhn*-dlay	*handle*
sport	sport/*i*-drreht	*sport/idrett*
the theatre	ti-*uh*-tehrr	*teater*
travelling	*rray*-sehrr	*reiser*
writing	*skrri*-vehrr	*skriver*

Festivals

Santa Lucia is celebrated on 13 December. Children dressed in white, the boys wearing cone-shaped hats and the girls with tinsel and glitter in their hair, take part in candlelight processions.

Jul (Christmas) is celebrated on the evening of 24 December, when gifts are exchanged. In the countryside, people mount sheaves of oats, julenek, on poles for the birds, and many people leave a bowl of porridge out for the nisse, a type of Christmas gnome traditionally thought to bring good luck to farmers.

At Easter, påske, the Sami people hold colourful celebrations in Karasjok and Kautokeino with concerts, joik (traditional chanting), reindeer races and other festivities.

Syttende maj (17 May) is Norway's Constitution Day. Everybody celebrates, and many wear traditional costume. In every city and town there are marching bands and parades of school children. The biggest celebrations take place in Oslo where you'll see thousands of school children march up Karl Johans gate to the palace, where they're greeted by the royal family.

Midsummer's Eve (Jonsok), is celebrated throughout the country, with bonfires and parties.

IN THE COUNTRY
Weather

What's the weather forecast?
vah arr *varr*-mehl-ling-uh? Hva er værmeldinga?

The weather is ...	va-*rrö* arr ...	Været er ...
today.	i-dahg	i dag.
Will it be ...	blee rdeh ...	Blir det ...
tomorrow?	i-*mo-rrn*?	i morgen?
cloudy	*or*-vö-shü-yeht	overskyet
cold	kuhlt	kaldt
foggy	*tor*-kö	tåke
frosty	*frrost*-va-rr	frostvær
hot	vuh-rnt	varmt
raining	rrayn	regn
snowing	sner	snø
sunny	mü-yö *sool*	mye sol
windy	mü-yö *vin*	mye vind

Camping

SIGNS	
KAMPING/LEIRPLASS	CAMPING GROUND

Am I allowed to camp here?
    for-rr yay lorv til o *shlor* op
    tehl-tö mit harr?
          Får jeg lov til å slå opp
          teltet mitt her?

Is there a campsite nearby?
    fins deh ehn *kam*-ping
    plass i *narr-hay*-tön?
          Finnes det en camping-
          plass i nærheten?

backpack	*rrüg*-sehk	ryggsekk
can opener	*boks*-or-pnörr	boksåpner
compass	kom-*puhs*	kompass
crampons	*brrod*-dör	brodder
firewood	veh	ved
gas cartridge	prru-*pahn*-bö-*hol*-lörr	propanbeholder
ice axe	*ees*-erks	isøks
mattress	muh-*drruhs*	madrass
penknife	*lum*-mö-kneev	lommekniv
rope	tohv	tau
tent	tehlt	telt
tent pegs	*tehlt*-plug-görr	teltplugger
torch (flashlight)	*lum*-mö-lükt	lommelykt
sleeping bag	*sor*-vö-poo-sö	sovepose
stove	*koo-kö*-uhp-puh-*rraht*	kokeapparat
water bottle	*vuhn*-fluhs-kö	vannflaske

FOOD
Some Useful Words & Phrases

breakfast	*frroo*-kost	*frokost*
lunch	*lernsh*	*lunsj*
dinner	*mid*-dahg	*middag*

Table for ..., please.
  eht *boo-rr* til ... tuhk — *Et bord til ..., takk.*
Can I see the menu please?
  kuhn yay for meh-*nü*-yön tuhk — *Kan jeg få menyen, takk.*
I'd like today's special, please.
  yay vil *ya*-rrnö hah *dah*-göns rreht takk — *Jeg vil gjerne ha dagens rett, takk.*
What does it include?
  vah in-kloo-*deh*-rreh rdeh? — *Hva inkluderer det?*
Is service included in the bill?
  arr bö-*vart*-ning-uh *ee*-bö-rray-nöt? — *Er bevertninga iberegnet?*
Not too spicy please.
  ik-kö fo *shtarrkt* krrüd-drruh tuhk — *Ikke for sterkt krydra, takk.*

NORWEGIAN

ashtray	*uhs*-kö-bay-görr	*askebeger*
the bill	*rray*-ning-ön	*regningen*
a cup	ehn *kop*	*en kopp*
dessert	deh-*sehrr*	*dessert*
a drink	ehn *drringk*	*en drink*
a fork	ehn *guhf*-föl	*en gaffel*
a glass	eht *gluhs*	*et glass*
a knife	ehn *kneev*	*en kniv*
a plate	ehn tuhl-larr-kön	*en tallerken*
spicy	starrkt (*krrüd*-rruh)	*sterkt (krydra)*
a spoon	ehn *shay*	*en skje*
stale	dor-*vönt*	*dovent*
starter	forr-reht	*forrett*
sweet	sayrr-t	*søt*
teaspoon	*tay*-sheh	*teskjed*
toothpick	*tuhn*-pirr-körr	*tannpirker*

NORWEGIAN

Vegetarian Meals

I'm a vegetarian.

yay arr veh-geh-tuh-rri-*ah-nörr*   *Jeg er vegetarianer.*

I don't eat meat.

yay *spi*-sörr ik-kö *cher-t*   *Jeg spiser ikke kjøtt.*

I don't eat chicken or fish or ham.

yay spee-sörr *varr*-kön *chül*-ling   *Jeg spiser verken kylling*
ehl-lörr *fisk* ehl-lö *shing*-kö   *eller fisk eller skinke.*

Breakfasts & Breads

biscuit	chehks	kjeks
brown bread	grrorv-brrer	grovbrød
crisp-bread	kneh-keh-brrer	knekkebrød
cured ham	speh-keh-shin-keh	spekeskinke
food on top of a sandwich, like cold cuts	por-lehg	pålegg
fried egg (sunny side up)	spayl-ehg	speilegg
hard-boiled	hahrr-kukt	hardkokt
honey	hun-ning	honning
jam	sül-teh-töy	syltetøy
oatmeal biscuits	huh-vrreh-chehks	havrekjeks
oatmeal porridge	huh-vrreh-grrert	havregrøt
open sandwich	smer-brrer	smørbrød
peanut butter	pi-a-nert-smer-rr	peanøttsmør
porridge, cereal	grrert	grøt
roll	rrun-stü-keh	rundstykke
rusk	kuh-vrring	kavring
scrambled eggs	ehg-eh-rreh-rreh	eggerøre
slice	shi-veh	skive
soft-boiled	blert-kukt	bløtkokt
white bread	loof	loff
wholemeal bread	hehl-koorrn-brrer	helkornbrød

MENU DECODER

Dairy Products

gammalost	*guh*-muhl-ust	semi-hard brown cheese with strong flavour
geitost	*yayt*-ust	sweet brown goat cheese
gudbrands dalsost	*gud*-brruhns-duhls-ust	cheese similar to geitost
mysost	*müs*-ust	brown whey cheese
normannaost	nor-*man*-nuh-ust	Danish Blue
pultost	*pült*-ust	soft fermented cheese, often with caraway seeds
riddarost	*rrid*-ehrr-ust	Munster cheese
remuladesaus	*rrehm*-u-luh-deh-sows	cream mayonnaise with chopped gherkins and parsley

Soups & Mixed Dishes

dagens rett	dah-gehns-*rreht*	today's special
fårikål	forr-ih-*korl*	lamb in cabbage stew
flatbrød	*fluht*-brrer	thin wafer of rye/barley
gryte(rett)	*grrü*-teh-(reht)	casserole
italiensk salat	it-uhl-i-*ehnsk*-sah-*luht*	salad of diced cold meat, potatoes, apples and vegetables in mayonnaise
lapskaus	*luhp*-skows	thick stew of diced meat, potatoes, onions and other vegetables
koldtbord	*korlt*-boorr	buffet of cold dishes (fish, meat, cheese, salad and a sweet)
pyttipanne	*püt*-i-*puh*-nö	chunks of meat and potatoes, fried with onions, etc
suppe	*su*-pö	soup
surkål	*surr*-korl	boiled cabbage flavoured with caraway seeds, sugar and vinegar

NORWEGIAN

NORWEGIAN

Meat

bankebiff	*ban*-keh-*bif*	slices/chunks of beef simmered in gravy
benløse fugler	behn-lor-sö-foo-lehrr	rolled slices of veal stuffed with minced meat
blodpudding	*bloo*-pud-ing	black pudding
bris/brissel	brris/*brri*-söl	sweetbread
dyrestek	dü-rreh-stayk	roast venison
fenalår	feh-nuh-lor-rr	cured leg of lamb
fleske pannekake	*fleh*-skeh-*puh*-neh *kah*-keh	thick pancake with bacon, baked in the oven
fleskepølse	*fleh*-skeh-*perl*-seh	pork sandwich spread
fyll	fül	stuffing, forcemeat
kålruletter	*korl*-rru-*leht*-ehrr	minced meat in cabbage leaves
kalvetunge	*kuhl*-veh-tung-eh	calf's tongue
kjøttdeig	*chert*-day	minced meat
kjøttkake	*chert*-kah-keh	small hamburger steak
kjøttpålegg	*chert*-por-lehg	cold meat cuts
kjøttpudding	*chert*-pud-ing	meat loaf
lam(mebog)	*luh*-meh-*boog*	(shoulder of) lamb
lever(postei)	*leh*-vehrr pu-*stay*	liver (pate)
medaljong	mehd-uhl-*yong*	small round fillet
pai	pai	pie
pinnekjøtt	*pi*-neh-*chert*	salted and fried lamb ribs
postei	pu-*stay*	meat pie
spekemat	*speh*-keh-maht	cured meat (lamb, beef, pork, reindeer, often served with scrambled eggs)
spekepølse	*speh*-keh-*perl*-seh	air-dried sausage
syltelabb	*sül*-teh-*lahb*	boiled, salt-cured pig's trotter

Seafood

fiskebolle	*fis*-keh-*bol*-eh	fish ball
fiskegrateng	*fis*-keh-grruh-*teng*	fish casserole
fiskekake	*fis*-keh-*kah*-keh	fried fishball

fiskepudding	*fis*-keh-pud-ing	fish pate fried in a pan
gaffelbitar	guh-fehl-*bee*-tehrr	salt- and sugar-cured sprat/herring fillets
gravlaks	grrahv-*luhks*	salt- and sugar-cured salmon with dill and a creamy sauce
kaviar	kuh-vi-*uhrr*	smoked cod-roe spread
klippfisk	*klip*-fisk	salted and dried cod
lutefisk	lu-teh-*fisk*	stockfish treated in lye solution, boiled
plukkfisk	*pluk*-fisk	poached fish in white sauce
rakefisk	*rrahk*-fisk	cured and fermented fish (often trout)
sildesalat	sil-deh-suh-*laht*	salad with slices of herring, cucumber, onions, etc
spekesild	*speh*-keh-*sild*	salted herring, often served with pickled beetroot, potatoes and cabbage

Desserts

arme riddere	*uhrr*-meh-*rri*-deh-rreh	slices of bread dipped in batter, fried and served with jam
bløtkake	*blert*-kah-keh	rich sponge layer cake with whipped cream
fløteis	fler-teh-*ees*	ice cream made of cream
fløtevaffel	fler-teh-*vuh*-fehl	cream-enriched waffle with jam
fromasj	frroo-*muhsh*	mousse/blancmange
fruktis	frrukt-ees/sorr-*beh*	sorbet/water ice
julekake	yu-leh-*kah*-keh	rich fruit cake
hvetebolle	veh-teh-*bor*-leh	bun; sweet roll
kransekake	krruhn-seh-*kah*-keh	pile of almond-macaroon rings
kringle	*krring*-leh	ring-twisted bread with raisins
lefse	*lehf*-seh	thin pancake (without eggs)
napoleonskake	nuh-pool-eh-uns-*kah*-keh	custard slice

NORWEGIAN

NORWEGIAN

riskrem	*rrees*-krrehm	boiled rice with whipped cream and raspberry jam
rislapp	*rrees*-luhp	small sweet rice cake
rødgrøt	*rrer*-grrert	fruit pudding with vanilla cream
rømmegrøt	*rrer*-meh-grrert	boiled sour cream porridge with cinnamon and sugar
rørte tyttebær	*rreh*-teh-*tü*-teh-*barr*	mashed uncooked cranberries
sirupsnipp	*si*-rrup-*snip*	ginger cookie
tilslørte	*til*-sler-teh-	layers of apple sauce and
bonde-piker	bon-deh-*pee*-kehrr	breadcrumbs, topped with whipped cream
vannbakkels	*vuhn*-buh-kehls	cream puff
vørterkake	*ver*-rr-teh-*kah*-keh	spiced malt bread
wienerbrød	*wee*-nehrr-*brrer*	Danish pastry

Non-Alcoholic Drinks

brus	brrus	fizzy fruit drink
kefir	*keh*-firr	fermented milk
kulturmelk	kul-*turr*-*mehlk*	cultured thick milk
vørterøl	*ver*-tehrr-*erl*	non-alcoholic beer

Alcoholic Drinks

akevitt	uh-*keh*-vit	kind of gin flavoured with spices
bokkøl	*buk*-erl	bock beer
dram	drrahm	drink/tot/shot
exportøl	ehks-*purt*-erl	strong, light-coloured beer
gløgg	glerg	kind of mulled wine, with schnapps and spices
hjemmebrent	*yeh*-meh-*brrehnt*	home-made brandy
lett-	leht	with little/less alcohol or sugar
pils	pils	lager
pjolter	*pyorl*-tehrr	long drink of whisky and soda water
toddi	to-di	mulled wine

Dairy Products

butter	smer-rr	smør
cheese	ust	ost
cream	fler-teh	fløte
cream cheese	fler-teh-ust	fløteost
sour cream	rrer-mö	rømme
whipped cream	krrehm; pis-keht-krrehm	krem; pisket krem

Meat

beef	uk-seh-chert	oksekjøtt
fillet of beef	uk-seh-fi-leh	oksefilet
game	vilt	vilt
ham	shin-keh	skinke
kidney	nü-rreh	nyre
lamb/mutton	sow-eh-chert	sauekjøtt
meat	chert	kjøtt
meatball	chert-bor-leh	kjøttbolle
pork	svi-neh-chert	svinekjøtt
pork chop	svi-neh-kort-eh-leht	svinekotelett
roast beef	uk-seh-stayk	oksestek
roast pork	svi-neh-stayk	svinestek
roast reindeer	rrayns-dürr-stayk	reinsdyrstek
rump steak	mer-brrahd	mørbrad
sausage	perl-seh	pølse
spare rib	svi-neh-rri-beh	svineribbe
veal	kuhl-veh-chert	kalvekjøtt

Seafood

anchovy	uhn-shoos	ansjos
catfish	stayn-bit	steinbit
coalfish	say	sei
cod	torshk	torsk
crab	krruh-beh	krabbe
crayfish	krrehps	kreps
eel	orl	ål

NORWEGIAN

NORWEGIAN

fish	fisk	*fisk*
flounder	*flün*-drreh	*flyndre*
frog fish/ angler fish	*brray*-fluhb	*breiflabb*
haddock	*hü*-seh/*korl*-yeh	*hyse/kolje*
herring	sil	*sild*
lobster	*hu*-mehrr	*hummer*
mackerel	muh-*krrel*	*makrell*
mussel	*blor*-shehl	*blåskjel(l)*
pickled/ marinated herring	*krrüd*-ehrr-sil/*sürr*-sil	*kryddersild/sursild*
plaice	*rrer-speh*-teh	*rødspette*
(rainbow) trout	(*rrayng*-büeh-)*er*-eht	*(regnbue)ørret*
roe	rrorrngn	*rogn*
sea trout	*sher-er*-rreht	*sjøørret*
shellfish	*skuhl*-dürr	*skaldyr*
shrimps	*rray*-kehrr	*reker*
(smoked) salmon	(*rrer-keh*-)*luhks*	*(røyke)laks*
sole	*sher-tun*-geh	*sjøtunge*
sprat/sardine	*brris*-ling	*brisling*
tuna	*tun*-fisk	*tunfisk*
whale steak	*vahl*-bif	*hvalbiff*

Poultry & Wildfowl

black grouse	*orr*-fool	*orrfugl*
chicken	*chül*-ling	*kylling*
chicken fricassee	*hern-seh-frri-kuh-seh*	*hønsefrikasse*
duck	uhn	*and*
goose	gors	*gås*
partridge	*rrap-hern*-eh	*rapphøne*
ptarmigan	*rrü*-peh	*rype*
quail	*vuhk*-tehl	*vaktel*
turkey	kuhl-*kun*	*kalkun*

Vegetables

beans	*bern-nehrr*	bønner
beetroot	rrrr-*beh*-tehrr	rødbeter
Brussels sprouts	*rroo*-sehn-*korl*	rosenkål
button mushroom	sham-pin-*yong*	sjampinjong
cabbage	korl	kål
carrots	*gu*-leh-rrer-tehrr	gulrøtter
cauliflower	*blorm-korl*	blomkål
chives	*grrehs*-lerk	gressløk
cucumber	uh-*gurrk*	agurk
horseradish	*peh*-pehrr-*rroot*	pepperrot
leek	*pu*-rreh	purre
lentils	*lin*-sehrr	linser
marrow/squash	*grrehs*-kahrr	gresskar
mashed potatoes	por-*teht*-mos	potetmos
mushroom	sop	sopp
onion	lerk	løk
peas	*at*-tehrr	erter
pickled gherkin	*sül*-teh-uh-*gurrk*	sylteagurk
potato dumplings	rruh-speh-*buh*-lehrr	raspeballer
potato pancake	*lum*-peh	lompe
radish	rreh-*dik* ˝	reddik
red cabbage	*rror*-korl	rødkål
spinach	spi-*naht*	spinat
sugar peas	*su*-kehrr-at-tehrr	sukkererter
swede	korl-rah-*bi*	kålrabi
tomato	too-*maht*	tomat
vegetables	*grrern*-suh-kehrr	grøn(n)saker

Spices, Herbs & Condiments

caraway seeds	*kuhrr*-veh	karve
cardamom	kuhrr-deh-*mum*-meh	kardemomme
cinnamon	kuh-*nehl*	kanel
curry	*kuh*-rri	karri
garlic	*veet*-lerk	hvitløk

NORWEGIAN

NORWEGIAN

mustard	*sehn*-ehp	*sennep*
parsley	pa-*shi*-leh	*persille*
pepper	*peh*-pehr	*pepper*
spices/herbs	krrü-*dehrr*	*krydder*
sugar	su-kehrr	*sukker*
tarragon	ehs-trruh-*gon*	*estragon*
thyme	*ti*-mi-uhn	*timian*
vinegar	*eh*-dik	*eddik*

Fruit

apple	*ehp*-leh	*eple*
apricot	uh-prri-*kus*	*aprikos*
banana	buh-*nahn*	*banan*
bilberries	*blor*-barr	*blåbær*
blackberries	*byer*-neh-*barr*	*bjørnebær*
blackcurrants	*sool*-barr	*solbær*
cherry	*shi*-sheh-*barr*	*kirsebær*
cranberries	*tü*-teh-*barr*	*tyttebær*
currant	kor-int	*korint*
fruit	frrukt	*frukt*
fruit salad	frrukt-suh-*laht*	*fruktsalat*
gooseberries	*sti*-kehls-*barr*	*stikkelsbær*
grapes	*drroo*-ehrr	*druer*
lemon	si-*trroon*	*sitron*
orange	uh-pehl-*seen*	*appelsin*
peach	*fa*-shkehn	*fersken*
pear	*pah*-rreh	*pære*
pineapple	*uh*-nuh-*nuhs*	*ananas*
plum	*plu*-meh	*plomme*
raisin	rroo-*sin*	*rosin*
raspberries	*brring*-eh-*barr*	*bringebær*
redcurrants	rrips	*rips*
rhubarb	rruh-*buhrr*-brruh	*rabarbra*
stewed plums	*plu*-meh-*grrert*	*plommegrøt*
stewed prunes	*svi*-skeh-*grrert*	*sviskegrøt*
strawberries	*yoorr*-barr	*jordbær*

Desserts, Cakes & Cookies

apple cake	*eh*-pleh-*kah*-keh	eplekake
biscuit/cookie	*smor*-*kah*-keh	småkake
cake	*kah*-keh	kake
chocolate	shoo-kor-*luh*-deh	sjokolade
ice cream	ees	is
meringue	muh-*rrehngs*	marengs
pancake	*puh*-neh-*kah*-keh	pannekake
sponge cake	suk-kehrr-*brrer*	sukkerbrød
tart	*tahrr*-teh	terte

Non-Alcoholic Drinks

apple juice	*eh*-pleh-*must*	eplemost
cocoa	kuh-*kuh*-oo	kakao
coffee	*kuh*-feh	kaffe
fruit juice	yoos	jus
ice	ees	is
milk	mehlk	melk
mineral water	*fuhrr*-is	farris
non-alcoholic	*uhl*-ku-hool-*frri*	alkoholfri
orangeade	*uh*-pehl-*seen*-brrus	appelsinbrus
squash	suhft	saft
tea	teh	te
water	vuhn	vann

Alcoholic Drinks

beer	erl	øl
brandy	*brrehn*-eh-vin	brennevin
cognac	*kon*-yuhk	konjakk
dark beer	*bah*-yehrr	bayer
double	*dor*-behl	dobbel
dry	ter-rr	tørr
liqueur	li-*ker*-rr	likør
port	*purrt*-vin	portvin
red/white wine	*rrer*-vin/*veet*-vin	rødvin/hvitvin
rum	rroom	rom
sparkling	mus-*sehrr*-ehn-deh	musserende

AT THE MARKET

NORWEGIAN

Basics

bread	brrer	*brød*
butter	smer-rr	*smør*
cheese	ust	*ost*
chocolate	shoo-kor-*luh*-deh	*sjokolade*
cooking oil	*ol*-yeh	*olje*
eggs	ehg	*egg*
flour (plain)	mehl	*mel*
jam	*sül*-teh-töy	*syltetøy*
milk	mehlk	*melk*
rice	rrees	*ris*
sugar	*su*-kehrr	*sukker*
mineral water	*fuhrr*-is	*farris*

Meat & Poultry

beef	*uk*-seh-*chert*	*oksekjøtt*
chicken	*chül*-ling	*kylling*
duck	uhn	*and*
ham	*shin*-keh	*skinke*
lamb/mutton	sow-eh-chert	*sauekjøtt*
meat	chert	*kjøtt*
pork	*svi*-neh-*chert*	*svinekjøtt*
sausage	*perl*-seh	*pølse*
turkey	kuhl-*kun*	*kalkun*
veal	kuhl-veh-*chert*	*kalvekjøtt*

Vegetables

beans	*bern*-nehrr	*bønner*
beetroot	rrrr-*beh*-tehrr	*rødbeter*
Brussels sprouts	*rroo*-sehn-*korl*	*rosenkål*
cabbage	korl	*kål*
carrots	*gu*-leh-rrer-tehrr	*gulrøtter*
cauliflower	*blorm*-korl	*blomkål*
cucumber	uh-*gurrk*	*agurk*
mushroom	sop	*sopp*

AT THE MARKET

onion	lerk	*løk*
peas	*at*-tehrr	*erter*
potato	por-*teht*	*potet*
red cabbage	rror-korl	*rødkål*
spinach	spi-*naht*	*spinat*
tomato	too-*maht*	*tomat*
vegetables	grrrern-suh-kehrr	*grøn(n)saker*

NORWEGIAN

Seafood

cod	torshk	*torsk*
crab	*krruh*-beh	*krabbe*
crayfish	krrehps	*kreps*
fish	fisk	*fisk*
herring	sil	*sild*
lobster	*hu*-mehrr	*hummer*
mackerel	muh-*krrel*	*makrell*
mussel	*blor*-shehl	*blåskjel(l)*
salmon	*luhks*	*laks*
shrimps	*rray*-kehrr	*reker*
whale steak	*vahl*-bif	*hvalbiff*

Fruit

apple	*ehp*-leh	*eple*
apricot	uh-prri-*kus*	*aprikos*
banana	buh-*nahn*	*banan*
bilberries	*blor*-barr	*blåbær*
fruit	frrukt	*frukt*
grapes	*drroo*-ehrr	*druer*
lemon	si-*trroon*	*sitron*
orange	uh-pehl-*seen*	*appelsin*
peach	*fa*-shkehn	*fersken*
pear	*pah*-rreh	*pære*
plum	*plu*-meh	*plomme*
strawberries	*yoorr*-barr	*jordbær*

SHOPPING

How much is it ...?
  vorr mü-yö *kos-törr* deh ...? *Hvor mye koster det ...?*

bookshop	*book*-huhn-dl	bokhandel
camera shop	*foo*-tu-fo-*rreht*-ning	fotoforretning
clothing store	*klays*-bu-tik	klesbutikk
delicatessen	deh-li-kuh-*tehs*-sö-fo-*rreht*-ning	delikatesse-forretning
general store; shop	*dah*-lig-vah-rrö-fo-*rreht*-ning	dagligvare-forretning
green grocer	*grrern*-sahks-*huhn*-dlörr	grøn(n)sakshandler
laundry	rrehn-sö-*rree*	renseri
market	*muhrr*-köd	marked
newsagency/ stationers	chyosk	kiosk
pharmacy	uh-pu-*tayk*	apotek
shoeshop	skoo-töy-fo-*rreht*-ning	skotøyforretning
souvenir shop	su-vö-*neerr*-shuhp	suvenirsjapp
supermarket	*snahrr*-cherp(s-bu-*tik*)	snarkjøp(sbutikk)

I'd like to buy ...
  yay kuhn *for* ... *Jeg kan få ...*
Do you have others?
  hah du uhn-drreh? *Har du andre?*
I don't like it.
  deh *lee*-körr yay *ik*-kö *Det liker jeg ikke.*
Can I look at it?
  kuhn yay for *say* po deh? *Kan jeg få se på det?*
I'm just looking.
  yay bah-rrö *sayrr* ma rrünt *Jeg bare ser meg rundt.*
Can you write down the price?
  kuhn du *skrree*-vö up prree-sn? *Kan du skrive opp prisen?*
Do you accept credit cards?
  tah du i-*moot* krray-*dit*-kort? *Tar du imot kredittkort?*

NORWEGIAN

Could you lower the price?
   kun-nö du seht-tö *ned prree*-sn?   *Kunne du sette ned prisen?*
I don't have much money.
   yay *hahrr* ik-kö mü-yö *pehng*-örr   *Jeg har ikke mye penger.*

Can I help you?
   kuhn yay *yehl*-pö day?   *Kan jeg hjelpe deg?*
Will that be all?
   vah rdeh sor noo *ahnt*?   *Var det så noe annet?*
Would you like it wrapped?
   skuhl yay puhk-kö deh   *Skal jeg pakke det*
   in forr *day*?   *inn for deg?*
Sorry, this is the only one.
   bö-*klah*-görr deht-tö arr   *Beklager, dette er*
   dehn *ay*-nehs-tö   *den eneste.*
How much/many do you want?
   voor *mü-yö/muhng*-ö   *Hvor mye/mange*
   vil du *hah*?   *veel du ha?*

NORWEGIAN

Essential Groceries

batteries	buh-teh-*ri*	batteri
bread	brrer	brød
butter	smer-rr	smør
cheese	ust	ost
chocolate	shoo-kor-*luh*-deh	sjokolade
cooking oil	*ol*-yeh	olje
eggs	ehg	egg
flour (plain)	mehl	mel
ham	*shin*-keh	skinke
honey	*hun*-ning	honning
jam	*sül*-teh-töy	syltetøy
matches	*für*-sti-kehr	fyrstikker
milk	mehlk	melk
pepper	*peh*-pehrr	pepper
rice	rrees	ris
salt	suhlt	salt

NORWEGIAN

shampoo	*shuhm*-poo	*sjampo*
soap	*sor*-pö	*såpe*
sugar	*su*-kehrr	*sukker*
toilet paper	*doo*-puh-pee-rr	*dopapir*
toothbrush	*tuhn*-ber-shtö	*tannbørste*

Souvenirs

earrings	*ohrr*-rrö-*dob*-börr	*øredobber*
glasswork	*gluhs*-töy	*glasstøy*
handicraft	*kunst*-huhn-varrk	*kunsthandverk*
necklace	*huhls*-chay-dö	*halskjede*
Norwegian vest	*kuf*-tö	*kofte*
pottery	*stayn*-töy	*steintøy*
ring	*rring*	*ring*
rug	*rrü*-yö	*rye*

Clothing

clothing	klarr	*klær*
coat	frruhk	*frakk*
dress	*choo*-lö	*kjole*
jacket	*yuhk*-kö	*jakke*
jumper (sweater, jersey)	*gehn*-sörr	*genser*
shirt	*shu*-rtö	*skjorte*
shoes	skoo	*sko*
skirt	sher-rt	*skjørt*
trousers	*buk*-sörr	*bukser*

It doesn't fit.	deh *puhs*-sörr ik-kö	*Det passer ikke.*

It's too ...	deh arr forr ...	*Det er for ...*
big	*shtoort*	*stort*
small	*lee*-tö	*lite*
short	kort	*kort*
long	*luhngt*	*langt*
tight	*teht*-sit-tuhn-nö	*tettsittande*
loose	lowst	*laust*

Materials

cotton	*bum*-ul	*bomull*
handmade	*hon-lah*-göt	*håndlaget*
leather	larr	*lær*
brass	*mehs*-sing	*messing*
gold	gul	*gull*
silver	serlv	*sølv*
silk	sil-kö	*silke*
wool	ul	*ull*

Toiletries

comb	kuhm	*kam*
condoms	kun-*doom*	*kondom*
deodorant	day-yu-du-*rruht*	*deodorant*
hairbrush	*hor-rr*-ber-shteh	*hårbørste*
razor	buhrr-*bayrr*-her-völ	*barberhøvel*
sanitary napkins	*dah*-mö-bin	*damebind*
shampoo	*shuhm*-poo	*sjampo*
shaving cream	buhrr-*bayrr*-krraym	*barberkrem*
soap	sor-pö	*såpe*
sunblock cream	*sern*-blok-ul-yö	*sunblock-olje*
tampons	tuhm-*pong*-örr	*tamponger*
tissues	puh-*peerr*-lum-mö-ter-rr-klö	*papirlommetørkle*
toilet paper	*doo*-puh-peerr	*dopapir*
toothpaste	*tuhn*-krraym	*tannkrem*

Stationery & Publications

map	kuhrt	*kart*
newspaper	uh-*vees*	*avis*
newspaper in English	*ehng*-ölsk-sprror-kli uh-*vees*	*engelskspråklig avis*
novels in English	*ehng*-öl-skö rru-*mah*-nörr	*engelske romaner*
paper	puh-*peerr*	*papir*
pen (ballpoint)	pehn (*kü*-lö-pehn)	*penn (kulepenn)*
scissors	suhks	*saks*

NORWEGIAN

NORWEGIAN

Photography

How much is it to process this film?

voor mü-yö *kos*-törr deh o *fruhm*-kuhl-lö dehn-nö *fil*-mön?	*Hvor mye koster det å framkalle denne filmen?*

When will it be ready?

norr arr dehn *fa*-rdi?	*Når er den ferdig?*

I'd like a film for this camera.

yay vil *ya*-rrnö hah ehn film til dehn-nö *kah*-mö-rruhn	*Jeg vil gjerne ha en film til denne kameraen.*

B&W (film)	svuhrt-vit	*svart-hvitt*
camera	*kah*-mö-rruh	*kamera*
colour (film)	*fuhrr*-gö(-film)	*farge(film)*
film	film	*film*
flash	blits	*blitz*
lens	*lin*-sö	*linse*
light meter	*lüs*-mor-lörr	*lysmåler*

Smoking

A packet of cigarettes, please.

ehn puhk-kö si-guh-*rreht*-törr tuhk	*En pakke sigaretter, takk.*

Are these cigarettes strong/mild?

arr dis-sö si-guh-rreht-tö-neh krruhf-ti-yö/*mil*-lö?	*Er disse sigarettene kraftige/milde?*

Do you have a light?

hah du *fürr*?	*Har du fyr?*

cigarette papers	rrul-lö-puh-pee-rr	rullepapir
cigarettes	si-guh-rreht-törr	sigaretter
filtered	fil-törr	filter
lighter	lai-törr	lighter
matches	für-stik-körr	fyrstikker
menthol	mehn-tol	mentol
pipe	pee-pö	pipe
tobacco (pipe)	(pee-pö)-tu-buhk	(pipe)tobakk

Colours

black	svuhrt	svart
blue	blor	blå
brown	brrun	brun
green	grrern	grønn
pink	rroo-suh	rosa
red	rrer	rød
white	veet	hvit
yellow	gul	gul

Sizes & Comparisons

small	lee-tn	liten
big	stoorr	stor
heavy	tung	tung
light	leht	lett
more	mehrr	mer
less	min-drrö	mindre
too much/many	forr mü-yö/muhng-ö	for mye/mange
many	muhng-ö	mange
enough	nok	nok
also	os-so	også
a little bit	lit	litt

NORWEGIAN

NORWEGIAN

HEALTH

Where is the ...?	voor arr ...?	Hvor er ...?
chemist	uh-pu-*tay*-kö	apoteket
dentist	*tuhn*-lay-gön	tannlegen
doctor	*lay*-gön	legen
hospital	*sü*-kö-hu-sö	sykehuset

I'm/My friend is sick.
yay arr/*vehn*-n min arr *sük*

Jeg er/Vennen min er syk.

Could I see a female doctor?
kuhn yay for *snuhk*-kö mayn
kvin-nö-li *lay*-gö?

Kan jeg få snakke med en kvinnelig lege?

What's the matter?
vah arr i *vay*-ön?

Hva er i veien?

Where does it hurt?
voor yer rdeh *vunt*?

Hvor gjør det vondt?

It hurts here.
deh yer-rr *vunt* harr

Dette gjør vondt.

My ... hurts.
deh yer-rr *vunt* i ...

Det gjør vondt i ...

Parts of the Body

ankle	*uhng*-kö-lön	ankelen
arm	*uhrr*-mön	armen
back	*rrüg*-gön	ryggen
chest	*brrüst*-kuhs-suh	brystkassa
ear	*ohrr*-rreh	øret
eye	*öy*-eh	øyet
finger	*fing*-ö-rrön	fingeren
foot	*foo*-tn	foten
hand	*hon*-nuh	hånda
head	*hoo*-deh	hodet
heart	*ya*-rteh	hjertet
leg	*bay*-neh	beinet
mouth	*mun*-n	munnen
nose	*nay*-suh	nesa
teeth	*tehn*-n-neh	tennene
throat	*strru*-pön	strupen

Ailments

I have (a/an) ...	yay hahr ...	Jeg har ...
allergy	ehn uhl-lehrr-*gee*	en allergi
anaemia	*bloo*-muhng-öl	blodmangel
burn	eht *brrehn*-sor-rr	et brennsår
cold	snu-ö	snue
constipation	fo-*shtop*-pölsö	forstoppelse
cough	*hoos*-tö	hoste
diarrhoea	*mah*-gö-show	magesjau
fever	*fay*-börr	feber
headache	*vunt* i *hoo*-dö	vondt i hodet
hepatitis	*gul*-sot	gulsott
indigestion	*dor*-rrli fo-*rdöy*-öl-sö	dårlig fordøyelse
infection	ehn beh-*tehn*-öl-sö	en betennelse
influenza	in-flu-*ehn*-suh	influensa
low/high blood	*lahft*/ *höyt*	lavt/høyt
pressure	*bloo*-trrük	blodtrykk
pain	*sma*-rtö	smerte
sore throat	*vunt* i *huhl*-sn	vondt i halsen
sprain	ehn fo*shtu*-ing	en forstuing
sunburn	*sool*-brrehnt-hayt	solbrenthet
venereal disease	*chern*-sük-dom	kjønnssykdom
worms	*in*-vols-muhrrk	innvollsmark

Some Useful Words & Phrases

I'm ...	yay hahr ...	Jeg har ...
asthmatic	*uhst*-muh	astma
diabetic	*suk*-kö-sük-eh	sukkersyke
epileptic	*fuhl*-lö-sük-eh	fallesyke

NORWEGIAN

I'm allergic to
antibiotics/penicillin.
    yay arr uh-*lehrr*-gisk moot
    uhn-ti-bi-*yoo*-ti-kuh/
    pehn-ni-si-*leen*
*Jeg er allergisk mot
antibiotika/
penicillin*

I'm pregnant.
    yay arr grruh-*veed*
Jeg er gravid.

I'm on the pill.
    yay tahrr *pay*-pil-lön
Jeg tar P-pillen.

I haven't had my
period for ... months.
    yay hahrr *ik*-kö huht
    mehns por ... *mor*-ntörr
*Jeg har ikke hatt
mens på ... måneder.*

I have been vaccinated.
    yay arr vuhk-si-*nay*-rt
Jeg er vaksinert.

I have my own syringe.
    yay hahrr min
    eh-gön *sprröy*-tö-spis
*Jeg har min
egen sprøytespiss.*

I feel better/worse.
    yay *fayrr*-lörr meh
    bay-drrö/*varr*-ö
*Jeg føler meg
bedre/verre.*

accident	*oo*-lük-kö	*ulykke*
addiction	ahv-*hehng*-i-hayt	*avhengighet*
aspirin	dis-*prril*	*dispril*
bandage	buhn-*dah*-shö	*bandasje*
blood test	*bloo*-prrer-vö	*blodprøve*
contraceptive	prray-vehn-*shoons*-midl	*prevensjonsmiddel*
injection	*sprröy*-tö	*sprøyte*
menstruation	mehns-trroo-uh-*shoon*/ mens	*menstruasjon/ mens*

At the Chemist

I need medication for ...
    yay trrehng-örr eht
    midl moot ...
*Jeg trenger et
middel mot ...*

I have a prescription.
    yay hahrr ehn rrö-*sehpt*
Jeg har en resept.

TIME & DATES

What time is it?	vah arr *klok-kuh*?	*Hva er klokka?*

It's ... (am/pm)	*klok*-kuh arr ...	*Klokka er ...*
in the morning	um *fo-rr-*mid-dah-gön	*om formiddagen*
in the afternoon	um *eht*-törr-mid-dah-gön	*om ettermiddagen*
in the evening	um *kvehl*-n	*om kvelden*

What date is it today?
vah *dah*-tu arr deh i-*dahg*?   *Hva dato er det i dag?*

NORWEGIAN

Days of the Week

Monday	*muhn*-dah(g)	*mandag*
Tuesday	*teesh*-dah(g)	*tirsdag*
Wednesday	*uns*-dah(g)	*onsdag*
Thursday	*toosh*-dah(g)	*torsdag*
Friday	*frreh*-dah(g)	*fredag*
Saturday	*ler*-rdah(g)	*lørdag*
Sunday	*sern*-dah(g)	*søndag*

NUTS ABOUT KNUT

Knut Hamsun is probably the best-known Norwegian writer since Henrik Ibsen. Often characterised as one of the most influential European writers of the 20th century, he is credited with inventing a new literary style. He was awarded the Nobel Prize for Literature in 1920 but is often shunned in Norway because of his support for Hitler and the Norwegian Nazi Party during WWII.

Months

January	yuh-noo-*wahrr*	*januar*
February	feh-brroo-*wahrr*	*februar*
March	mahsh	*mars*
April	uh-*prril*	*april*
May	*mah*-i	*mai*
June	*yoo*-ni	*juni*
July	*yoo*-li	*juli*
August	ow-*gust*	*august*
September	sehp-*tehm*-börr	*september*
October	uk-*too*-börr	*oktober*
November	no-*vehm*-börr	*november*
December	deh-*sehm*-börr	*desember*

Seasons

summer	*som*-mörr	*sommer*
autumn	herst	*høst*
winter	*vin*-törr	*vinter*
spring	vor-rr	*vår*

Present

today	i-*dahg*	*i dag*
this morning	i-*morr*-ös	*i morges*
tonight (evening)	i-*kvehl*	*i kveld*
this week	dehn-nö *u*-kuh	*denne uka*
this year	i-*yor*-rr	*i år*
now	nor	*nå*

Past

yesterday	i-*gor*-rr	*i går*
day before yesterday	i *forr*-gor-sh	*i forgårs*
yesterday morning	i-*gor*-rr *forr*-mid-dahg	*i går formiddag*
last night	i-*nuht*	*i natt*
last week/month	sis-tö *u*-kö/*mor*-nt	*siste uke/måned*
last year	i-*fyoorr*	*i fjor*

Future

tomorrow (morning)	i-*mor-rrn*	*i morgen*
day after tomorrow	i-*or*-vörr-mor-rrn	*i overmorgen*
next week/year	*nehs*-tö u-kö/*or*-rr	*neste uke/år*

During the Day

afternoon	*eht*-törr-mid-dahg	*ettermiddag*
dawn, very early morning	*dahg*-grrü	*daggry*
day	dahg	*dag*
early	*tee*-li	*tidlig*
midnight	*mit*-nuht	*midtnatt*
morning	*forr*-mid-dahg	*formiddag*
night	nuht	*natt*
noon	klok-kuh *tol*	*klokka tolv*

NUMBERS & AMOUNTS

0	nul	*null*
1	ehn	*en*
2	too	*to*
3	trreh	*tre*
4	*fee*-rrö	*fire*
5	fehm	*fem*
6	sehks	*seks*
7	shu/süv	*sju/syv*
8	*ot*-tö	*åtte*
9	nee	*ni*
10	tee	*ti*

NORWEGIAN

11	*el*-vö	elleve
12	tol	tolv
13	*trreh*-tehn	tretten
14	*fyor*-tehn	fjorten
15	*fehm*-tehn	femten
16	*sehks*-tehn	seksten
17	*sü*-tehn	sytten
18	*at*-tehn	atten
19	*ni*-tehn	nitten
20	*chu*-ö	tjue
21	*chu*-ehn	tjueen
30	*trreht*-te/*trrehd*-vö	trettil tredve
40	*fer*-rti	førti
50	*fem*-ti	femti
60	*sehks*-ti	seksti
70	*ser*-ti	sytti
80	*ot*-ti	åtti
90	*nit*-ti	nitti
100	*hun*-drrö	hundre
1000	*tus*-ön	tusen
one million	ehn mi-li-*yoon*	en million

1/4	ehn *kvuh-rt*	en kvart
1/3	ehn *trray*-dayl	en tredel
1/2	ehn *huhl*	en halv
3/4	*trreh*-kvuh-rt	trekvart
1st	*fersh*-tö	første
2nd	*ahn*-drreh	andre
3rd	*trreh*-dyö	tredje

Some Useful Words

Enough!	nok!	*Nok!*
a little (amount)	lit	*litt*
double	*dob*-bölt	*dobbelt*
a dozen	tol	*tolv*
few	for	*få*
less	*min*-drrö	*mindre*
many	*muhng*-ö	*mange*
more	may-rr / *flay*-rrö	*mer/flere*
once	ehn guhng	*en gang*
a pair	eht puhrr	*et par*
percent	prru-*sehnt*	*prosent*
some	*noo*-n	*noen*
too much	forr *mü*-yö	*for mye*
twice	*too* guhng-örr	*to ganger*

NORWEGIAN

ABBREVIATIONS

AS	company
EF	EC
e.Kr./f.Kr.	AD/BC
FN	UN
f.o.m.	from (eg. today)
gt./vn.	St/Rd
hovudpostkontor	GPO
Herr/Fru	Mr/Mrs/MS
m.o.h.	metres above sea level
NAF	AA (Automobile Association)
nord/sør	Nth/Sth
NSB	Norwegian Railway Company
postnummer	ZIP-code
Storbritannia	UK

EMERGENCIES

Help!
yehlp!   *Hjelp!*

It's an emergency!
deht-tö arr eht uh-*kut*-til-fehl-lö!   *Dette er et akutt-tilfelle!*

There's been an accident!
deh hah shehd ehn *oo*-lük-kö!   *Det har skjedd en ulykke!*

Call a doctor!
rring ehn *lay*-gö!   *Ring en lege!*

Call an ambulance!
rring eht-törr ehn *sü*-kö-beel!   *Ring etter en sykebil!*

I've been raped.
yay arr *vol*-tuht   *Jeg er voldtatt.*

I've been robbed.
yay arr *rrah*-nuh   *Jeg er rana.*

Call the police!
rring pu-li-*tee*-ö!   *Ring politiet!*

Where is the police station?
voor arr pu-li-*tee*-stuh-shoon-n?   *Hvor er politistasjonen?*

Go away!/Buzz off!
fo-*shvin*!/stik-*ahv*!   *Forsvinn!/Stikk av!*

I'll call the police!
ya *til*-kuhl-lörr pu-li-*tee*-ö!   *Jeg tilkaller politiet!*

SIGNS	
POLITI	**POLICE**
POLITISTASJON/ LENSMANNSKONTOR	**POLICE STATION**

Thief!
  tüv!   *Tyv!*

I'm ill.
  yay arr *sük*   *Jeg er syk.*

I'm lost.
  yay hahrr got meh *vil*   *Jeg har gått meg vill.*

Where are the toilets?
  voor arr too-uh-*leht-tö*-nö/veh-seh?   *Hvor er toalettene/wc?*

Could you help me please?
  kuhn du *yehl*-pö meh
  kuhn-shö?   *Kan du hjelpe meg
                                            kanskje?*

Could I please
use the telephone?
  kuhn yay for *lor*-nö   *Kan jeg få låne
  teh-leh-*foon*-n?   telefonen?*

I'm sorry.
  yay arr *lay* fo *rdeh*   *Jeg er lei for det.*

I didn't realise I was doing
anything wrong.
  yay vahrr ik-kö *klahrr* or-vörr   *Jeg var ikke klar over
  uht yay yoo-rrö noo-ö *gahlt*   at jeg gjorde noe galt.*

I didn't do it.
  yay hahrr *ik*-kö yurt deh   *Jeg har ikke gjort det.*

I wish to contact my
embassy/consulate.
  va-sho-*snil* o lah meh for   *Vær så snill å la meg få
  kon-*tuhk*-tö min   kontakte min
  uhm-buh-*sah*-dö/mit kon-su-*laht*   ambassade/mitt konsulat.*

I speak English.
  yay snuh-körr *ehng*-ölsk   *Jeg snakker engelsk.*

I have medical insurance.
  yay hah *sü*-kö-fo-*shik*-rring   *Jeg har sykeforsikring.*

My possessions are insured.
  ay-ön-day-lö-nö mee-nö   *Eiendelene mine
  arr fo-*shik*-rröt   er forsikret.*

NORWEGIAN

My ... was stolen.	... arr styor-löt	... er stjålet.
I've lost my ...	yay hahrr *mis*-teht ...	*Jeg har mistet ...*
bags	buh-*gah*-shön min	*bagasjen min*
handbag	*vehs*-kuh mee	*vesken min*
money	*pehng*-eh-nö mee-nö	*pengene mine*
travellers cheques	*rray*-sö-shehk-kuh-neh mee-nö	*reisesjekkene mine*
passport	*puhs*-sö mit	*passet mitt*

SWEDISH

QUICK REFERENCE

Hello.	hay	Hej.
Goodbye.	uh-*yer*!/ hay dor!	Adjö!/Hej då!
Yes./No.	yah/nay	Ja./Nej.
Excuse me.	ü-*shehk*-tuh may	Ursäkta mig.
Sorry.	fer-*lort*	Förlåt.
Please.	*tuhk*	Tack.
Thank you.	tuhk	Tack.
You're welcome.	vuh-sho-*goo*	Varsågod.

I'd like a...	yuh *skul*-leh vil-yuh *hah* ehn ...	Jag skulle vilja ha en ...
one-way ticket	*ehn*-kehl-bil-*yeht*	enkelbiljett
return ticket	rreh-*türr*-bil-*yeht*	returbiljett

I (don't) understand.
yuh fer-*shtor*-rr (*in*-teh)
Jag förstår (inte).

Do you speak English?
tah-luhrr du *ehng*-ehls-kuh?
Talar du engelska?

Where is ...?
vahrr *air*/ *lig*-gehrr ...?
Var är/ligger ...?

Go straight ahead.
gor *rrahkt frruhm*
Gå rakt fram.

Turn left/right.
svehng til *vehns*-tehrr/ *her*-gehrr.
Sväng till vänster/ höger.

Do you have any rooms available?
fins deh nor-grruh *lea*-di-guh *rrum*?
Finns det några lediga rum?

I'm looking for a public toilet.
yuh *lea*-tuhrr ehf-tehrr ehn oo-*fehnt*-li too-uh-*leht*
Jag letar efter en offentlig toalett.

SWEDISH

1	eht	*ett*	6	sehx	*sex*
2	tvor	*två*	7	fhü	*sju*
3	trrea	*tre*	8	ot-tuh	*åtta*
4	*fü-rruh*	*fyra*	9	nee-oo	*nio*
5	fehm	*fem*	10	tee-oo	*tio*

Swedish belongs to the Nordic branch of the Germanic languages. It's spoken by the Swedes, who number close to nine million, and by the Finnish-Swedish minority in southern Finland, including the island of Åland. The language is very closely related to Danish and Norwegian. In fact, Scandinavians can usually make themselves understood in their sister countries. Outside this northern outpost, however, it's a different matter, so most Swedes speak at least some English, which is a compulsory subject on school curriculums. Many Swedes actually enjoy practising their English on tourists.

Since English and Swedish have common roots in ancient Germanic, there are many similarities between the languages. Many words were also borrowed from Old Norse into the English language during the Viking period, which ended about a thousand years ago, making the language connection even stronger. In modern times the borrowing is going in the opposite direction, with Swedish borrowing mainly from American English.

There are also quite a few differences between English and Swedish. For a start, you will notice that there are three extra letters in Swedish: å, ä and ö. These are the last three letters of the alphabet, so if you want to look up Åkesson in the telephone directory, you have to look near the end.

Even though you won't have too much difficulty getting around with English, making the effort to learn a few common phrases in Swedish will definitely pay off, as it will be greatly appreciated by the Swedes, who are not used to foreign visitors speaking their language.

PRONUNCIATION

There's a great variety of dialects in Sweden. The pronunciation guide in this book reflects a neutral Swedish, rikssvenska, but don't be surprised if you're given a slightly different pronunciation from a Swede. It all depends on where they come from!

It's important to get the stress right in words. Swedish can have a single or a double accent on a word, giving it its sing-song quality, and sometimes the difference of meaning between two identical-looking words can be huge depending on which accent is used. A good example is anden '*uhn-dehn*' and anden '*uhn-dehn*' where the former is 'the duck' and the latter is 'the spirit/ghost'. In this guide we have used italic letters to denote stressed syllables.

Pronunciation is given in the pronunciation guide in the front of this book, with the following exceptions:

Vowels

Most Swedish vowels have a long and a short variant. In a stressed syllable, a vowel is short if it's followed by two consonants and (generally) long when followed by only one consonant. The unstressed syllables have short vowel sounds.

The letter e is always pronounced in Swedish, even at the end of words, and the letter y is always a vowel.

The vowels are divided into two groups, the hard vowels are a, o, u, å and the soft vowels are e, i, y, ä, ö. They help determine the pronunciation of certain preceding consonants.

Diphthongs

SWEDISH	GUIDE	SOUNDS
e	ea	as in British English 'fear'

Consonants

Some consonants have different sounds depending on whether the following vowel is hard or soft (see *Vowels* above).

SWEDISH	GUIDE	SOUNDS
g	g	as in 'get' in front of hard vowels and consonants
	y	as in 'yet' in front of soft vowels
j	y	as in 'yet'. This sound can be spelled *dj*, *g*, *gj*, *hj*, *lj* at the beginning of words.
k	k	as 'c' in 'cap' in front of hard vowels and consonants
	ch	as *tj* in front of soft vowels
tj	ch	as the 'ch' in 'cheap' but without the slight 't' sound initially. Can also be spelled *ch*, *k*, *kj*.
sj	fh	not unlike 'sh' in 'ship' but try touching the inside of your lower lip with your front teeth while saying it. Can be spelled *ch sch*, *skj*, *stj*.
sk	fh	in front of soft vowels as *sj*, in other positions each letter is pronounced separately

SWEDISH

PRONOUNS		
SG		
I	yahg	*jag*
you	dü/nee	*du/ni*
he/she/it	huhn/hoon/dea	*han/hon/det*
PL		
we	vee	*vi*
you	nee	*ni*
they	dom	*de*

GREETINGS & CIVILITIES
Top Useful Phrases

Hello.	hay	*Hej.*
Goodbye.	uh-*yer!/ hay dor!*	*Adjö!/Hej då!*
Yes./No.	yah/nay	*Ja./Nej.*
Excuse me.	ü-*shehk*-tuh *may*	*Ursäkta mig.*
May I?	*for* yuh?	*Får jag?*
Do you mind?	*yer-rr* deh *nor*-got?	*Gör det något?*
Sorry.	fer-*lort*	*Förlåt.*
Please.	tuhk	*Tack.*
		(at the end of a request)
	snehl-luh!	*Snälla!* (when pleading)
Thank you.	tuhk	*Tack.*
Many thanks.	*tuhk* sor *mü*-keh	*Tack så mycket.*
That's fine.	dea air *brrah*	*Det är bra.*
You're welcome.	*vuh*-sho-goo	*Varsågod.*

Greetings

Good morning.	goo-*mo-rr-on*	*Godmorgon.*
Good afternoon.	goo-*mid*-duh	*Godmiddag.*
Good evening/	goo-*kvehl*/	*Godkväll/*
night.	goo-*nuht*	*Godnatt.*
How are you?	*hürr* stor rde *til*?	*Hur står det till?*
Well, thanks.	*brrah* tuhk	*Bra, tack.*

Forms of Address

you (sg)	dü	*du*
you	nee	*ni*
(pol sg & pl)		
Mrs	frrü	*fru*
Mr	harr	*herr*
Miss	*frrer*-kehn	*fröken*
companion	kuhm-*rraht*/ kom-pis	*kamrat/kompis*
friend	veh-*nin-nuh*/vehn	*väninna/vän* (f/m)

SWEDISH

SMALL TALK
Meeting People

What is your name?
vuh *hea*-tehrr du?   *Vad heter du?*

My name is ...
yuh *hea*-tehrr ...   *Jag heter ...*

I'd like to introduce you to ...
for-rr yuh prreh-sehn-*tea*-rra ...   *Får jag presentera ...*

I'm pleased to meet you.
trreav-lit uht *trrehf*-fuhs/   *Trevligt att träffas./*
uhn-yeh-*nairmt*   *Angenämt.* (pol)

Nationalities

Where are you from?
vahrr-i-frrorn *kom*-mehrr doo?   *Varifrån kommer du?*

I'm from ...   yuh *kom*-mehrr   *Jag kommer*
           frrorn ...   *från ...*

Australia	uh-u-*strrah*-lee-ehn	*Australien*
Canada	*kuh*-nuh-duh	*Kanada*
England	*ehng*-luhnd	*England*
Ireland	*eer*-luhnd	*Irland*
New Zealand	nü-uh *sea*-luhnd	*Nya Zealand*
Scotland	*skot*-luhnd	*Skottland*
Sweden	*svarr*-yeh	*Sverige*
the USA	*ü*-ehs-ah	*USA*
Wales	wayls	*Wales*

Age

How old are you?
hürr *guh*-muhl air du?   *Hur gammal är du?*

I'm ... years old.
yuh air ... *or-rr guh*-mal   *Jag är ... år gammal.*

Occupations

What is your profession?
vuh *hahrr* du fer-rr *ürr-keh?*   *Vad har du för yrke?*

I'm (a/an) ...	yuh air ...	*Jag är ...*
artist	*konst-naer*	*konstnär*
business person	uh-*faesh-muhn*	*affärsman*
computer expert	*dah*-to-rr-ehks-*part*	*datorexpert*
doctor	*lair-kuh-rreh*	*läkare*
engineer	in-fhehn-*yer-rr*	*ingenjör*
farmer	*boon*-deh	*bonde*
handyman	*huhnt-varr*-kuh-rreh	*hantverkare*
journalist	fhoo-nuh-*list*	*journalist*
lawyer	uhd-voo-*kaht*	*advokat*
manual worker	krrops-uhrr-*bea*-tuh-rreh	*kroppsarbetare*
mechanic	meh-*kahn*-i-kehrr	*mekaniker*
nurse	*fhük-fher*-tehsh-kuh	*sjuksköterska*
office worker	kon-too-*rrist*	*kontorist*
scientist	nuh-*türr-vea*-tuh-rreh	*naturvetare*
student	stoo-*dea*-rruhn-deh	*studerande*
teacher	*laer*-uhrr-eh	*lärare*
waiter	sehrr-vi-*trrees/* sehrr-vi-*ter-rr*	*servitris/ servitör* (f/m)
writer	fer-rr-*fuht*-tuh-rreh	*författare*

Religion

What is your religion?
| *vil*-kehn rreh-li-*yoon* | Vilken religion |
| *til*-her-rr du? | tillhör du? |

I'm not religious.
| yuh air *in*-teh rreh-li-*fhers* | Jag är inte religös. |

I'm ...	yuh air ...	Jag är ...
Buddhist	bu-*dist*	buddist
Catholic	kuh-too-*leek*	katolik
Christian	*krris-tehn*	kristen
Hindu	hin-*dü*	hindu
Jewish	*yü-deh*	jude
Muslim	mus-*leem*	muslim
Protestant	prroo-tehs-*tuhnt*	protestant

Family

Are you married?	air du *yift*?	Är du gift?

I'm ...	yuh air ...	Jag är ...
married	*yift*	gift
single	*ü-yift*	ogift

How many children do you have?
| hürr mong-uh | Hur många |
| *bahrn* hahrr du? | barn har du? |

I don't have any children.
| yuh *hahrr* ing-uh *bahrn* | Jag har inga barn. |

I have a daughter/son.
| yuh hahrr ehn *dot-ehrr/sorn* | Jag har en dotter/son. |

How many brothers/
sisters do you have?
| hürr mong-uh *brrer*-dehrr/ | Hur många bröder/ |
| *süs-trruhrr* hahrr du? | systrar har du? |

SWEDISH

Do you have a ...?	harr doo non ...?	*Har du någon ...?*
boyfriend	*poyk-vehn/kil-leh*	*pojkvän/kille (col)*
girlfriend	*flik-vehn/chehy*	*flickvän/tjej (col)*
brother/s	brroorr/*brrer*-dehrr	*bror/bröder*
children	bahrn	*barn*
daughter/s	*dot-tehrr/dert-rruhrr*	*dotter/döttrar*
de facto husband/wife	*suhm-boo*	*sambo*
family	fuh-*mily*	*familj*
father	fahrr/*puh-puh*	*far/pappa*
grandparents (maternal)	*moorr-moorr* o *moorr-fuhrr*	*mormor och morfar*
grandparents (paternal)	*fuhrr-moorr* o *fuhrr-fuhrr*	*farmor och farfar*
husband	muhn	*man*
mother	moorr/*muh-muh*	*mor/mamma*
sister/s	*süs-tehrr/süs-trruhrr*	*syster/systrar*
son/s	sorn/*ser-nehrr*	*son/söner*
wife	frrü	*fru*

Kids' Talk

How old are you?
    hürr *guh*-muhl *air* du?   *Hur gammal är du?*

When's your birthday?
    naer fül-ler du *or-rr*?   *När fyller du år?*

What do you do after school?
    vuh *yer-rr* du ehf-tehrr *skoo-luhn*?   *Vad gör du efter skolan?*

Do you have a pet at home?
    hahrr du nor-rruh *hüs-yürr*?   *Har du några husdjur?*

SWEDISH

I have a ...	yuh hahrr ...	Jag har ...
bird	ehn *for*-gehl	en fågel
budgerigar	ehn un-du-*laht*	en undulat
canary	ehn kuh-*nah*-rree-eh-*for*-gehl	en kanariefågel
cat/pussycat	ehn *kuht*/*kis*-seh-kuht	en katt/kissekatt
dog/bow-wow	ehn *hund*/*voov*-veh	en hund/vovve
fish	*fis*-kuhrr	fiskar
frog	ehn *grroo*-duh	en groda
guinea pig	eht *mah*-shveen	ett marsvin
hamster	ehn *huhm*-stehrr	en hamster
horse	ehn *hehst*	en häst

Feelings

I (don't) like ...

yuh tük-kehrr (*in*-teh) om ...   Jag tycker (inte) om ...

I'm ...	yuh hahrr ...	Jag har ...
in a hurry	*brrot*-tom	bråttom
right/wrong	*rreht*/*feal*	rätt/fel

I'm ...	yuh air ...	Jag är ...
grateful	*tuhk*-suhm	tacksam
hot	*vuhrrm*	varm
hungry/thirsty	*hung*-rri/*ter*-shti	hungrig/törstig
angry	*uhrry*	arg
happy/sad	*glahd*/*leh*-sehn	glad/ledsen
tired	*trrert*	trött
worried	*oo*-rroo-li	orolig

I'm cold.	yuh *frrü*-sehrr	Jag fryser.
I'm well.	yuh *mor*-rr *brrah*	Jag mår bra.
I'm sorry. (condolence)	yuh beh-*klah*-guhrr	Jag beklagar.

SWEDISH

BREAKING THE LANGUAGE BARRIER

Do you speak English?
    tah-luhrr du *ehng*-ehls-kuh?   *Talar du engelska?*

Does anyone speak English?
    fins deh *non* hair som   *Finns det någon här som*
    tah-luhrr *ehng*-ehls-kuh?   *talar engelska?*

I speak a little ...
    yuh *tah*-luhrr *lee*-teh ...   *Jag talar lite ...*

I don't speak ...
    yuh *tah*-luhrr *in*-teh ...   *Jag talar inte ...*

I (don't) understand.
    yuh fer-*shtor-rr* (*in*-teh)   *Jag förstår (inte).*

Could you speak more
slowly please?
    kuhn du vuh *snehl* o *tah-luh*   *Kan du vara snäll och tala*
    lee-teh *long-suhm*-muh-rreh?   *lite långsammare?*

Could you repeat that?
    kuhn doo *up-rrea*-puh deh?   *Kan du upprepa det?*

How do you say ...?
    hürr *say*-ehrr muhn ...?   *Hur säger man ...?*

What does that mean?
    vuh beh-*tü*-dehrr dea?   *Vad betyder det?*

I speak ...	yuh *tah*-luhrr ...	*Jag talar ...*
Danish	*duhn-skuh*	*danska*
Dutch	*hol-lehn*-skuh	*holländska*
English	*ehng*-ehl-skuh	*engelska*
Finnish	*fin-skuh*	*finska*
French	*frruhn-skuh*	*franska*
German	*tüs-kuh*	*tyska*
Italian	i-tuhl-*yean*-skuh	*italienska*
Norwegian	*nosh-kuh*	*norska*
Swedish	*svehn-skuh*	*svenska*

Some Useful Phrases

Sure.	yuh-*vist*	*Javisst.*
Just a minute.	eht *er*-gon-*blik!*	*Ett ögonblick!*
It's (not) important.	deh air (*in*-teh) *vik-tit*	*Det är (inte) viktigt.*
It's (not) possible.	deh air (*oo*-)*mey-lit*	*Det är (o-)möjligt.*
Good luck!	*lük*-kuh til!	*Lycka till!*

BODY LANGUAGE

Swedes aren't very different from other westerners when it comes to body language. They nod their head for yes and shake it for no. An unarticulated little uhuh or umh always means 'yes' and is often accompanied by nodding. 'No' is nej or nähä or a plain shake of the head without a sound.

You'll find that the Swedes will want to shake hands with you every time you meet, men and women alike. Kissing on the cheek is becoming more common among close friends, but the old hand shake is still the most common form of greeting.

SIGNS

BAGAGEINLÄMNING	BAGGAGE COUNTER
DAMER/HERRAR	LADIES/GENTLEMEN
EJ INGÅNG	NO ENTRY
FÖRBJUDET	PROHIBITED
GRATIS INTRÄDE	FREE ADMISSION
INCHECKNING	CHECK-IN COUNTER
INFORMATION/UPPLYSNINGAR	INFORMATION
INGÅNG	ENTRANCE
NÖDUTGÅNG	EMERGENCY EXIT
RESERVERAD	RESERVED
RÖKNING FÖRBJUDEN	NO SMOKING
TELEFON	TELEPHONE
TOALETTER	TOILETS
TULL	CUSTOMS
UTGÅNG	EXIT
VARM/KALL	HOT/COLD
ÖPPET/STÄNGT	OPEN/CLOSED

SWEDISH

PAPERWORK

address	uh-*drrehs*	*adress*
age	*ol*-dehrr	*ålder*
birth certificate	pa-*shoon*-beh-*vees*	*personbevis*
border	grrehns	*gräns*
date of birth	*fer*-dehl-seh-*dah*-tum	*födelsedatum*
driver's licence	*cher*-rr-*koort*	*körkort*
identification	leh-gi-ti-muh-*fhoon*	*legitimation*
immigration	*puhs*-kont-*rrol*	*passkontroll*
marital status	si-*veel*-stond	*civilstånd*
name	nuhmn	*namn*
nationality	nuht-fhoo-nuh-li-*teat*	*nationalitet*
passport (number)	*puhs*(-*num*-mehrr)	*pass(nummer)*
place of birth	*fer*-dehl-seh-*oort*	*födelseort*
profession	*ürr*-keh	*yrke*
reason for travel	*rrea*-suhns	*resans*
	ehn-duh-*morl*	*ändamål*
religion	rreh-li-*yoon*	*religon*
sex	chern	*kön*
tourist card	tu-*rrist*-*koort*	*turistkort*
visa	*vee*-sum	*visum*

GETTING AROUND

What time does the ... leave/arrive?	hürr duhks *gor-rr*/ *kom-mehrr* ...?	*Hur dags går/ kommer* ...?
(aero)plane	(*flüg-*)*plah*-neht	(*flyg*)*planet*
boat	*bor*-tehn	*båten*
bus	*bu*-sehn	*bussen*
ferry	*farr*-*yuhn*	*färjan*
train	*tor*-geht	*tåget*
tram	*spor-rr-vuhng*-nehn	*spårvagnen*

Directions

Where is ...?
    vahrr *air/lig*-gehrr ...?   *Var är/ligger ...?*

How do I get to ...?
    hürr *kom*-mehrr muhn til ...?   *Hur kommer man till ...?*

Is it near here?
    air deh *longt* haer-i-*frrorn*?   *Är det långt härifrån?*

Can I walk there?
    kuhn muhn *gor deet*?   *Kan man gå dit?*

Can you show me (on the map)?
    kuhn du *vee*-suh may   *Kan du visa mig*
    (po *kah-rtuhn)*?   *(på kartan)?*

Are there other means of
getting there?
    kuhn muhn kom-muh   *Kan jag komma dit*
    deet po *uhn-nuht seht*?   *på annat sätt?*

Go straight ahead.
    gor *rrahkt frruhm*   *Gå rakt fram.*

SIGNS	
ANKOMST	ARRIVALS
AVGÅNG	DEPARTURES
BAGAGEUTLÄMNING	LUGGAGE PICKUP
BILJETTKONTOR	TICKET OFFICE
BUSSHÅLLPLATS	BUS STOP
FLYGBUSS	AIRPORT BUS
GÅNGTUNNEL	SUBWAY (pedestrian)
JÄRNVÄGSSTATION	TRAIN STATION
PASSKONTROLL	IMMIGRATION
SPÅR	PLATFORM
SPÅRVAGNSHÅLLPLATS	TRAM STOP
TIDTABELL	TIMETABLE
TUNNELBANA	SUBWAY (metro)
VÄXEL	CHANGE (for coins)

SWEDISH

Turn left/	*svehng* til *vehns*-tehrr/	Sväng till vänster/
right at the ...	*her*-gehrr veed ...	höger vid ...
next	*nehst*-uh	nästa
corner	*her*-rn	hörn
traffic lights	trruh-*feek*-yü-seht	trafikljuset

behind	*bah-kom*	bakom
in front of	*frruhm-fer-rr*	framför
far	longt	långt
near	*nae-rruh*	nära
opposite	*mit* eh-*moot*	mitt emot

Booking Tickets

Where can I buy a ticket?
vahrr kuhn yuh *ker*-puh
ehn bil-*yeht*?

*Var kan jag köpa
en biljett?*

I want to go to ...
yuh vil *or*-kuh til ...

Jag vill åka till ...

Do I need to book?
mos-teh muhn *boo*-kuh?

Måste man boka?

I'd like to book a seat to ...
yuh *skul*-leh vil-yuh *boo*-kuh
ehn *pluhts* til ...

*Jag skulle vilja boka
en plats till ...*

I'd like (a) ...	yuh *skul*-leh vil-yuh *hah* ...	Jag skulle vilja ha ...
one-way ticket	ehn *ehn*-kehl-bil-*yeht*	en enkelbiljett
return ticket	ehn rreh-*türr*-bil-*yeht*	en returbiljett
two tickets	tvor bil-*yeht*-ehr	två biljetter
student's fare	ehn stu-*dehnt*-bil-*yeht*	en studentbiljett
child's fare	ehn *bahrn*-bil-*yeht*	en barnbiljett
pensioner's fare	puhn-fhoo-*naesh*-bil-*yeht*	en pensionärs-biljett

1st class	*fersh*-tuh kluhs	första klass
2nd class	*uhn*-drruh kluhs	andra klass

Is it completely full?
    arr deat *uhl*-deh-lehs *fult*?   *Är det alldeles fullt?*
Can I get a stand-by ticket?
    fins deh non *vehn*-teh-*lis*-tuh?   *Finns det någon väntelista?*

Air

Is there a flight to ...?
    fins deh not *flüg* til ...?   *Finns det något flyg till ...?*
How long does the flight take?
    hürr long teed *tahrr* flü-geht?   *Hur lång tid tar flyget?*
What is the flight number?
    vil-keht *flight-num-mehrr*   *Vilket flightnummer*
    air deh?   *är det?*

airport tax	*flüg*-pluhts-*skuht*	*flygplatsskatt*
boarding pass	*boo*-rding-*kahrd*	*boardingcard*
customs	tul	*tull*

Bus

Where is the bus/tram stop?
    vahrr air *bus*-hol-*pluht*-sehn/   *Var är busshållplatsen/*
    spor-rr-vuhngns-hol-*pluht*-sehn?   *spårvagnshållplatsen?*
Which bus goes to ...?
    vil-kehn *bus* gor-rr til ...?   *Vilken buss går till ...?*
Could you let me know when
we get to ...?
    kuhn du seh-ya *til* naer   *Kan du säga till när*
    vi *kom*-mehrr til ...?   *vi kommer till ...?*
I want to get off!
    yuh vil gor *ahv*!   *Jag vill gå av!*

What time is	naer	*När*
the ... bus?	gor-rr ...?	*går ...?*
next	*nehs*-ta *bus*	*nästa buss*
first	*fersh*-tuh *bu*-sehn	*första bussen*
last	*sis*-tuh *bu*-sehn	*sista bussen*

Metro

Which line takes me to ...?
| vil-kehn *leen*-yeh gor-rr til ...? | *Vilken linje går till ...?* |

What is the next station?
| vil-kehn air *nehs*-tuh stuh-*fhoon*? | *Vilken är nästa station?* |

Train

Is this the right platform for the train to/from ...?
| air deh *haer* rreht pa-*rrong* fer-rr *tor*-geht til/frrorn ...? | *Är det här rätt perrong för tåget till/från ...?* |

Passengers for ... must change trains in ...
| *rrea*-suhn-deh moot ... mos-teh *bü*- tuh *torg* i ... | *Resande mot ... måste byta tåg i ...* |

The train leaves from platform ...
| *torg*-eht *ahv-gor-rr* frrorn *spor-rr* ... | *Tåget avgår från spår ...* |

dining car	rrehs-tu-*rruhng-vuhngn*	*resturangvagn*
express	ehx-*prrehs-torg*	*expresståg*
local	loo-*kahl-torg*	*lokaltåg*
sleeping car	sorv-*vuhngn*	*sovvagn*

Taxi

Can you take me to ...?
| kuhn doo *cher*-rruh may til ...? | *Kan du köra mig till ...?* |

How much does it cost to go to ...?
| vuh *kos*-tuhrr deh til ...? | *Vad kostar det till ...?* |

Here is fine, thank you.
| *haer* bleer *brrah* tuhk | *Här blir bra, tack.* |

The next corner, please.
| *nehs*-tuh *her*-rn tuhk | *Nästa hörn, tack.* |

Continue!
| *foort-sheht*! | *Fortsätt!* |

SWEDISH

Stop here!
    stuhm-uh haer!   Stanna här!
Please slow down.
    kuhn du suhk-tuh nearr?   Kan du sakta ner?
Please wait here.
    kuhn du vehn-tuh haer?   Kan du vänta här?

Some Useful Phrases
The train is delayed/cancelled.
    tor-geht air fer-shea-nuht/   Tåget är försenat/
    in-stehlt   inställt.
How long will it be delayed?
    hurr mük-keh air deh   Hur mycket är det
    fer-shea-nuht?   försenat?
How long does the trip take?
    hurr long teed tuhrr rrea-suhn?   Hur lång tid tar resan?
Is it a direct route?
    air deh ehn   Är det en
    di-rrehkt-fer-rr-bin-dehl-seh?   direktförbindelse?
Is that seat taken?
    air deh up-tah-geht haer?   Är det upptaget här?
I want to get off at ...
    yuh vil gor ahv ee ...   Jag vill gå av i ...
Where can I hire a bicycle?
    vahrr kuhn yuh hü-rruh   Var kan jag hyra
    ehn sük-kehl?   en cykel?

SWEDISH

HOW FAR?

In Sweden, all road signs show distance in kilometres,
but the Swedes prefer to use the term mil (meel) for 10
km when they talk about how far away a place is, eg.
50 km is fem mil.

Car

Where can I rent a car?
vahrr kuhn yuh
hü-rruh ehn beel?

*Var kan jag
hyra en bil?*

How much is it daily/weekly?
hurr mük-keh kos-tuhrr
deh parr *dahg*/parr *vehk-kuh?*

*Hur mycket kostar
det per dag/per vecka?*

Does that include insurance/mileage?
in-gor-rr fer-shaek-rring/
free-uh meel?

*Ingår försäkring/
fria mil?*

Where's the next petrol station?
vahrr air *nehs*-tuh
behn-*seen*-stuh-*fhoon?*

*Var är nästa
bensinstation?*

How long can I park here?
hurr *lehng*-eh for-rr muhn
puhrr-*kea*-rruh *haer?*

*Hur länge får man
parkera här?*

Does this road lead to?
gor-rr dehn *haer*
vair-gehn til ...?

*Går den här
vägen till ...?*

SIGNS	
BILMEKANIKER	MECHANIC
BILUTHYRNING	CAR RENTAL
BILVERKSTAD/GARAGE	GARAGE
BLYFRI BENSIN	UNLEADED
EJ INFART	NO ENTRY
ENKELRIKTAT	ONE WAY
FÖRBJUDET ATT STANNA	NO STANDING
MOTORVÄG	FREEWAY
PARKERING FÖRBJUDEN	NO PARKING
REPARATIONER	REPAIRS
SJÄLVBETJÄNING	SELF SERVICE
STOPP	STOP
SUPER/HÖGOKTANIG BENSIN	SUPER
VÄJNINGSPLIKT	GIVE WAY

SWEDISH

air (for tyres)	luft	*luft*
battery	buh-teh-*rree*	*batteri*
brakes	*brrom-suhrr*	*bromsar*
clutch	*kop-ling*	*koppling*
driver's licence	*cher-rr-koort*	*körkort*
engine	*moo-to-rr*	*motor*
fan belt	*flehkt-rrehm*	*fläktrem*
lights	*lü-seh*	*lyse*
oil	*ol-yuh*	*olja*
puncture	punk-*tea*-rring	*punktering*
radiator	*chü*-luh-rreh	*kylare*
road map	*vairg-kah*-rtuh	*vägkarta*
studded winter tyres	*dub-dehk*	*dubbdäck*
tyres	dehk	*däck*
windscreen	vind-rrü-tuh	*vindruta*
windscreen wipers	*vind*-rrü-teh-to-rr-kuh-rreh	*vindrutetorkare*
windscreen washer fluid	spoo-luhrr-*vehts*-kuh	*spolarvätska*

SWEDISH

I need a mechanic.
yuh beh-*her*-vehrr ehn
meh-*kah*-ni-kehrr

*Jag behöver en
mekaniker.*

The battery is flat.
buh-teh-*rree*-eht air *slüt*

Batteriet är slut.

The radiator is leaking.
chü-luh-rrehn *lehk*-kehrr

Kylaren läcker.

I have a flat tyre.
yuh hahrr fot punk-*tea*-rring

Jag har fått punktering.

It's overheating.
moo-to-rn *koo-kuhrr*

Motorn kokar.

It's not working.
dehn *gor-rr* in-teh

Den går inte.

ACCOMMODATION

Where is	vahrr *fins* deh	*Var finns det*
a ... hotel?	eht ... hoo-*tehl*?	*ett ... hotell?*
cheap	*bil*-lit	*billigt*
good	*brrah*	*bra*
nearby	*naer*-lig-guhn-deh	*närliggande*

What is the address?
vil-kehn uh-*drrehs* air deh?   *Vilken adress är det?*

Could you write the address, please?
kuhn du skrree-vuh   *Kan du skriva*
nearr uh-*drrehs*-sehn?   *ner adressen?*

At the Hotel

Do you have any rooms available?
fins deh nor-grruh   *Finns det några*
lea-di-guh *rrum*?   *lediga rum?*

I'd like to share a dorm.
yuh *skul*-leh vil-yuh   *Jag skulle vilja*
boo ee *sorv*-sahl   *bo i sovsal.*

I'd like a ...	yuh *skul*-leh	*Jag skulle*
	vil-yuh *hah* ...	*vilja ha ...*
single room	eht *ehn*-kehl-*rrum*	*ett enkelrum*
double room	eht *dub*-behl-*rrum*	*ett dubbelrum*
bed	ehn *sehng*	*en säng*

I want a room	yuh vil *hah*	*Jag vill ha*
with a ...	eht *rrum* meh ...	*ett rum med ...*
balcony	buhl-*kong*	*balkong*
bathroom	*bahd*	*bad*
shower	*dufh*	*dusch*
television	*tea-vea*	*teve*
window	*fern*-stehrr	*fönster*

I'm going to	yuh tehn-kehrr	*Jag tänker*
stay for ...	*stuhn-nuh ...*	*stanna ...*
one day	*ehn dah*	*en dag*
two days	*tvor dah-guhrr*	*två dagar*
one week	*ehn veh-kuh*	*en vecka*

Do you have identification?
  hahrr du leh-gi-ti-muh-*fhoon?* *Har du legitimation?*
Your membership card, please.
  dit *mead*-lehms-*koort tuhk* *Ditt medlemskort, tack.*
Sorry, we're full.
  tü-*varr* air deh *ful*-beh-*luhkt* *Tyvärr är det fullbelagt.*
How long will you be staying?
  hurr lehng-eh *stuhn*-nuhrr *ni?* *Hur länge stannar ni?*
It's ... per day/per person.
  deh *kos-tuhrr* ... parr *dahg/* *Det kostar ... per dag/*
  parr pa-*shoon* *per person.*
How much is it per night/
per person?
  hurr mük-keh *kos*-tuhrr *Hur mycket kostar*
  deh parr *nuht/*parr pa-*shoon?* *det per natt/per person?*
Can I see the room?
  kuhn yuh for *sea rrum*-meht? *Kan jag få se rummet?*
Are there any other/cheaper rooms?
  fins deh nor-grruh *uhnd*-rruh/ *Finns det några andra/*
  bil-li-guh-rreh *rrum?* *billigare rum?*
Is there a reduction for students/
children?
  fins deh stu-*dehnt*-rruh-*buht/* *Finns det studentrabatt/*
  bahrn-rruh-*buht?* *barnrabatt?*
Does it include breakfast?
  in-*gor-rr frru*-kost i *prree*-seht? *Ingår frukost i priset?*
It's fine, I'll take it.
  deht bleer *brrah* yuh *tahrr* deh *Det blir bra, jag tar det.*

I'm not sure how long I'm staying.
> yuh *veat* in-teh hurr *lehng*-eh
> yuh *stuhm*-uhrr

Jag vet inte hur länge
jag stannar.

Is there a lift?
> fins deh *his*?

Finns det hiss?

Where is the bathroom?
> vahrr air *bahd-rrum*-meht?

Var är badrummet?

Do you have a safe where
I can leave my valuables?
> *hahrr* ni non
> fer-rr-*vah*-rrings-*boks* daer
> yuh kuhn *lehm*-nuh mee-nuh
> *vaer*-deh-*sah*-kehrr?

Har ni någon
förvaringsbox där
jag kan lämna mina
värdesaker?

Is there somewhere to wash clothes?
> *fins* deh non *tveht-stü*-guh?

Finns det någon tvättstuga?

Can I use the kitchen?
> kuhn yuh *uhn-vehn*-duh
> *ker*-keht?

Kan jag använda
köket?

May I use the telephone?
> for-rr yuh *lor*-nuh
> teh-leh-*for*-nehn?

Får jag låna
telefonen?

Requests & Complaints

Please wake me up at ...
> kuhn ni *vehk*-kuh may
> klok-kuhn ...?

Kan ni väcka mig
klockan ...?

The room needs to be cleaned.
> *rrum*-meht beh-her-vehrr
> *stair-duhs*

Rummet behöver
städas.

I can't open/close the window.
> yuh kuhn in-teh *erp-nuh*/
> *stehng-uh fernst*-rreht

Jag kan inte öppna/
stänga fönstret.

I've locked myself out of my room.
> yuh hahrr lorst may *ü-teh*

Jag har låst mig ute.

The toilet won't flush.
> too-uh-*leht*-tehn
> *spoo*-luhrr *in*-teh

Toaletten
spolar inte.

I (don't) like this room.
    yuh tük-kehrr (*in*-teh) *om*   *Jag tycker inte om*
    deh *haer* rrum-meht   *det här rummet.*

It's too ...	deh air fer-rr ...	*Det är för ...*
dark	*mer*-rrkt	*mörkt*
expensive	*dürt*	*dyrt*
noisy	*bul*-rrit	*bullrigt*
small	*lee*-teht	*litet*

Some Useful Words & Phrases

I'm/We're leaving now.
    yah/*vee* skuh *or*-kuh *nü*   *Jag/Vi ska åka nu.*
I'd like to pay the bill.
    yuh *skul*-leh vil-yuh   *Jag skulle vilja*
    beh-*tah*-luh rrairk-ning-*ehn*   *betala räkningen.*

name	nuhmn	*namn*
surname	*ehf*-tehrr-*nuhmn*	*efternamn*
address	uh-*drrehs*	*adress*
room number	*rrums*-num-mehrr	*rumsnummer*
air-conditioning	*luft*-kon-di-fhoo-*nea*-rring	*luftkonditionering*
balcony	buhl-*kong*	*balkong*
bathroom	*bahd*-rrum	*badrum*
bed	sehng	*säng*
blanket	filt	*filt*
chair	stool	*stol*
clean (adj)	rreant	*rent*
cot	*bahrn*-sehng	*barnsäng*
cupboard	skorp	*skåp*
dirty	*smut*-sit	*smutsigt*
double bed	*dub*-behl-*sehng*	*dubbelsäng*
electricity	ehl-ehk-trri-si-*teat*	*elektricitet*
excluded	*in*-gor-rr *ay*	*ingår ej*
fan	flehkt	*fläkt*
heater	varr-meh-eh-leh-*mehnt*	*värmeelement*

SWEDISH

included	*in*-beh-*rraek*-nuht/	*inberäknat/*
	in-gor-rr	*ingår*
key	*nük-kehl*	*nyckel*
lift (elevator)	hiss	*hiss*
light bulb	*glerd-luhm-*puh	*glödlampa*
a lock	lors	*lås*
mattress	muh-*drruhs*	*madrass*
mirror	*spea-gehl*	*spegel*
padlock	*hehng-lors*	*hänglås*
pillow	*kud-deh*	*kudde*
quiet	tüst	*tyst*
quilt	*teh-keh*	*täcke*
refrigerator	*chül-skorp*	*kylskåp*
room (in hotel)	rrum	*rum*
sauna	*buhs-tu*	*bastu*
sheet	*lah-kuhn*	*lakan*
shower	dufh	*dusch*
soap	tvorl	*tvål*
suitcase	*rreas-vehs-*kuh	*resväska*
swimming pool	*sim-*buh-*sehng*	*simbassäng*
table	boord	*bord*
toilet (paper)	too-uh-*leht*(-*puhp*-pehrr)	*toalett(papper)*
towel	*huhn-dook*	*handduk*
(hot/cold) water	(*vuhrrm-/kuhl-*)*vuht*-ehn	*(varm/kall)vatten*
window	*fern*-stehrr	*fönster*

SWEDISH

SIGNS

CAMPINGPLATS	CAMPING GROUND
FULLBELAGT/	FULL/
INGA LEDIGA RUM	NO VACANCIES
GÄSTGIVERI/PENSIONAT	GUESTHOUSE
HOTELL	HOTEL
MOTELL	MOTEL
LEDIGA RUM/RUM ATT HYRA	ROOMS AVAILABLE
VANDRARHEM	YOUTH HOSTEL

AROUND TOWN

I'm looking for (the/a) ...	yuh *lea*-tuhrr ehf-tehrr ...	*Jag letar efter ...*
art gallery	*konst*-mu-*sea*-eht	*konstmuséet*
bank	ehn *buhnk*	*en bank*
cathedral	*doom*-chürr-kuhn	*domkyrkan*
church	*chürr-kuhn*	*kyrkan*
city centre	*sehnt*-rrum	*centrum*
... embassy	... uhm-buh-*sah*-dehn	*... ambassaden*
hotel	mit hoo-*tehl*	*mitt hotell*
market (outdoor)	*sah*-lu-to-rr-yeht	*salutorget*
market (indoor)	*sah*-lu-*huhl*-lehn	*saluhallen*
museum	mu-*sea*-eht	*muséet*
police	poo-*lee*-sehn	*polisen*
post office	*pos*-tehn	*posten*
public toilet	ehn oo-*fehnt*-li too-uh-*leht*	*en offentlig toalett*
public telephone	ehn teh-leh-*forn*-chosk	*en telefonkiosk*
tourist information office	tu-*rrist* in-for-muh-*fhoon*-ehn	*turist- informationen*

What time does it open/close?
narr *erp*-nuhrr/
stehng-ehrr dom?

*När öppnar/
stänger de?*

What ... is this?	vuh air deh *haer* fer-rr ...	*Vad är det här för ...?*
road	*vairg*	*väg*
street	*gah*-tuh	*gata*
suburb	*stuhts-deal*/ *fer*-rr-oort	*stadsdel/ förort*

For directions, see the Getting Around section, page 319.

At the Post Office

I'd like to send a ...	yuh *skul*-leh vil-yuh *fhik*-kuh eht ...	*Jag skulle vilja skicka ett ...*
letter	*brreav*	*brev*
postcard	*vü-koort*	*vykort*
parcel	puh-*keat*	*paket*
telegram	teh-leh-*grruhm*	*telegram*

I'd like some stamps.
| yuh skul-leh vil-yuh *hah* nor-grruh *free-marr*-kehn | *Jag skulle vilja ha några frimärken.* |

How much does it cost to send this to ...?
| hurr *mük*-keh *kos*-tuhrr deh uht *fhik*-uh deh *haer* til ...? | *Hur mycket kostar det att skicka det här till ...?* |

an aerogram	eht ae-rroo-*grruhm*	*ett aerogram*
airmail	*flüg*-post	*flygpost*
envelope	ku-*vaer*	*kuvert*
mailbox	*brreav*-lor -duh	*brevlåda*
registered mail	rreh-kom-mehn-*dea*-rruht *brreav*	*rekommenderat brev*
surface mail	*üt*-post	*ytpost*

Telephone & Internet

Can I use the telephone, please?
| kuhn *yah* fo *lor*-nuh teh-leh-*for*-nehn? | *Kan jag få låna telefonen?* |

I want to ring ...
| yuh vil *rring*-uh til ... | *Jag vill ringa till ...* |

The number is ...
| *num*-rreht air ... | *Numret är ...* |

How much does a
three-minute call cost?

   hurr mük-keh *kos*-tuhrr eht   *Hur mycket kostar ett*
   trrea-mi-*nü*-tehsh-suhm-*tahl*?   *treminuterssamtal?*

How much does each extra
minute cost?

   hurr mük-keh *kos*-tuhrr   *Hur mycket kostar*
   vuhrr-yeh *ehks*-trruh mi-*nüt*?   *varje extra minut?*

I'd like to speak to
(Göran Persson).

   yuh *skul*-leh vil-yuh *tah*-luh   *Jag skulle vilja tala*
   meh (yer-rruhn *pae*-shon)   *med (Göran Persson).*

I want to make a reverse-charges
phone call.

   yuh *skul*-leh vil-yuh *yer*-rruh   *Jag skulle vilja göra*
   eht *bea-ah*-suhm-*tahl*   *ett ba-samtal.*

What is the area code for ...?

   vuh air *rrikt-num*-rreht til ...?   *Vad är riktnumret till ...?*

It's engaged.

   deh air *up-tah*-geht   *Det är upptaget.*

I've been cut off.

   suhm-tahl-eht *brrerts*   *Samtalet bröts.*

Is there an Internet cafe nearby?

   fihns deh not *in*-tehrr-neht-   *Finns det något Internet-*
   kuh-*fea* i *naer-hea*-tehn?   *kafé i närheten?*

Can I access the Internet from here?

   kuhn yuh kop-luh *up* may por   *Kan jag koppla upp mig på*
   in-tehrr-neht *haer*-i-*frrorn*?   *Internet härifrån?*

I'd like to check my e-mail.

   yuh *skul*-leh vil-yuh-*kol*-luh   *Jag skulle vilja kolla*
   min *ea-mail*   *min e-mail.*

computer	*dah-to-*rr	*dator*
public telephone	teh-leh-*forn-chosk*	*telefonkiosk*
telephone directory	teh-leh-*forn-*	*telefonkatalog*
	kuh-tuh-*lorg*	

SWEDISH

At the Bank

I want to exchange some money/
travellers cheques.

yuh *skul*-leh vil-yuh *vehks*-luh *Jag skulle vilja växla*
pehng-uhrr/*rrea*-seh-*chehk*-kuhrr *pengar/resecheckar.*

What is the exchange rate?

vuh air *vehks*-ehl-*ku*-shehn? *Vad är växelkursen?*

How many kronor per dollar?

hurr mong-uh *krroo*-ner *Hur många kronor*
parr *dol*-luhrr? *per dollar?*

automatic teller machine	buhn-koo-*maht*	bankomat
bank draft	*post*-vehk-sehl	postväxel
bank notes	*sead*-luhrr	sedlar
cashier	*kuhs*-suh/*kuh*-ser	kassa/kassör
coins	münt	mynt
credit card	krreh-*deet*-koort	kreditkort
to exchange	*vehks*-luh	växla
foreign exchange	*üt*-lehnsk vuh-*lü*-tuh	utländsk valuta
loose change	*smor*-pehng-uhrr	småpengar
signature	*un*-dehrr-*skrrift*	underskrift

INTERESTS & ENTERTAINMENT
Sightseeing

Do you have a guidebook/map of ...?

hahrr ni ehn *rrea*-seh-huhnd-*book*/ *Har ni en resehandbok/*
kah-rtuh er-vehrr ...? *karta över ...?*

What are the main attractions?

vilk-uh air *Vilka är*
hü-vud-uht-rruhk-*fhoon*-ehrr-nuh? *huvudattraktionerna?*

What is that?

vuh air *dea*? *Vad är det?*

How old is it?

hurr *guhm*-muhl *air* dehn? *Hur gammal är den?*

May I take photographs?

    for-rr yuh foo-too-grruh-*fea*-rruh?   *Får jag fotografera?*

What time does it open/close?

    hurr *duhks erp*-nuhrr/   *Hur dags öppnar/*
    stehng-ehrr dom?   *stänger de?*

ancient	*foo-rn-tee*-duh	*forntida*
archaeological	uhrr-keh-o-*lor*-gisk	*arkeologisk*
beach	strruhnd	*strand*
bridge	brroo	*bro*
building	*büg-nuhd*	*byggnad*
castle	slot	*slott*
cathedral	*doom-chürr*-kuh	*domkyrka*
church	*chürr-kuh*	*kyrka*
concert hall	kon-*saer-hüs*	*konserthus*
island	er	*ö*
lake	fher	*sjö*
library	bib-lee-oo-*teak*	*bibliotek*
the main square	*stoorr-to-rr-yeht*	*stortorget*
market (outdoor)	*to-rry-huhn*-dehl	*torghandel*
market (indoor)	*sah*-lu-*huhl*	*saluhall*
monastery	*klos*-tehrr	*kloster*
monument	mo-nu-*mehnt*	*monument*
mosque	mos-*kea*	*moské*
the old city	guhm-luh *stahn*	*gamla stan*
palace	puh-*luhts*/slot	*palats/slott*
opera house	*oo*-peh-rruh-*hüs*	*operahus*
river	or/ehlv	*å/älv*
ruins	rru-*ee*-nehrr	*ruiner*
the sea	*hah*-veht	*havet*
square	*to*-rry	*torg*
stadium	ee-drrots-*pluhts*	*idrottsplats*
statues	stuh-*tü*-ehrr	*statyer*
synagogue	*sü*-nuh-*goo*-guh	*synagoga*
temple	*tehm*-pehl	*tempel*
university	u-ni-va-shi-*teat*	*universitet*

Going Out

What's there to do in the evenings?

vuh fins deh uht yer-rruh
po kvehl-luhrr-nuh?

Vad finns det att göra
på kvällarna?

Are there places where you can
hear Swedish folk music?

fins deh not stehl-leh daer
muhn kuhn her-rruh
svehnsk folk-mu-seek?

Finns det något ställe där
man kan höra
svensk folkmusik?

How much does it cost to get in?

hurr mük-keh kos-tuhrr
deh ee in-trrair-deh?

Hur mycket kostar
det i inträde?

cinema	*bee-oo*	*bio*
concert	*kon-saer*	*konsert*
discotheque	*dis-koo-teak*	*diskotek*
nightclub	*nuht-klub*	*nattklubb*
theatre	*teh-ah-tehrr*	*teater*

Sports & Interests

What sports do you play?

vil-kuh spo-rtehrr
üt-er-vuhrr du?

Vilka sporter
utövar du?

What are your interests?

vuh hahrr du fer-rr
in-trrehs-sehn?

Vad har du för
intressen?

SWEDISH

art	konst	konst
bandy	*buhn*-dü	bandy
(team sport on ice)		
basketball	*bahs*-keht	basket
canoeing	uht *puh*-dluh kuh-*noot*	att paddla kanot
chess	fhuhk	schack
collecting ...	yuh *suhm*-luhrr ...	Jag samlar ...
computer games	*dah*-to-rr-*speal*	datorspel
dancing	duhns	dans
fishing	uht *fis*-kuh	att fiska
football	*foot*-boll	fotboll
hiking/trekking	uht *vuhn*-drruh	att vandra
horse riding	uht *rree-duh*	att rida
icehockey	*ees-hok*-kü	ishockey
martial arts	*kuhmp-spo*-rtehrr	kampsporter
meeting	uht trrehf-fuh	att träffa
(new) friends	(*nü*-uh) vehn-nehrr	(nya) vänner
movies	film	film
music	mu-*seek*	musik
photography	foo-too-grruh-*fea*-rring	fotografering
reading	uht *lair*-suh	att läsa
running	uht *sprring-uh/yog-guh*	att springa/jogga
sailing	uht *seag-luh*	att segla
shopping	uht *shop-puh*	att shoppa
skating	uht or-kuh *skrri*-sker	att åka skridskor
(downhill)	uht or-kuh	att åka
skiing	(*slah*-lom)/*fhee-der*	(slalom)/skidor
swimming	uht *sim-muh/ bah-duh*	att simma/bada
tennis	*tehn*-nis	tennis
travelling	uht *rrea-suh*	att resa
visiting friends	uht gor *hehm* til	att gå hem till
	kom-pi-suhrr	kompisar
walking	uht gor *üt* o *gor*	att gå ut och gå

SWEDISH

Festivals

Lucia is celebrated 13 December, which was the longest night in the old calendar. During the dark ages it was vital to make sure the evil forces of darkness didn't get a foothold, so people feasted with lots of food and bright lights. These days, Lucia, a young woman wearing a crown of candles, and her followers all dressed in white and carrying candles, sing traditional songs and serve golden saffron buns in the early morning hours.

On the first Sunday of Advent the first of four candles, one for every Sunday of Advent, is lit in every home. The big Christmas celebrations take place on julafton, the evening of 24 December. The tree, julgranen, is decorated with candles, tinsel, home-made crackers, hearts and a star on top and the Christmas table is laden with food.

On Christmas Day morning, the churches are lit with candles for the pre-dawn service, Julottan. In central Sweden you may see people arrive at church in a horse drawn sleigh. To wish someone a merry Christmas, you say God Jul!

In some cultures Lent (Fastan) is observed as a time of fasting, but not in Sweden! Instead the Swedes indulge in traditional Shrove Tuesday fare of delicious fastlagsbullar or semlor (sweet buns with almond paste and cream) after a meal of bruna bönor och fläsk (brown beans and pork). The home is decorated with fastlagsris, small birch or willow branches with coloured feathers tied to them.

Easter, Påsk, is in the beginning of spring – daffodils are called påskliljor (Easter lilies) in Swedish. Eggs are painted in delicate patterns before being served and some are blown empty and hung in the påskris, small birch branches decorated with fluffy chickens, eggs and feathers.

The påskkärringar, Easter hags, are said to fly off to Blåkulla (the Blue Hill) on Maundy Thursday to party with the devil and on påskafton, Easter Saturday, they return home. To prevent the witches landing in their community, people light bonfires and shoot firecrackers to scare them off. Children dress up as påskkärringar and go around with Easter letters to their neighbours calling out Glad Påsk!

On 30 April, Valborgsmässsoafton (Walpurgis Night), Sweden celebrates the coming of spring with predominantly male choirs singing traditional songs by huge bonfires.

Perhaps the most exotic of all Swedish festivals, Midsommar (Midsummer) is celebrated all over the country. The maypole, majstången, decorated with leaves and flowers, is erected in an open space. People who have a traditional costume wear it, and girls wear wreaths of flowers in their hair. Everyone dances around the maypole and sings traditional songs until late into the night that never really goes beyond dusk.

Throughout the year there are also many local cultural festivals and events all over Sweden. To mention but a few:

Jokkmokk Winter Market in Lapland since 1602. Meet the Same people and their reindeer at this unique cultural event.

Vasaloppet is 85 km of skiing from Sälen to Mora in Dalecarlia, following the tracks of King Gustav Vasa in the 1520s.

Himlaspelet in Leksand, Dalecarlia is an open air theatre performance in traditional costumes which has been on stage since 1941.

Stockholm Water Festival is a huge event with all sorts of activities including sports, music and fireworks.

Medieval Week, Visby, Gotland. The medieval city goes back to the 1300s with historical re-enactments, markets and a medieval banquet.

IN THE COUNTRY

Sweden offers unique possibilities for trekking, canoeing and camping as Allemansrätten 'Everyman's right' allows you to use all land, regardless of ownership, as long as you are careful and don't cause any damage or bother the owner. You can even pitch a tent for one night without permission, but for a caravan or a longer stay, ask the land owner first. And remember to clean up before you leave!

Weather

What's the weather like?

hürr air *vaird*-rreht?		*Hur är vädret?*

It's ...	deh air ...	*Det är ...*
cloudy	*mol-nit*	*molnigt*
cold	*kuhlt*	*kallt*
foggy	*dim-mit*	*dimmigt*
frosty	*frost ü*-teh	*frost ute*
warm	*vuhrrmt*	*varmt*

It's raining.	deh *rrehng-nuhrr*	*Det regnar.*
It's snowing.	deh *sner-uhrr*	*Det snöar.*
It's sunny.	*soo*-lehn *fhee*-nehrr	*Solen skiner.*
It's windy.	deh *blor*-sehrr	*Det blåser.*

Camping

Am I allowed to camp here?

for-rr yuh *kuhm*-puh *haer?*		*Får jag campa här?*

Is there a campsite nearby?

fins deh non *kuhm*-ping-*pluhts*		*Finns det någon campingplats*
ee *naer-hea*-tehn?		*i närheten?*

backpack	*rrüg-sehk*	*ryggsäck*
can opener	kon-*sehrrv-erp*-nuh-rreh	*konservöppnare*
compass	kom-*puhs*	*kompass*
crampons	*ees-brrod*-duhrr	*isbroddar*
firewood	vead	*ved*
gas cartridge	guh-*sorl-fluhs*-kuh	*gasolflaska*

gas cylinder	guh-*sol*-tüb	*gasoltub*
hammock	hehng-*muht*-tuh	*hängmatta*
ice axe	*ees-ük*-suh	*isyxa*
mattress	muh-*drruhs*	*madrass*
mosquito repellent	*müg*-ol-yuh	*myggolja*
padlock	hehng-*lors*	*hänglås*
penknife	*fik-kneev*	*fickkniv*
rope	rreap	*rep*
tent (pegs)	*tehlt(-pin*-nuhrr)	*tält(pinnar)*
torch/flashlight	*fik-luhm*-puh	*ficklampa*
sleeping bag	*sorv-sehk*	*sovsäck*
stove (for camping)	guh-*sorl-cherk*	*gasolkök*
water bottle	*vuht*-ehn-*fluhs*-kuh	*vattenflaska*

FOOD

The Swedish smörgåsbord is famous throughout the world for its great variety of cold and hot dishes, but there's more to Swedish food than that. Many dishes are associated with different seasons and may be difficult to find at other times.

SPRING

The first sign of spring is the semla, a sweet bun filled with almond paste and whipped cream, traditionally served on Tuesdays during Lent. Some prefer it in a bowl with hot milk and then it's called hetvägg. Following Lent is Easter with its tradition of brightly painted Easter eggs which are eaten with ham or fish dishes like gravad lax (cured salmon).

SUMMER

During summer the Swedes eat light food, with many cold meals like salads and smoked ham, lots of fish and for dessert a variety of berries (bär) with cream (grädde) or ice cream (glass).

During the Midsummer celebrations, inlagd sill (pickled herring) with sour cream and chives and new potatoes boiled with dill is a must and it's accompanied by a cold beer and a snaps (shot of akvavit) or two. Jordgubbar (strawberries) are most likely served as dessert. Ideally, this meal should be eaten outdoors.

AUTUMN

Towards the end of August the crayfish season is in full swing with kräftskivor (crayfish parties) all over the country. People wearing bibs and party hats, get together to eat kräftor (crayfish) boiled with dill, and drink quite a few glasses of snaps in between singing well-known drinking songs, snapsvisor.

If you're in the north, you might try their autumn specialty, surströmming (fermented herring), which tastes somewhat better than it smells. It's eaten with raw onion on tunnbröd (thin bread) or knäckebröd (crisp bread), and quite a few snapsar.

Autumn also sees an abundance of funghi, svamp, in the woods. Try kantareller, which should be available at markets and well-stocked grocery stores throughout the season.

More berries appear in autumn such as lingon (lingonberries) and the northern delicacy hjortron (cloudberries), and apples, pears and plums are ripe on the trees.

WINTER

The cold weather requires substantial meals. The traditional Thursday dinner is ärter med fläsk (yellow peasoup with pork) and for dessert pannkakor med lingonsylt (pancakes with lingonberry jam).

December 13 is Lucia when lussekatter (saffron-flavoured sweet buns), pepparkakor (ginger snaps) and glögg (mulled wine) are served by Lucia, and her followers.

At Christmas, a special smörgåsbord called julbord is the tradition. On the julbord you will find ham, different sorts of pickled herring, sausages, kalvsylta (brawn), patés, red cabbage, vörtbröd (rye bread flavoured with wort, a kind of herb) lutfisk (dried ling soaked in lye before being boiled), mustard, cheese, risgrynsgröt (sweet rice pudding) and more. A special Christmas beer, julöl, is served and the children get julmust, a sweet dark-brown soft drink which forms a head like beer when poured.

SWEDISH

Some Useful Words & Phrases

breakfast	*frroo*-kost	*frukost*
lunch	lunfh	*lunch*
dinner	*mid*-duh	*middag*
supper	su-*peal kvehls-morl*	*supé/kvällsmål*

Table for ..., please.
eht *boord* fer-rr ... tuhk   *Ett bord för ..., tack!*
Can I see the menu, please?
kuhn yuh for *sea* meh-*nün*?   *Kan jag få se menyn?*
What does it include?
vuh *in-gor-rr* i *dea*?   *Vad ingår i det?*
Is service included in the bill?
air sehrr-*vea*-rrings-ahv-*yif-tehm*   *Är serveringsavgiften*
in-rraek-nuhd?   *inräknad?*

ashtray	eht *uhsk-faht*	*ett askfat*
the bill	*noo-tuhn*	*notan*
a cup	ehn *kop*	*en kopp*
dessert	dehs-*saer*	*dessert*
a drink	nor-got uht *drrik-kuh*	*något att dricka*
a fork	ehn *guhf*-fehl	*en gaffel*
fresh	faeshk	*färsk*
a glass	eht *glahs*	*ett glas*
a knife	ehn *kneev*	*en kniv*
a plate	ehn *tuhl-rrik*	*en tallrik*
spicy	*vairl-krrüd*-duht	*välkryddat*
a spoon	ehn *fhead*	*en sked*
stale (bread)	tort	*torrt*
sweet	sert	*söt*
teaspoon	ehn *tea-fhead*	*en tesked*
toothpick	ehn *tuhnd-pea*-tuh-rreh	*en tandpetare*

Vegetarian Meals

I'm a vegetarian.
yuh air veh-geh-tuh-rri-ahn   *Jag är vegetarian.*
I don't eat meat.
yuh ae-tehrr in-teh chert   *Jag äter inte kött.*
I don't eat chicken, or fish, or ham.
yuh ae-tehrr vuhrr-kehn chük-ling   *Jag äter varken kyckling*
ehl-lehrr fisk ehl-lehrr fhing-kuh   *eller fisk eller skinka*

Spices, Herbs & Condiments

allspice	*krrüd-pehp-puhrr*	*kryddpeppar*
chives	*grraes-lerk*	*gräslök*
dill	dil	*dill*
garlic	*veet-lerk*	*vitlök*
herbs	*errt-krrü-der*	*örtkryddor*
mustard	*sea-nuhp*	*senap*
parsley	*pa-shil-yuh*	*persilja*
pepper	*pehp-puhrr*	*peppar*
salt	suhlt	*salt*
soy sauce	*soh-yuh*	*soja*
spices	*krrüd-der*	*kryddor*
sugar	*sok-kehrr*	*socker*
tomato sauce	*keht-chup*	*ketchup*
vinegar	*vi-nae-gehrr/*	*vinäger/*
	veen-eh-ti-kuh	*vinättika*

Vegetables

asparagus	*spuhrr-rris*	*sparris*
beans	*ber-ner; huh-rri-koo-vaer*	*bönor; haricot vert*
beetroot	*rrerd-beht-ter*	*rödbetor*
Brussels sprouts	*brrüs-sehl-korl*	*brysselkål*
cabbage	*veet-korl*	*vitkål*
capsicum	*puhp-rri-kuh*	*paprika*
carrot	*moo-rroot*	*morot*
cauliflower	*bloom-korl*	*blomkål*
cucumber	*gurr-kuh*	*gurka*
leek	*purr-yoo-lerk*	*purjolök*

lettuce	*suhl*-luhd	sallad
mushrooms	svuhmp/	svamp/
	fham-pin-*yoo*-nehrr	champinjoner
onion	lerk	lök
parsnip	*puhls*-tehrr-*nuhk*-kuh	palsternacka
peas	a-*rtehrr*	ärter
potato	poo-*tah*-tis	potatis
spinach	speh-*naht*	spenat
tomato	too-*maht*	tomat
turnip	korl-*rroot*	kålrot

Fruit & Berries

apple	*ehp-leh*	äpple
banana	buh-*nahm*	banan
blackberries	*bjer-rn*-baer	björnbär
black/ red currants	*svuh*-rtuh/	svarta/
	rrer-duh *veen*-baer	röda vinbär
blueberries	*blor*-baer	blåbär
cherries	*chersh*-baer/	körsbär/
	bi-guh-*rror*-ehrr	bigarråer
cloudberries	*yoort*-rron	hjortron
cranberries	*trrahn*-baer	tranbär
gooseberries	*krrüs*-baer	krusbär
grapefruit	*grreyp*-ffrukt	grapefrukt
grapes	*veen-drrü*-ver	vindruvor
lemon	sit-*rroon*	citron
lingonberries	*ling-on*	lingon
orange	uh-pehl-*seen*	apelsin
peach	pa-shi-*kuh*	persika
pear	*pae-rron*	päron
pineapple	*uh*-nuh-nuhs	ananas
plum	*ploo-mon*	plommon
raspberries	*huhl-lon*	hallon
rhubarb	rruh-*buhrr*-behrr	rabarber
strawberries	*yoord-gub*-buhrr	jordgubbar
wild strawberries	*smult*-rron	smultron

SWEDISH

Breakfast

bread	brrerd	bröd
bread roll	*smor-frruhns-kuh/ frru-kost-bul-leh*	*småfranska/ frukostbulle*
butter	smer-rr	smör
boiled egg	*kookt ehg*	*kokt ägg*
cereal	*fling-er/müs-li*	*flingor/müsli*
cheese	oost	ost
coffee	*kuh-feh*	*kaffe*
fried egg	*steakt ehg*	*stekt ägg*
jam/marmalade	*sült/muhrr-meh-lahd*	*sylt/marmelad*
milk	mjerlk	mjölk
orange juice	*uh-pehl-seen-yoos*	*apelsinjuice*
scrambled eggs	*oo-meh-leht*	*omelett*
sugar	*sok-kehrr*	*socker*
tea	tea	te
toast	*rros-tuht brrerd*	*rostat bröd*
yoghurt	*yorg-urt*	*yoghurt*

Soup

broth	bul-*yong*	*buljong*
chicken soup	*herns-sop-puh*	*hönssoppa*
fish soup	*fisk-sop-puh*	*fisksoppa*
mushroom soup	*svuhmp-sop-puh*	*svampsoppa*
vegetable soup	*grrern-sahks-sop*-puh	*grönsakssoppa*

Meat

beef	*nert-chert*	*nötkött*
casserole	*grrü-tuh*	*gryta*
chicken	*chük-ling*	*kyckling/broiler*
fillet of beef	*ooks-fi-lea*	*oxfilé*
ham	*fhing-kuh*	*skinka*
lamb chops	*luhm-kot-leht*-tehrr	*lammkotletter*
liver paté	*lea-vehrr-puhs-tehy*	*leverpastej*
meatballs	*chert-bul-luhrr*	*köttbullar*
minced beef	*chert-fash*	*köttfärs*
minced beef and pork	*bluhnd-fash*	*blandfärs*

pork (lean)	grrees-chert	griskött
pork (with fat)	flehsk	fläsk
pork chops	flehsk-kot-leht-tehrr	fläskkotletter
roast beef	ooks-steak/rrost-bif	oxstek/rostbiff
roast lamb	luhm-steak	lammstek
sausage/salami	ko-rrv/suh-lah-mi	korv/salami
spare ribs	rreav-beans-spyehl	revbensspjäll
steak	bif/uhn-trreh-kor	bifflentrecote
turkey	kuhl-koon	kalkon
veal	kuhlv-chert	kalvkött

Fish & Seafood

baltic herring	strrer-ming	strömming
caviar	rrüsk kuhv-yuhrr	rysk kaviar
cod (roe)	toshk(-rrom)	torsk(rom)
cod roe cream	kuhv-yuhrr	kaviar
crab	krruhb-buh	krabba
crayfish	krrehf-ter	kräftor
eel	orl	ål
fish	fisk	fisk
haddock	kol-yuh	kolja
halibut	hehl-leh-flund-rruh	hälleflundra/helgeflundra
herring	sil	sill
lobster	hum-mehrr	hummer
mackerel	muhk-rril	makrill
mussels	mus-ler	musslor
oysters	oost-rron	ostron
perch	uhb-bor-rreh	abborre
pike	yehd-duh	gädda
plaice	rrerd-speht-tuh	rödspätta
prawns	huhfs-krrehf-ter	havskräftor
salmon	luhks	lax
shrimps	rrair-ker	räkor
sole	fher-tung-uh	sjötunga
trout	fo-rrehl	forell
whiting	vit-ling	vitling

SWEDISH

Desserts & Pastries

apple pie	*ehp*-pehl-*puhy*	*äppelpaj*
cake (with cream)	*tor-rtuh*	*tårta*
cake (no cream)	*myük kah-kuh*	*mjuk kaka*
cheese cake	*oost-kah-*kuh	*ostkaka*
mousse	frroo-*mahsh*	*fromage*
custard	vuh-*nily-krrairm/*	*vaniljkräm/*
	muhy-*sea-nuh*	*maizena*
fruit salad	*frrukt-suhl*-luhd	*fruktsallad*
ginger snaps	*pehp*-puhrr-*kah*-ker	*pepparkakor*
ice cream	gluhs	*glass*
pancakes	*puhn-kah-*ker/	*pannkakor/*
	pleht-tuhrr	*plättar*
whipped cream	visp-*grrehd*-deh	*vispgrädde*

Non-Alcoholic Drinks

apple juice	*ehp*-pehl-*must*	*äppelmust*
coffee	*kuhf-feh*	*kaffe*
herbal tea	*errt-tea*	*örtte*
hot chocolate	*vuhrrm* fhook-*lahd*	*varm choklad*
milk	myerlk	*mjölk*
orange juice	uh-pehl-*seen-yoos*	*apelsinjuice*
punch	*frrukt-borl*	*fruktbål*
soft drink (carbonated)	lehsk	*läsk*
cordial	suhft	*saft*
tea	tea	*te*
water	*vuht-*tehn	*vatten*

Alcoholic Drinks

beer	erl/*pils*-nehrr	*öl/pilsner*
fortified wine	*stuhrrk-veen*	*starkvin*
liqueur	li-*ker-rr*	*likör*
red/white wine	*rrerd-veen*; vit veen	*rödvin; vitt vin*

MENU DECODER

Breakfast

filmjölk	*feel-myerlk*	cultured milk, similar to buttermilk, eaten with cereal and a sprinkle of sugar
gröt	*grrert*	porridge made of rolled oats
knäckebröd	*knehk-keh-brrerd*	crisp bread, usually rye
välling	*vehl-ling*	gruel (Try it, you'll like it!)

Breads and Sandwiches

tunnbröd   *tun-brrerd*
   very thin crisp or soft bread made from barley
vörtbröd   *verrt-brrerd*
   rye bread flavoured with wort (a kind of herb)

franskbröd	*frruhnsk-brrerd*	white French loaf
fullkornsbröd	*ful-koonsh-brrerd*	whole grain loaf
grahamsbulle	*grrah-huhms-bul-leh*	brown bread roll
kavring	*kahv-rring*	dark sweetened rye bread
limpa	*lim-puh*	loaf of bread
rågbröd	*rrorg-brrerd*	rye bread
sötlimpa	*sert-lim-puh*	sweetened brown loaf

Swedish sandwiches are always open and if they're very elaborate you eat them with a knife and fork. In winter you may be served grilled open sandwiches, varma smörgåsar, for an evening snack. You can make a smörgås with any sort of bread, a thin spread of butter and some pålägg (any kind of sandwich topping).

landgång	'gangplank' – long gourmet sandwich with a variety of pålägg
räksmörgås	shrimps on lettuce, hardboiled egg, mayonnaise and lemon
sillmörgås	pickled herring on cold boiled potato
smörgåstårta	a large layered sandwich with lots of different fillings, cut like a cake

SWEDISH

Soup

kålsoppa	*korl-sohp*-puh
med frikadeller	meh frri-kuh-*dehl*-lehrr

   cabbage soup with boiled meatballs (usually pork)

köttsoppa	*chert-sop*-puh

   beef broth with meat and vegetables

nässelsoppa	*neh*-sehl-*sop*-puh

   nettle soup with a hardboiled egg (spring only)

ärtsoppa	*art-sop*-puh

   yellow pea soup with pork

Meat

Meat is quite expensive in Sweden and the Swedes have come up with a host of different ways of making a little meat go a long way. Casseroles are common, as are dishes made with minced meat like köttbullar (Swedish meatballs), but perhaps the most famous Swedish meat product is the sausage, korv, which comes in all shapes and forms.

biff á la Lindström	bif uh-luh *lin-strrerm*

   patties of minced meat mixed with beetroot and served
   with a fried egg

blodpudding med lingon	*blood-pud*-ding meh *ling-on*

   black pudding with lingonberry jam

bruna bönor och fläsk	brrü-nuh *ber*-ner o *flehsk*

   brown beans in a sweet sauce with bacon

falukorv	*fah*-lu-*ko-rrv*

   a lean sausage cut in thick slices and fried

SWEDISH

isterband   *is*-tehrr-*buhnd*
  sausage of pork, beef and barley grains
kalops   kuh-*lops*
  meat casserole with onions and allspice
pannbiff med lök   *puhn-bif* meh *lerk*
  minced beef patties with lots of fried onion
pytt i panna   *püt*-i-*puhn-nuh*
  diced meat, boiled potatoes and onion fried and served with
  beetroot and a fried egg
rotmos och fläskkorv   *rroot-moos* o *flehsk-ko-rrv*
  boiled pork sausage with mashed turnips
varm korv   *vuhrrm ko-rrv*
  hot dog on a breadroll, the special comes with mashed
  potatoes – Swedish fast food!
viltgryta   *vilt-grrü*-tuh
  game casserole – try älg, elk, in October

kåldolmar	*korl-dol*-muhrr	stuffed cabbage leaves
lövbiff	*lerv-bif*	very thinly sliced beef
renskav	*rrean-skahv*	thinly sliced reindeer meat

Fish & Seafood

Sweden has an enormous coastline and thousands of lakes and fish is an important part of the diet. Kräftor (crayfish) are caught in creeks and lakes from late August and many other types of seafood are brought ashore all year round.

inlagd sill   *in*-luhgd *sil*
  pickled herring which comes in a great number of varieties
lutfisk   *lüt-fisk*
  dried ling soaked in lye before being boiled. Served with a
  white sauce with allspice. (Christmas only)
sotare   *soo-tuh-rreh*
  'chimney sweep' – lightly salted herring grilled over an open fire

böckling	*berk-ling*	smoked herring
gravad lax	*grrah*-vuhd *luhks*	cured salmon

Potatoes

Swedes eat potatoes with just about everything and there's a great number of ways to prepare them for the table.

Janssons frestelse   *yahn*-sons *frrehs*-tehl-*seh*
  'Jansson's Temptation' – potato, onion and anchovy, oven-baked with lots of cream
raggmunkar/rårakor   *rruhg*-mung-kuhrr/*rror-rrah*-ker
  pancakes made from grated potatoes
råstekt potatis   *rror-steakt* poo-*tah*-tis
  raw potato slices fried in oil
skalpotatis   *skahl*-poo-*tah*-tis
  potatoes boiled in their jackets
stekt potatis   *steakt* poo-*tah*-tis
  fried pre-boiled potatoes
stuvad potatis   *stü*-vuhd poo-*tah*-tis
  potatoes in white sauce

potatismos	poo-*tah*-tis-*moos*	mashed potatoes
potatissallad	poo-*tah*-tis-*suhl*-luhd	potato salad
färskpotatis	*fashk*-poo-*tah*-tis	new potatoes

Desserts & Pastries

chokladpudding   fhook-*lahd-pud*-ding
  chocolate mousse
kanelbulle   kuh-*neal-bul*-leh
  sweet roll with cinnamon and cardamon
kräm och mjölk   krrairm-o-*myerlk*
  thickened berry juice with milk
mazarin   muh-suh-*rreen*
  pastry with almond paste filling

SWEDISH

nyponsoppa   *nü*-pon-*sop*-puh
   rose hip soup, eaten with a dollop of cream
prinsesstårta   prrin-*sehs*-*tor*-rtuh
   layered sponge cake with jam, cream and custard filling
   covered with green marzipan
ris á la malta   *rees* uh-luh *muhl*-*tuh*
   rice with whipped cream and orange
schwartzwaldstårta   *shvuhrtsh*-vuhlds-*tor*-rtuh
   meringue, cream and chocolate cake
småländsk ostkaka   *smor*-lehnsk *oost*-*kah*-kuh
   baked curd cake with almonds
sockerkaka   *sok*-kehrr-*kah*-kuh
   sponge cake, usually flavoured with lemon

skorpor	*skohrr*-per	rusks
småkakor	*smor*-*kah*-ker	biscuits/cookies
wienerbröd	*vee*-nehrr-*brrerd*	Danish pastries

Alcoholic Drinks

Alcohol can only be purchased by those over 20 at special shops called Systembolaget. If a Swede asks you if you would like 'a drink', they probably have alcohol in mind as the word drink in Swedish denotes an alcoholic drink, usually a cocktail.

brännvin   *brrehn*-*veen*
   spirit distilled from potatoes, may be flavoured with herbs
   and berries or plain
glögg   glerg
   mulled wine with raisins and almonds, served in winter
punsch   punfh
   a sweet liqueur flavoured with arrack
snaps   snuhps
   a shot of *brännvin*. With the word Skål! a shot glass is
   emptied in one go.
vinbål   *veen*-*borl*
   a punch based on wine

SWEDISH

SHOPPING

bookshop	*book-huhn-dehl*	*bokhandel*
camera shop	*foo-too-uh-faer*	*fotoaffär*
clothing store	*moo-deh-bu-teek*	*modebutik*
delicatessen	deh-li-kuh-*tehs*-uh-faer	*delikatessaffär*
general store	di-*veh*-sheh-*huhn*-dehl	*diversehandel*
laundry/laundrette	tveht/tveh-too-*maht*	*tvätt/tvättomat*
market (indoor)	*sah*-lu-*huhl*	*saluhall*
market (outdoor)	to-rry-*huhn*-dehl	*torghandel*
newsagency	*prrehs*-bü-rro/	*pressbyrå/*
	too-buhks-uh-faer	*tobaksaffär*
pharmacy	uh-poo-*teak*	*apotek*
shoeshop	*skoo*-uh-faer	*skoaffär*
shop	uh-*faer*	*affär*
souvenir shop	soo-veh-*neer*-uh-faer	*souveniraffär*
stationers	*puhp*-pehsh-*huhn*-dehl	*pappershandel*
supermarket	*snuhb*-cherp	*snabbköp*
vegetable shop	*grrern*-sahks-uh-*faer*	*grönsaksaffär*

I'd like to buy ...
  yuh *sku*-leh vil-yuh *hah* ...   *Jag skulle vilja ha ...*
Do you have others?
  hahrr ni nor-rruh *uhn*-drruh?   *Har ni några andra andra?*
I (don't) like it.
  yuh tük-*kehrr* (*in*-teh)   *Jag tycker (inte)*
  om dehn/deh   *om den/det.*
I'm just looking.
  yuh *tit*-tuhrr *bah*-rruh   *Jag tittar bara.*
How much is it?
  hurr *mük*-keh *kos*-tuhrr deh?   *Hur mycket kostar det?*
Can you write down the price?
  kuhn doo skrree-vuh   *Kan du skriva*
  nearr prree-seht?   *ner priset?*
Do you accept credit cards?
  tahrr ni krreh-*deet*-koort?   *Tar ni kreditkort?*
Could you lower the price?
  kuhn du gor *nearr* i *prrees*?   *Kan du gå ner i pris?*

Can I help you?
kuhn yuh *yehl*-puh *day*? *Kan jag hjälpa dig?*
Will that be all?
vahrr deh *uhlt*? *Var det allt?*
Sorry, this is the only one.
tü-*varr* deh *haer* air *Tyvärr, det här är*
dehn *ehn-duh* *den enda.*
How much/many do you want?
hurr *mük*-keh/ *Hur mycket/*
mong-uh vil du *hah*? *många vill du ha?*

Essential Groceries

batteries	buh-teh-rree-ehrr	batterier
bread	brrerd	bröd
butter	smer-rr	smör
cheese	oost	ost
chocolate	fhook-*lahd*	choklad
cooking oil	*maht-ol*-yuh	matolja
dishwashing liquid	*disk-mea*-dehl	diskmedel
eggs	ehg	ägg
flour (plain)	*vea*-teh-*myerl*	vetemjöl
ham	*fhing-kuh*	skinka
honey	*hor-nung*	honung
marmalade	muhrr-meh-*lahd*	marmelad
matches	*tehnd-stik*-korr	tändstickor
milk	myerlk	mjölk
pepper	*pehp-puhrr*	peppar
rice	rrees	ris
salt	suhlt	salt
shampoo	*fham*-poo	schampo
soap	tvorl	tvål
sugar	*sok*-kehrr	socker
toilet paper	too-uh-*leht-puhp*-pehrr	toalettpapper
toothpaste	*tuhn-krrairm*	tandkräm
washing powder	*tveht-mea*-dehl	tvättmedel

SWEDISH

SWEDISH

AT THE MARKET

Basics

bread	brrerd	bröd
butter	smer-rr	smör
cereal	*fling-er/müs*-li	flingor/müsli
cheese	oost	ost
chocolate	fhook-*lahd*	choklad
cooking oil	*maht-ol*-yuh	matolja
eggs	ehg	ägg
flour (plain)	*vea*-teh-*myerl*	vetemjöl
marmalade	muhrr-meh-*lahd*	marmelad
milk	myerlk	mjölk
pasta	*pahs-tah/ nood-lahr*	pasta/nudlar
rice	rrees	ris
sugar	*sok*-kehrr	socker
water	*vuht*-tehn	vatten
yoghurt	*yorg*-urt	yoghurt

Meat & Poultry

beef	*nert-chert*	nötkött
chicken	*chük-ling*	kyckling/broiler
ham	*fhing-kuh*	skinka
lamb	luhm	lamm
meat	chert	kött
pork	*grees-chert/*	griskött (lean)/
(with fat)	*flehsk*	fläsk
sausage/salami	ko-rrv/suh-*lah*-mi	korv/salami
turkey	kuhl-*koon*	kalkon
veal	*kuhlv-chert*	kalvkött

Vegetables

beans	*ber-ner*; huh-rri-koo-*vaer*	bönor; haricot vert
beetroot	rrerd-*beht*-ter	rödbetor
cabbage	*veet-korl*	vitkål
capsicum	*puhp*-rri-*kuh*	paprika

carrot	moo-rroot	morot
cauliflower	bloom-korl	blomkål
cucumber	gurr-kuh	gurka
lettuce	suhl-luhd	sallad
mushrooms	svuhmp/ fham-pin-yoo-nehrr	svamp/ champinjoner
onion	lerk	lök
peas	a-rtehrr	ärter
potato	poo-tah-tis	potatis
spinach	speh-naht	spenat
tomato	too-maht	tomat
vegetables	grrern-sahk-ehrr	grönsaker

Seafood

cod	toshk	torsk
crayfish	krrehf-ter	kräftor
fish	fisk	fisk
herring	sil	sill
lobster	hum-mehrr	hummer
mussels	mus-ler	musslor
oysters	oost-rron	ostron
salmon	luhks	lax

Fruit

apple	ehp-leh	äpple
banana	buh-nahn	banan
fruit	frrukt	frukt
grapes	veen-drrü-ver	vindruvor
lemon	sit-rroon	citron
orange	uh-pehl-seen	apelsin
peach	pa-shi-kuh	persika
pear	pae-rron	päron
plum	ploo-mon	plommon
strawberries	yoord-gub-buhrr	jordgubbar

SWEDISH

Souvenirs

earrings	*er-rr-hehng-ehn*	*örhängen*
glassware	glahs	*glas*
handicraft	*hehm-sleyd*	*hemslöjd*
necklace	*huhls-buhnd*	*halsband*
pottery	cheh-ruh-*meek*	*keramik*
ring	*rring*	*ring*

Clothing

bathers	*bahd-drrehkt/*	*baddräkt/*
	*bahd-bük-*sorr	*badbyxor* (f/m)
clothing	*klae-*dehrr	*kläder*
coat	*kuhp-puh/*rrok	*kappa/rock* (f/m)
dress	*klehm-*ning	*klänning*
jacket	*yak-kuh*	*jacka*
jumper (sweater)	*trrer-yuh*	*tröja*
shirt	*fhoo-rtuh*	*skjorta*
shoes	skoorr	*skor*
skirt	chool	*kjol*
trousers/pants	*bük-ser*	*byxor*

It doesn't fit.
  dehn *puhs-uhrr in-*teh   *Den passar inte.*

It's too ...	dehn air fer-rr ...	*Den är för ...*
big/small	*stoorr/lee-tehn*	*stor/liten*
long/short	*long/kort*	*lång/kort*
loose/tight	*veed/trrong*	*vid/trång*

Materials

brass	*mehs-sing*	*mässing*
cotton	*boom-ul*	*bomull*
fabric	tüg	*tyg*
flax	leen	*lin*
gold	guld	*guld*
handmade	*huhnd-yoord*	*handgjord*
hand woven	*hehm-vairvd*	*hemvävd*

leather	*lair*-dehrr	*läder*
linen	*lin-neh*	*linne*
silk	*sil-keh/see-dehn*	*silke/siden*
silver	*sil*-vehrr	*silver*
wood	trrair	*trä*
wool	*ül-leh*	*ylle*

Colours

black	svuhrt	*svart*
blue	blor	*blå*
brown	brrün	*brun*
green	grrern	*grön*
orange	o-*rruhnsh*	*orange*
pink	*rror*-suh/fhaer	*rosa/skär*
purple	*lee*-luh	*lila*
red	rrerd	*röd*
white	veet	*vit*
yellow	gül	*gul*

Toiletries

comb	kuhm	*kam*
condoms	kon-*dor*-mehrr	*kondomer*
deodorant	dea-oo-doo-*rruhnt*	*deodorant*
hairbrush	*hor-rr-bosh*-teh	*hårborste*
moisturising cream	*hüd-krrairm*	*hudkräm*
mosquito repellent	*müg-ohl*-yuh	*myggolja*
razor	*rrahk-hü*-vehl	*rakhyvel*
razor blades	*rrahk-blahd*	*rakblad*
sanitary napkins	*dahm-bin*-der	*dambindor*
shampoo	*fham*-poo	*schampo*
shaving cream	*rrahk-tvorl*	*raktvål*
soap	tvorl	*tvål*
sunblock cream	*sool-krrairm*	*solkräm*
tampons	tuhm-*pong*-ehrr	*tamponger*
tissues	*nairs-dü*-kuhrr	*näsdukar*
toilet paper	too-uh-*leht-puh*-pehrr	*toalettpapper*
toothbrush	*tuhn-bosh*-teh	*tandborste*

Stationery & Publications

envelope	ku-*vaer*	*kuvert*
map	*kah-rtuh*	*karta*
newspaper (in English)	(*ehng*-ehlsk) *tee*-ning	(*engelsk*) *tidning*
novels in English	*ber*-kehrr po *ehng*-ehls-kuh	*böcker på engelska*
paper	*puh-pehrr*	*papper*
pen	*pehn-nuh*	*penna*
scissors	suhks	*sax*

Photography

How much is it to process this film?
hurr mük-eht *kost*-uhrr deh uht *ffruhm*-kuhl-luh dehn *haer fil*-mehn?
Hur mycket kostar det att framkalla den här filmen?

When will it be ready?
naer air dehn *klahrr*?
När är den klar?

I'd like a film for this camera.
yuh skool-leh vil-yuh *hah* ehn *film* til dehn *haer kahm*-rruhn.
Jag skulle vilja ha en film till den här kameran.

B&W (film)	*svuhrt-veet film*	*svart-vit film*
battery	buh-teh-*rree*	*batteri*
camera	*kahm*-rruh	*kamera*
colour (film)	*farry-film*	*färgfilm*
copy	ko-*pee-uh*	*kopia*
film	film	*film*
flash	blikst	*blixt*
lens	ob-yehk-*teev*	*objektiv*
light meter	*yüs-mair*-tuh-rreh	*ljusmätare*

SWEDISH

Smoking

A packet of cigarettes, please.
    eht puh-*keat*   *Ett paket*
    si-guh-*rreht*-tehrr *tuhk*   *cigarretter, tack.*

Are these cigarettes strong/mild?
    air dom *haer*   *Är de här*
    si-guh-*rreht*-tehrr-nuh   *cigarretterna*
    stuhrr-kuh/*mil-duh?*   *starka/milda?*

Do you have a light?
    hahrr du *ehld?*   *Har du eld?*

May I smoke here?
    for-rr yuh *rrer*-kuh *haer?*   *Får jag röka här?*

cigarette papers	si-guh-*rreht*-puhp-pehrr	*cigarrettpapper*
cigarettes	si-guh-*rreht*-tehrr	*cigarretter*
filtered	*fil*-tehrr	*filter*
lighter	*tehn*-duh-*rreh*	*tändare*
matches	*tehnd-stik*-korr	*tändstickor*
menthol	mehn-*torl*	*mentol*
pipe	pee-*puh*	*pipa*
tobacco (pipe)	(*peep*-)*too*-buhk	(*pip*)*tobak*

Sizes & Comparisons

small	lee-*tehn*	*liten*
big	stoorr	*stor*
heavy	tung	*tung*
just right	*lah*-gom	*lagom*
light (not heavy)	leht	*lätt*
more	mearr	*mer*
less	*min*-drreh	*mindre*
too much/many	fer-rr *mük*-keh/ *mong*-uh	*för mycket/ många*
many	*mong*-uh	*många*
enough	*til-rrehk*-lit	*tillräckligt*
also	*ok*-so	*också*
a little bit	lee-teh *grruhn*	*lite grand*

HEALTH

Where is the ...?	vahrr air ...?	Var är ...?
chemist	uh-poo-*tea*-keht	*apoteket*
dentist	*tuhnd-lair*-kuh-rrehn	*tandläkaren*
doctor	*dok*-to-rn	*doktorn*
hospital	*fhük-hü*-seht	*sjukhuset*

I'm/My friend is sick.
    yuh air/min *vehn* air *fhük*   *Jag är/Min vän är sjuk.*

Could I see a female doctor?
    kuhn yuh for *trrehf*-fuh   *Kan jag få träffa*
    ehn *kvin*-li *lair*-kuh-rreh?   *en kvinnlig läkare?*

What's the matter?
    vuh air deh fer-rr *feal* po *day*?   *Vad är det för fel på dig?*

Where does it hurt?
    vahrr yer-rr deh *oont*?   *Var gör det ont?*

I have ...	yuh hahrr ...	*Jag har ...*
It hurts here.	deht yer-rr *oont haer*	*Det gör ont här.*

Parts of the Body

ankle	*vrris*-tehn	*vristen*
arm	*uhrr*-men	*armen*
back	*rrüg*-gehn	*ryggen*
chest	*brrerst*-eht	*bröstet*
ear	*er-rruht*	*örat*
eye	*er-guht*	*ögat*
finger	*fing*-rreht	*fingret*
foot	*foo*-tehn	*foten*
hand	*huhn*-dehn	*handen*
head	*hü-veht*	*huvudet*
heart	*yarr-tuht*	*hjärtat*
leg	*bea*-neht	*benet*
mouth	*mun*-nehn	*munnen*
nose	*nair-suhm*	*näsan*
ribs	*rreav-bea*-nehn	*revbenen*
skin	*hü*-dehn	*huden*

SWEDISH

spine	*rrüg-rrah*-dehn	*ryggraden*
stomach	*mah-gehn*	*magen*
teeth	*tehn*-dehrr-nuh	*tänderna*
throat	*huhl*-sehn	*halsen*
wrist	*huhnd-lea*-dehn	*handleden*

Ailments

an allergy	ehn uh-lehrr-*gee*	*en allergi*
anaemia	*blood-brrist*	*blodbrist*
a blister	ehn *blor-suh*	*en blåsa*
a burn	eht *brrehn-sor-rr*	*ett brännsår*
a cold	ehn fer-*chül*-ning	*en förkylning*
constipation	fer-*shtop*-ning	*förstoppning*
a cough	*hoos-tuh*	*hosta*
diarrhoea	dee-uh-*rrea*	*diarré*
fever	*fea*-behrr	*feber*
glandular fever	*ker*-rtehl-*fea*-behrr	*körtelfeber*
headache	*hü*-vud-*varrk*	*huvudvärk*
hepatitis	heh-puh-*teet/gül-soot*	*hepatit/gulsot*
indigestion	*dor-li*	*dålig*
	maht-smehlt-ning	*matsmältning*
an infection	ehn in-fehk-*fhoon*	*en infektion*
influenza	in-flu-*ehn*-suh	*influensa*
lice	lers	*löss*
low/high	*lorgt/hergt*	*lågt/högt*
blood pressure	*blood-trrük*	*blodtryck*
motion sickness	*ork-fhü*-kuh	*åksjuka*
a pain	oont	*ont*
sore throat	oont i *huhl*-sehn	*ont i halsen*
sprain	*stük*-ning	*stukning*
a stomachache	oont i *mah*-gehn	*ont i magen*
sunburn	*sool-brrehn*-nuh	*solbränna*
urinary tract infection	*blors*-kuh-*tuhrr*	*blåskatarr*
venereal disease	*cherns*-fhük -*doom*	*könssjukdom*
worms	*muhsk* i *mah*-gehn	*mask i magen*

Some Useful Words & Phrases

I'm ...	yuh air ...	*Jag är ...*
asthmatic	uhst-*mah*-ti-kehrr	*astmatiker*
diabetic	dee-uh-*bea*-ti-kehrr	*diabetiker*
epileptic	eh-pi-*lehp*-ti-kehrr	*epileptiker*

I'm allergic to antibiotics/penicillin.
　yuh air uh-*lehrr*-gisk moot 　　*Jag är allergisk mot*
　uhn-ti-bi-*or*-ti-kuh/pehn-i-si-*leen* 　*antibiotika/penicillin.*
I'm pregnant.
　yuh air grruh-*veed* 　　*Jag är gravid.*
I'm on the pill.
　yuh air-tehrr *pea-pil*-lehrr 　　*Jag äter p-piller.*
I haven't had my period for ... months.
　yuh hahrr *in*-teh huhft 　　*Jag har inte haft*
　mehns por ... mor-nuh-dehrr 　*mens på ... månader.*
I have been vaccinated.
　yuh air vuhk-si-*nea*-rruhd 　*Jag är vaccinerad.*
I have my own syringe.
　yuh hahrr min *ea*-gehn 　　*Jag har min egen*
　sprrü-tuh 　　*spruta.*
I feel better/worse.
　yuh mor-rr *beht*-rreh/*sehm*-rreh 　*Jag mår bättre/sämre.*

accident	*oo-lük*-kuh	*olycka*
addiction	*mis-brrük*	*missbruk*
antiseptic	uhn-ti-*sehp*-tisk	*antiseptisk*
aspirin	mang-neh-*sül*	*magnecyl*
bandage	fer-rr-*buhnd*	*förband*
band-aid	*plos*-tehrr	*plåster*
a bite	eht *beht*	*ett bett*
blood pressure	blood-*trrük*	*blodtryck*
blood test	blood-*prroov*	*blodprov*
contraceptive	prreh-vehn-*teev-mea*-dehl	*preventivmedel*
injection	*sprrü*-tuh	*spruta*
injury	*skah*-duh	*skada*
itch	*klor*-duh	*klåda*

medicine	meh-di-*seen*	*medicin*
menstruation	mehns	*mens*
nausea	il-luh-*mor*-ehn-deh	*illamående*
oxygen	*sü*-rreh	*syre*
panadol	puh-noo-*deel*	*panodil*
vitamins	vi-tuh-*mee*-nehrr	*vitaminer*
wound	sor-rr	*sår*

At the Chemist

I need medication for ...
  yuh beh-*her*-vehrr eht
  mea-dehl moot ...

*Jag behöver ett
medel mot ...*

I have a prescription.
  yuh *hahrr* eht rreh-*sehpt*

Jag har ett recept.

At the Dentist

I have a toothache.
  yuh hahrr *tuhnd-varrk*

Jag har tandvärk.

I've lost a filling.
  yuh hahrr *tuhp*-puht
  ehn *plomb*

*Jag har tappat
en plomb.*

I've broken a tooth.
  yuh hahrr slah-git *ahv*
  ehn *tuhnd*

*Jag har slagit av
en tand.*

My gums hurt.
  yuh hahrr *oont* i
  tuhnd-cher-teht

*Jag har ont i
tandköttet.*

I don't want it extracted.
  yuh vil *in*-teh hah dehn
  üt-drrah-gehn

*Jag vill inte ha den
utdragen.*

Please give me an anaesthetic.
  yuh vil hah be-*derv*-ning

Jag vill ha bedövning.

SWEDISH

TIME & DATES

What date is it today?

vil-keht *dah*-tum air deh i-*dah?*		*Vilket datum är det idag?*

What time is it?

hürr *mük*-keh air *klok*-kuhn?		*Hur mycket är klockan?*

It's ...	hun air ...	*Hon är ...*
in the morning (early)	por *mo*-rro-*nehn*	*på morgonen*
in the morning (later on)	por *fer*-rr-*mid*-duhn	*på förmiddagen*
in the afternoon	por *ehf*-tehrr-*mid*-duhn	*på eftermiddagen*
in the evening	por *kvehl*-lehn	*på kvällen*
at night	por *nuht*-tehn	*på natten*

Days of the Week

Monday	*mon*-duh	*måndag*
Tuesday	*tees*-duh	*tisdag*
Wednesday	*oons*-duh	*onsdag*
Thursday	*toosh*-rduh	*torsdag*
Friday	*frrea*-duh	*fredag*
Saturday	*ler*-rduh	*lördag*
Sunday	*sern*-duh	*söndag*

Months

January	yuh-nu-*ah*-rri	*januari*
February	feb-rru-*ah*-rri	*februari*
March	muhsh	*mars*
April	uhp-*rril*	*april*
May	muhy	*maj*
June	*yü*-ni	*juni*
July	*yü*-li	*juli*
August	uh-*gus*-ti	*augusti*
September	sehp-*tehm*-behrr	*september*
October	ok-*too*-behrr	*oktober*
November	noo-*vehm*-behrr	*november*
December	deh-*sehm*-behrr	*december*

Seasons

summer	*som-muhrr*	*sommar*
autumn	herst	*höst*
winter	*vin*-tehrr	*vinter*
spring	vor-rr	*vår*

Present

today	i-*dah*	*idag*
this morning	i-*dah* po mo-rro-*nehn*	*idag på morgonen*
tonight (evening)	i-*kvehl*	*i kväll*
tonight (very late)	i-*nuht*	*i natt*
this week	dehn *haer* vehk-kuhn	*den här veckan*
this year	i *or-rr*	*i år*
now	nü	*nu*

Past

yesterday	i-*gor-rr*	*igår*
day before yesterday	i-*fer*-rr-*gor*-rr	*i förrgår*
this morning	i-*mo-sheh*	*i morse*
yesterday morning	i-gor-rr *mosh-eh*	*igår morse*
last night	i-gor-rr kvehl	*igår kväll*
last week	i fer-rruh *vehk*-kuhn	*förra veckan*
last year	fer-rruh *or*-rreht	*förra året*

Future

tomorrow (morning)	i-*mo-rron* (bit-ti)	*i morgon (bitti)*
day after tomorrow	i *er*-vehrr-*mo*-rron	*i övermorgon*
tomorrow	i mo-rron	*i morgon*
afternoon/	*ehf*-tehrr-*mid*-duh/	*eftermiddag/*
evening	kvehl	*kväll*
next week/year	*nehs*-tuh veh-kuh/or-rr	*nästa vecka/år*

SWEDISH

WHAT TIME IS IT?

Swedes often use the 24-hour system for telling the time.

During the Day

afternoon	*ehf-tehrr-mid-duh*	*eftermiddag*
dawn	*grrü-ning*	*gryning*
day	*dahg*	*dag*
dusk	*fhüm-ning*	*skymning*
early	*tee-dit*	*tidigt*
evening	kvehl	*kväll*
late	seant	*sent*
late morning	*fer-rr-mid-duh*	*förmiddag*
midnight	*meed-nuht*	*midnatt*
morning	*mo-rron*	*morgon*
night	nuht	*natt*
noon	*mit po dahn;*	*mitt på dagen;*
	klo-kuhn *tolv*	*klockan tolv*

NUMBERS & AMOUNTS

0	nol	*noll*
1	eht	*ett*
2	tvor	*två*
3	trrea	*tre*
4	*fü-rruh*	*fyra*
5	fehm	*fem*
6	sehx	*sex*
7	fhü	*sju*
8	*ot-tuh*	*åtta*
9	*nee-oo*	*nio*
10	*tee-oo*	*tio*
11	*ehl-vuh*	*elva*
12	tolv	*tolv*
13	*trreh-ton*	*tretton*
14	*fyoo-rton*	*fjorton*
15	*fehm-ton*	*femton*
16	*sehx-ton*	*sexton*
17	*fhu-ton*	*sjutton*
18	*ah-rton*	*arton*
19	*ni-ton*	*nitton*

SWEDISH

20	*chü*-goo	tjugo
21	chü-goo-*eht*	tjugoett
30	*trreh*-ti	trettio
40	*fer*-rti	fyrtio
50	*fehm*-ti	femtio
60	*sehx*-ti	sextio
70	*fhu*-ti	sjuttio
80	*ot*-ti	åttio
90	*ni*-ti	nittio
100	eht *hun*-drruh	ett hundra
101	hun-drruh-*eht*	hundraett
1000	eht *tü*-sehn	ett tusen
one million	ehn mil-*yoon*	en miljon
one billion	ehn mil-*yahrd*	en miljard

1st	*fersh*-rtuh	första
2nd	*uhnd*-rruh	andra
3rd	*trread*-yeh	tredje

1/4	ehn *fyae*-rdeh-*deal*/ehn *kvartsh*	en fjärdedel/en kvarts
1/3	ehn *trrea*-dyeh-*deal*	en tredjedel
1/2	ehn *huhlv*	en halv
3/4	*trrea fyae*-rdeh-*dea*-luhrr/	tre fjärdedelar/
	trrea kvartsh	tre kvarts

Some Useful Words

| Enough! | deh *rrehk*-kehrr! | Det räcker! |

a little (amount)	lee-teh *grruhn*	lite grand
double	*dub*-behl	dubbel
a dozen	eht *dus*-sin	ett dussin
few	nor-grruh *for*	några få
just right	*lah*-gom	lagom
less	*min*-drreh	mindre
many	*mong*-uh	många
more	*mea*-rruh	mera
once	*ehn gong*	en gång
a pair	eht *pahrr*	ett par

SWEDISH

percent	**prroo-*sehnt***	*procent*
some	*nor-grruh*	*några*
too much	**fer-rr** *mük-keh*	*för mycket*
twice	*tvor gong-ehrr*	*två gånger*

ABBREVIATIONS

AB	limited corporation
avd	department
dl	decilitre (100 ml)
e Kr/f Kr	AD/BC
EU	European Union
exkl	excluded
FN	United Nations
fr o m	from and including
Gbg	Göteborg (Gothenburg)
hg	hecto (100 grams)
Hr/Fr/Frk	Mr/Mrs/Miss
inkl	included
jvgstn	railway station
kg	kilogram
kl	at (about time)
km	kilometre
kr	kronor (Swedish currency)
M	Motorists' National Organisation
moms	VAT/GST – sales tax
N/S/Ö/V	north/south/east/west
Obs!	Important
osv	and so on
Rea	Sale
SAS	Scandinavian Airlines System
SJ	Swedish railways
STF	Swedish Tourism Organisation
Sthlm	Stockholm
T-bana	underground, metro
t o m	until and including
tr	stairs (in an address)

SWEDISH

EMERGENCIES

English	Pronunciation	Swedish
Help!	*yehlp!*	*Hjälp!*
Fire!	*ehl-dehn air lers!*	*Elden är lös!*
Thief!	tuh *fuhst chü-vehn!*	*Ta fast tjuven!*
Call the police!	rring poo-*lee*-sehn!	*Ring polisen!*
I'm lost.	yuh hahrr got *vil-seh*	*Jag har gått vilse.*

It's an emergency!
  deh air ehn
  nerd-si-tu-uh-*fhoon!*

*Det är ett
nödsituation!*

There's been an accident!
  deh hahrr *hehnt* ehn *oo-lük*-kuh!

Det har hänt en olycka!

Call a doctor/an ambulance!
  rring ehf-tehrr ehn *dok*-to-rr/
  ehn uhm-boo-*luhns!*

*Ring efter en doktor/
en ambulans!*

I've been raped.
  yuh hahrr blee-vit *vold-tah*-gehn

Jag har blivit våldtagen.

I've been robbed!
  yuh hahrr blee-vit *rror-nuhd!*

Jag har blivit rånad!

Where is the police station?
  vahrr air poo-*lees*-stuh-*fhoo*-nehn?

Var är polisstationen?

Go away!
  fer-*shvin!*; gor din *vairg!*

Försvinn!; *Gå din väg!*

I'll call the police!
  yuh *kuhl*-luhrr po poo-*lees!*

Jag kallar på polis!

I'm/My friend is ill.
  yuh air/min *vehn* air *fhook*

Jag är/Min vän är sjuk.

Where are the toilets?
  vahrr air too-uh-*leht*-tehn?

Var är toaletten?

Could you help me please?
  kuhn du *yehl*-puh *may?*

Kan du hjälpa mig?

Could I please use the telephone?
  kuhn yuh for *lor*-nuh
  teh-leh-*for*-nehn?

*Kan jag få låna
telefonen?*

I'm sorry. I apologise.
  fer-*lort.* yuh bearr om *ü-shehkt*

Förlåt. Jag ber om ursäkt.

I didn't realise I was doing
anything wrong.

 yuh fer-*shtood* in-teh uht   *Jag förstod inte att*
 yuh yoo-rdeh *feal*   *jag gjorde fel.*

I didn't do it.

 yuh *yoo*-rdeh deh *in-teh*   *Jag gjorde det inte.*

I wish to contact my embassy/
consulate.

 yuh vil kon-*tuhk*-tuh min   *Jag vill kontakta min*
 uhm-buh-*sahdl*mit kon-su-*laht* *ambassad/mitt konsulat.*

I speak English.

 yuh tah-luhrr *ehng*-ehl-skuh   *Jag talar engelska.*

I have medical insurance.

 yuh hahrr *fhük*-fer-*shairk*-rring *Jag har sjukförsäkring.*

My possessions are insured.

 yuh hahrr fer-*shairk*-rring   *Jag har försäkring.*

My ...	min ... hahrr	*Min ... har*
was stolen.	blee-vit *stü-lehn*	*blivit stulen.*
I've lost my ...	yuh hahrr fer-*loo*-rruht ...	*Jag har förlorat ...*
bags	mee-nuh *vehs-korr*	*mina väskor*
handbag	min *huhnd-vehs-*kuh	*min handväska*
money	mee-nuh *pehng*-uhrr	*mina pengar*
travellers	mee-nuh	*mina*
cheques	rrea-seh-*chehk*-kuhrr	*resecheckar*
passport	mit *puhs*	*mitt pass*

INDEX

ICELANDIC 197

SWEDISH 307

I
N
D
E
X

379

don't just stand there, say something!

to see the full range of our language products, go to:

www.lonelyplanet.com

What kind of traveller are you?

A. You're eating chicken for dinner *again* because it's the only word you know.

B. When no one understands what you say, you step closer and shout louder.

C. When the barman doesn't understand your order, you point frantically at the beer.

D. You're surrounded by locals, swapping jokes, email addresses and experiences – other travellers want to borrow your phrasebook.

If you answered A, B, or C, you NEED Lonely Planet's phrasebooks.

- **Talk to everyone everywhere**
  Over 120 languages, more than any other publisher

- **The right words at the right time**
  Quick-reference colour sections, two-way dictionary, easy pronunciation, every possible subject

- **Lonely Planet Fast Talk** – essential language for short trips and weekends away

- **Lonely Planet Phrasebooks** – for every phrase you need in every language you want

'Best for curious and independent travellers' – Wall Street Journal

Lonely Planet Offices

Australia
90 Maribyrnong St, Footscray,
Victoria 3011
☎ 03 8379 8000
fax 03 8379 8111
email: talk2us@lonelyplanet.com.au

USA
150 Linden St, Oakland,
CA 94607
☎ 510 893 8555
fax 510 893 8572
email: info@lonelyplanet.com

UK
72-82 Rosebery Ave,
London EC1R 4RW
☎ 020 7841 9000
fax 020 7841 9001
email: go@lonelyplanet.co.uk

France
1 rue du Dahomey, 75011 Paris
☎ 01 55 25 33 00
fax 01 55 25 33 01
email: bip@lonelyplanet.fr
website: www.lonelyplanet.fr

www.lonelyplanet.com